J.K. LASSER'S™
HOMEOWNER'S TAX BREAKS 2005

Look for these and other titles from J.K. Lasser™—Practical Guides for All Your Financial Needs

J.K. Lasser's Year-Round Tax Strategies by David S. De Jong and Ann Gray Jakabin

J.K. Lasser's Taxes Made Easy for Your Home-Based Business by Gary W. Carter

J.K. Lasser's Pick Winning Mutual Funds by Jerry Tweddell with Jack Pierce

J.K. Lasser's Your Winning Retirement Plan by Henry K. Hebeler

J.K. Lasser's Strategic Investing After 50 by Julie Jason

J.K. Lasser's Small Business Taxes by Barbara Weltman

J.K. Lasser's 1001 Deductions by Barbara Weltman

J.K. Lasser's Homeowner's Tax Breaks by Gerald Robinson

J.K. LASSER'S™
HOMEOWNER'S TAX BREAKS 2005

Your Complete Guide to Finding Hidden Gold in Your Home

Gerald J. Robinson

John Wiley & Sons, Inc.

Copyright © 2005 by Gerald J. Robinson. All rights reserved.

Published by John Wiley & Sons, Inc., Hoboken, New Jersey.
Published simultaneously in Canada.

No part of this publication may be reproduced, stored in a retrieval system, or transmitted in any form or by any means, electronic, mechanical, photocopying, recording, scanning, or otherwise, except as permitted under Section 107 or 108 of the 1976 United States Copyright Act, without either the prior written permission of the Publisher, or authorization through payment of the appropriate per-copy fee to the Copyright Clearance Center, Inc., 222 Rosewood Drive, Danvers, MA 01923, 978-750-8400, fax 978-646-8600, or on the web at www.copyright.com. Requests to the Publisher for permission should be addressed to the Permissions Department, John Wiley & Sons, Inc., 111 River Street, Hoboken, NJ 07030, 201-748-6011, fax 201-748-6008.

Limit of Liability/Disclaimer of Warranty: While the publisher and author have used their best efforts in preparing this book, they make no representations or warranties with respect to the accuracy or completeness of the contents of this book and specifically disclaim any implied warranties of merchantability or fitness for a particular purpose. No warranty may be created or extended by sales representatives or written sales materials. The advice and strategies contained herein may not be suitable for your situation. You should consult with a professional where appropriate. Neither the publisher nor author shall be liable for any loss of profit or any other commercial damages, including but not limited to special, incidental, consequential, or other damages.

For general information on our other products and services, or technical support, please contact our Customer Care Department within the United States at 800-762-2974, outside the United States at 317-572-3993, or fax 317-572-4002.

Wiley also publishes its books in a variety of electronic formats. Some content that appears in print may not be available in electronic books.

For more information about Wiley products, visit our web site at www.wiley.com.

ISBN 0-471-64771-3

Printed in the United States of America.

10 9 8 7 6 5 4 3 2 1

About the Author

Gerald J. Robinson, Esq., tax counsel to the New York City law firm of Carb, Luria, Cook & Kufeld, is a member of the New York and Maryland bars. He received his BA degree from Cornell University, an LLB from the University of Maryland, and an LLM in Taxation from New York University. Prior to entering private practice, he served in the Office of Chief Counsel, Internal Revenue Service. He is the author of the treatise, *Federal Income Taxation of Real Estate*, now in its sixth edition, and wrote the monthly newsletter, "Real Estate Tax Ideas," both published by Warren, Gorham & Lamont. He is also a frequent lecturer and contributor to various professional journals.

He hates to pay taxes.

Acknowledgments

The author is indebted to colleagues and friends for their encouragement and help in moving the idea of a homeowner's tax guide from concept to reality.

Two of them deserve special thanks for their willingness to review the manuscript and offer helpful suggestions: Arnold Y. Kapiloff, Esq., of the New York City law firm of Schwartzman, Garelik Walker Kapiloff & Mann, P.C., and Richard Sonet, C.P.A., a tax accountant associated with the New York City accounting firm of Marks, Paneth & Shron LLP. Their willingness to bring their knowledge and expertise to a review of the manuscript is much appreciated.

The professionalism and helpfulness of the J.K. Lasser staff in the preparation of the book also merits acknowledgment. Working with them was a pleasure and their suggestions have made the book both more comprehensive and readable. Particular thanks are due to my editor, David Pugh.

For all of these contributions, my sincere thanks.

Taxes reflect a continuing struggle among contending interests for the privilege of paying the least.

> Tax philosopher Louis Eisenstein, in
> *The Ideologies of Taxation*

Homeowners *won*.

> Tax Attorney Gerald J. Robinson, author,
> *J.K. Lasser's Homeowner's Tax Breaks*

Contents

Preface xvii

Part I Sheltering Your Income with Home Deductions

1 Deductions in Year You Buy Your Home   3

   1.1 Overview   3
   1.2 Real Estate Taxes in the Year You Buy: Get Your Proper Share   4
   1.3 Mortgage Points: How to Assure Deduction   7
   1.4 Moving Expenses: Does Your Move Qualify for Deduction?   10
   1.5 How Should Married Couples Take Title to Their Home?   12
   1.6 Purchase Expenses: The Importance of Records   13
   1.7 Helping with the Down Payment: First-Time Homebuyer's IRA Break   14
   1.8 Purchaser's Tax-Planning Checklist   16

2 Recurring Deductions Every Year You Own Your Home   18

   2.1 Overview   18
   2.2 Planning to Maximize Deductions   19
   2.3 Deduct All Your Real Estate Taxes   20
   2.4 Tax Magic of Home Mortgages: Your Interest Deductions   21

- 2.5 Refinanced Home Mortgage—Watch Out for Interest Deduction and Points 22
- 2.6 Home Damaged? Let the IRS Help Pay! 24
- 2.7 How to Boost Your Damage Loss Deduction 29
- 2.8 When Your Damage Is from a Presidentially Declared Disaster 31
- 2.9 How to Deduct Your Home Office Expenses 33
- 2.10 Eligibility of Employees 33
- 2.11 Eligibility of Business Owners 35
- 2.12 Figuring the Deduction 37
- 2.13 If You Work outside Your Home: How to Get Home Office Deductions 46
- 2.14 How Home Office Makes Commuting Costs Deductible 47
- 2.15 Deduct Your Home Office Equipment Cost—Up Front 49

3 Special-Situation Deductions for Homeowners 51

- 3.1 Overview 51
- 3.2 How to Get Tax-Free Income from Short-Term Rental 51
- 3.3 How to Make Your Credit Card and Car Loan Interest Deductible 53
- 3.4 How to Deduct Cost of Medical Home Improvements 57
- 3.5 Deductible Home Improvements for the Disabled 60
- 3.6 How an Employee Gets a Tax Break for a "Sideline" Business 61
- 3.7 Deduction of Fees for Home Tax Advice 64
- 3.8 Tax-Wise Borrowing against Your Home for Business 65
- 3.9 Renting a Part of Your Home 67
- 3.10 Renting Your Entire Home 68
- 3.11 Your Home as a Retirement Nest Egg 73
- 3.12 Battling Condo or Co-op Board 73
- 3.13 Suing the Builder: Tax-Free Proceeds 73

Part II Tax Shelter When You Sell Your Home

4 How to Sell Your Home with No Tax on Gain 77

- 4.1 Overview 77
- 4.2 How to Plan for the Sale 78
- 4.3 Exclusion of Up to $250,000 or More of Gain 79
- 4.4 How to Qualify for the Exclusion 80

4.5 Exceptions to the Two-Year Rule: Job Change, Health Problems, or Unforeseen Circumstances   83
4.6 Married Couples: How to Get the $500,000 Exclusion   87
4.7 Is Your Home Your "Principal Residence"?   91
4.8 Your Home Office: Does It Qualify?   93
4.9 Vacant Land Can Qualify   93
4.10 Snowbirds: How to Deal with the Southern Home Trap   94
4.11 Gain in Excess of the Exclusion   96
4.12 How to Cope with a Depressed Market by Rental before Sale   98
4.13 How to Avoid Reporting to the IRS   99
4.14 Seller's Tax-Planning Checklist   103

5 The High-Priced Home: How to Avoid Tax When Gain Will Exceed the $250,000 or $500,000 Ceiling   104

5.1 Overview   104
5.2 Upper-Middle-Class Victims   105
5.3 Tax Time Bomb   106
5.4 Tax Idea 1: Deferred Sale Approach   107
5.5 Tax Idea 2: The Leasehold Carve-Out   108
5.6 Tax Idea 3: The Installment Sale   111
5.7 Tax Idea 4: Conversion to Rental and Exchange   115
5.8 Summing Up   116

6 When Spouses Split   124

6.1 Overview   124
6.2 Don't Lose the Exclusion on Principal Residence Sale!   124
6.3 Transfer of Home to Spouse   125
6.4 Is It Smart to Sell Prior to Divorce?   126
6.5 How to Avoid Gain on a Vacation Home   127
6.6 Splitting Up Marital Property: Beware the Tax Trap   128

Part III Tax Shelter from Homeowner Loopholes and Vacation Homes

7 Little-Known Loopholes Can Provide Big Savings   133

7.1 Overview   133
7.2 The Super Loophole: How to Use Home Sale Exclusion to Shield Gain on Other Real Estate from Tax   133

7.3 How to Buy a Vacation Home with Tax-Free Dollars from Sale of Rental Property 136
7.4 Avoiding Tax When Your Land Includes Both House and Investment Property 140
7.5 Your Appreciated Residence Is a Tax Treasure: How to Trade Up and Get Tax-Free Cash 142
7.6 Home Improvements: Handyman's Special Tax Shelter 143
7.7 Home Improvement Business: Tax-Free Income for Renovators 145
7.8 When a House Is Not a Home: How to Deduct Loss on Sale of Home 146
7.9 How to Get a Charitable Deduction for Your Home—And Still Live in It 148
7.10 Every Homeowner's Hidden Loophole: Nontaxable "Imputed" Income 152

8 Your Vacation Home Is a Tax Shelter 153

8.1 Overview 155
8.2 Scenario 1: Use of Vacation Home Exclusively as Vacation Home 156
8.3 Scenario 2: Use for Vacation and Rent for 14 Days or Less 157
8.4 Scenario 3: Use for Vacation and Rent for More Than 14 Days 158
8.5 Tax Loss from Rental Not Allowed 158
8.6 Figuring the Amount Deductible 161
8.7 Scenario 4: Rent to Others for the Entire Year 165
8.8 Need for Profit Motive 165
8.9 Figuring Amount of Tax Shelter 166
8.10 Hidden Nugget: A Little Personal Use 168
8.11 Depreciation: The Deduction without Cash Outlay 168
8.12 Tax Shelter Rules 172

Part IV Retirement Benefits and Estate Planning

9 How to Get Tax-Free Dollars in Retirement from Your Home 177

9.1 Overview 177
9.2 Tax-Free Trading Down 178
9.3 How Trading Down Increases Cash Flow 178

9.4 How Much Cash from Trading Down? 179
9.5 The Tax Benefit 180
9.6 Tax-Free Reverse Mortgages 181
9.7 What Is a Reverse Mortgage, Anyway? 181
9.8 The Tax Benefit 182
9.9 How Much Cash Flow Can You Get? 183
9.10 What Type of Reverse Mortgage Is Best for You? 184

10 Reducing Estate Tax on Home 186

10.1 Overview 186
10.2 Should Spouses Own Home Jointly? 187
10.3 Do You Need Estate Tax Planning? 188
10.4 Larger Estates: How Not to Lose the Second Exemption 190
10.5 How Parent Can Cut Taxes on Vacation Home 192
10.6 Estate Planning for a Parent's Home: Using Sale–Leaseback to Shift Appreciation in Value 195
10.7 How Parents Can Escape Estate Tax on Their Homes: The Qualified Personal Residence Trust 199

Epilogue 203

Appendix A

Instructions for Form 8829 207

Appendix B

IRS Publication 521: Moving Expenses 213

Appendix C

IRS Publication 530: Tax Information for First-Time Homeowners 235

Index 247

Preface

This is a book of revelations.

Tax revelations. It reveals a multitude of little-known tax-saving ideas for homeowners that can put substantial dollars in their pockets. In fact, it is packed with the largest collection in print of tax-planning ideas for the homeowner.

Beyond the garden variety deductions for mortgage interest and real estate taxes, homeowners have a cornucopia of tax opportunities. These include such little-known breaks as getting tax-free rent from a short-term home rental, using the generous $250,000/$500,000 home sale exclusion to shelter gain from the sale of other real estate, and pocketing tax-free mortgage proceeds when trading up to a more expensive home.

Divided into four parts, each part of the book provides a concise, plain-language explanation of tax rules for homeowners *and* a discussion of how these rules can be turned to your tax advantage and financial benefit.

- *Part I: Sheltering Your Income with Home Deductions* includes an explanation of how you can legitimately boost the amount of your casualty loss deductions, get deductions for household expenses when you have a home office, write off home office equipment such as computers and printers, make commuting costs from home deductible, make your credit card and car loan interest deductible . . . and more.
- *Part II: Tax Shelter When You Sell Your Home* includes a discussion of how to qualify to exclude up to $250,000 of gain on the sale of your home,

or up to $500,000 if you are married, how to escape tax on gain in excess of the $250,000 or $500,000 ceilings, how to cope with a depressed housing market by getting deductions for renting your home before you sell it, how to escape tax on the sale of a vacation home when you're splitting with your spouse . . . and more.

- *Part III: Tax Shelter from Homeowner Loopholes and Vacation Homes* shows you how to buy a vacation home with tax-free dollars from the sale of rental property, how you can create tax-free income from renovating your home and selling it at a profit, how to get a charitable deduction for your home while you still live in it, how to get deductions for the expenses of maintaining your vacation home when you rent it out . . . and more.

- *Part IV: Retirement Benefits and Estate Planning* explains how you can make your home a retirement nest egg that generates tax-free dollars from trading down or using it for a reverse mortgage, how to minimize estate taxes by using your spouse's "lifetime exemption," how a parent can cut estate tax on a vacation home, how to eliminate estate tax on your principal residence by use of a personal residence trust . . . and more.

Both the tax rules and the tax-saving ideas are explained in quick-to-the-point, nontechnical language, with plenty of illustrations. You don't have to read it all: You can quickly locate areas of particular interest to you in either the table of contents or index.

The tax-saving ideas described are strictly legit. This book will not suggest cutting any corners or taking questionable positions on your tax return. But it will suggest numerous legitimate strategies for saving taxes. There's nothing to be embarrassed about when it comes to the desire to save taxes. Judge Learned Hand in a famous statement put the matter in perspective.

> Over and over again the courts have said that there is nothing sinister in so arranging one's affairs as to keep taxes as low as possible. Everybody does so, rich or poor; and all do right, for nobody owes any public duty to pay more than the law demands: taxes are enforced exactions, not voluntary contributions. To demand more in the name of morals is mere cant.

This book shows homeowners how to do what the courts have blessed: "so arranging one's affairs as to keep taxes as low as possible."

PART I

Sheltering Your Income with Home Deductions

CHAPTER 1

Deductions in Year You Buy Your Home

> Next to being shot at and missed, nothing is so satisfying as avoiding a tax.
>
> **Anonymous**

1.1 OVERVIEW

It's often said the only thing you get from renting an apartment is rent receipts. It's an overstatement, of course, but it highlights the great preference Americans have for owning their own homes. The preference is understandable: In addition to being your own landlord and owning an asset that historically has been a stellar investment, home ownership provides you with unique tax benefits.

Home Ownership vs. Apartment Rental. As a homeowner, you enjoy a collection of tax breaks not afforded to rental apartment dwellers. For example, as a homeowner you can deduct your payments of real estate taxes and mortgage interest. If you rent an apartment, however, the rent you pay is a wholly nondeductible "personal" expense, even though part of your rent is used by the landlord to pay taxes on the building and mortgage interest. Similarly, home ownership is rewarded with a unique tax break when you sell your home at a gain. Tax on the gain may be completely avoided under exclusion provisions that exempt gain on the sale of your home. As explained in Chapter 4, you can exclude up to $250,000 of gain if you are single or up to $500,000 if you are married. No other asset is favored with exemption from taxation when it is sold at a gain.

The good tax news extends even to costs you pay in the year you purchase your home.

- *Deduction for real estate taxes.* In the year you purchase your home, the deduction for real estate taxes for the year is split between you and the seller. You should take steps to make sure you get your proper share.

4 SHELTERING YOUR INCOME WITH HOME DEDUCTIONS

- *Deduction for mortgage points.* Mortgage costs referred to as "points" may be treated as deductible interest in the year you purchase your home. But you have to meet IRS requirement to get the deduction.
- *Deduction for moving expenses.* If you are purchasing your home as a result of a job-related move, part of your moving expenses may be deductible. Again, you have to meet IRS requirements.

This chapter shows you how to nail down your share of the real estate tax deduction for the year of your purchase and how to meet the IRS requirements for the deduction of mortgage points and moving expenses.

> **Co-ops and Condos**
>
> While each of the tax factors noted should be considered by purchasers of single-family houses, they are equally relevant for purchasers of cooperative or condominium units.

Of course, when you purchase your home you ordinarily don't focus on factors that may affect your tax liability in the distant future. You have other things on your mind.

But there are other tax matters you should consider. How you take title is important. You should be aware of both the practical implications and the income and estate tax consequences if you take title to your home jointly with your spouse. (See Sections 1.5 and 10.2.) You also should be aware of the importance of keeping permanent records showing the "tax cost" of your home, including not just the purchase price but also brokerage commissions, legal fees, and other closing costs. These records can be critical if you sell your home later at a gain in excess of the home sale exclusion. (See Section 1.6.)

First we discuss real estate taxes in the year you buy.

1.2 Real Estate Taxes in the Year You Buy: Get Your Proper Share

When purchasing a home, buyers usually don't think much about the real estate taxes they're paying in the year of purchase. But buyers are entitled to deduct their share of real estate taxes on the home for the year in which the purchase occurs. As a purchaser, you should make sure you get your proper share of this valuable deduction.

DEDUCTIONS IN YEAR YOU BUY YOUR HOME

Just as important, you should make sure the seller gets *charged* for the seller's proper share of the year's real estate taxes. Otherwise, you could be paying part of the seller's real estate tax even though you can't deduct the payment.

Seller's and Your Share. The contract of sale for the property controls how real estate taxes for the year of sale are apportioned between the seller and the purchaser. In the part of the contract dealing with closing adjustments, it should be clearly stated how the real estate taxes for the year are to be prorated between you and the seller. The seller should be charged with the amount of tax from the beginning of the real property tax year to the date of closing, and you should be charged with the balance of the tax to the end of the real property tax year. That way, each of you is responsible for the taxes for the portion of the real property tax year during which you own the property.

If real estate taxes for the real property tax year have not yet been paid on the date you close the purchase of your home and the contract doesn't provide for prorating at the closing, then, since you will own the property when the taxes become due, you will have a problem. You will have to pay the real estate taxes in full, even though part of the taxes are attributable to the part of the year the seller owned the property. To add insult to injury, the seller will be able to deduct the share *you* pay. In other words, if the seller doesn't get charged at the closing for the seller's share of the taxes and you pay all the taxes sometime after the closing, you lose twice: The seller gets a free ride for the seller's share of the taxes and, as illustrated below, you can deduct only your share, not the entire amount you paid.

Pro Rata Sharing Required. The tax rules are specific as to how the seller and the purchaser are to deduct real estate taxes for the real property tax year

> **Caution**
>
> ***Check the Contract.*** If real estate taxes on the property you are purchasing have not been paid before your closing, you will pay the tax bill sometime after the closing. Accordingly, you should make sure the seller gets charged in the contract of sale or in the closing statement with the seller's portion of the tax, and that the adjustments at the closing reflect the charge to the seller.

6 SHELTERING YOUR INCOME WITH HOME DEDUCTIONS

the home is purchased. The rules require that, for deduction purposes, the real estate taxes are to be split between the seller and purchaser based on the number of days each of them owns the property. The real estate tax for the part of the year that ends on the day before the sale is treated as a tax imposed on the seller, and the tax for the part of the year that begins on the date of the sale is treated as a tax imposed on the purchaser. This rule applies whether or not the seller and purchaser actually make an allocation of the real estate tax in the contract of sale, and regardless of who pays the tax.

The following example, in which Mr. Sharp sells you his house, shows how the seller should be charged for the tax for the portion of the real property tax year during which the seller owns the property.

Example

The real property tax year is April 1 to March 31. Mr. Sharp, who owns the property on April 1, 2003, sells it to you on June 30, 2003. You own the property from June 30, 2003, through March 31, 2004. The real property tax for the real property tax year April 1, 2003, to March 31, 2004, is $3,650, and you pay the entire tax when it becomes due in 2004. Under these facts, $900 (90/365 × $3,650, April 1, 2003, to June 29, 2003) of the real property tax is treated as imposed on Mr. Sharp. Similarly, $2,750 (275/365 × $3,650, June 30, 2003, to March 31, 2004) of the real property tax is treated as imposed on you.

Since Mr. Sharp owned the property for part of the tax year for which you have paid the *entire* tax, he should have been charged for his share of the tax at the closing. If not, you paid part of Mr. Sharp's tax. To add insult to injury, while your payment of $3,650 in taxes included part of *his* tax, $900, you can deduct only the part treated as imposed on you, $2,750.

Observation

An ounce of prevention can prevent this problem. Simply be sure the purchase contract or closing statement is reviewed by your lawyer to verify that the seller is charged with the proper portion of the year's real property tax.

> **Caution**
>
> Transfer taxes paid on the sale of a home are not deductible. If the buyer pays the taxes, the amount of the taxes is added to the cost of the home for purposes of determining the buyer's tax basis for the home. If the seller pays the taxes, they are considered an expense of sale that reduces the amount realized on the sale by the seller.

1.3 Mortgage Points: How to Assure Deduction

Mortgage points are like cholesterol: There are good points and bad points. Only the good points are deductible.

Here's the story.

Charges you pay your lender for getting your home mortgage loan are expressed as a percentage of the loan and are called "points," each point being equal to 1 percent of the loan. For example, if you are obtaining a $150,000 mortgage, one point is $1,500. Can you deduct points you pay for your mortgage loan in the year you pay the points?

It depends.

Service Charges vs. Interest. When making a loan, the lender may perform various services for you as a borrower, such as securing appraisals, preparing documents, and processing applications. Points that you pay for such services by the lender in a personal residential transaction are nondeductible "personal expenses." On the other hand, if the points are additional interest charged by the lender on your home mortgage, they are currently deductible as home mortgage interest if they meet IRS guidelines. So it is important to determine whether the points are a charge for services or additional interest. You should try to make sure any points you pay are for interest, not services of the lender.

Get Your Lender's Help. Sometimes the purpose for which points are charged by the lender is not clearly stated, so that it is difficult to tell whether the points are being charged for services or as additional interest. However, the IRS says that an allocation of points between service charges and additional interest in your loan contract normally will be respected if the allocation is based on an honest agreement between you and the lender. If it's unclear that the points charged by your lender are for interest, ask your lender to clarify their purpose in your loan contract.

SHELTERING YOUR INCOME WITH HOME DEDUCTIONS

> **Tax Tip**
>
> *Cash Basis Taxpayers.* The guidelines apply to "cash basis" taxpayers. These are individuals who report income when received and expenses when paid. Individual homeowners are cash basis taxpayers.

How Do You Qualify to Deduct Points as Interest?   Assuming the points are for interest and not service charges, are they deductible? Again, it depends. According to IRS guidelines, the points you pay your lender can be deducted in the year you buy your home if the following five requirements are met. While the guidelines are needlessly complex and annoying, the cautious home purchaser will make sure they are complied with.

1. *Designation on Uniform Settlement Statement.* The Uniform Settlement Statement you get at the closing must clearly designate the amounts involved as points payable in connection with the loan. For example, the amount should be shown as "loan origination fees," "loan discount," "discount points," or "points."
2. *Figured as a percentage of the amount borrowed.* The amount paid must be computed as a percentage of the principal amount of your mortgage loan.
3. *Charged under established business practice.* The amount you pay must conform to an established business practice of charging points for loans for home purchases in your local area, and the amount of points you pay must not exceed the amount generally charged in your area. When you were shopping for your loan, you probably found that the amount of points your lender was charging was more or less standard in your area.
4. *Paid for acquisition or improvement of principal residence.* You must pay the points in connection with the purchase of your principal residence, and the loan must be secured by the residence. The guidelines don't cover points paid on a loan used to purchase or improve a second residence or other property that is not your principal residence.
5. *Paid directly by you.* The points generally must be "paid directly" by you to your lender from your *separate* funds, not from the mortgage money. Your check to the lender on preexisting funds in your checking account is one way to handle this requirement.

> **Caution**
>
> *Disguises Not Permitted.* If amounts labeled points are paid in lieu of amounts that usually are stated separately on the settlement statement, such as appraisal fees, inspection fees, title fees, attorney fees, and property taxes, such amounts are not interest and, accordingly, are not deductible as points.

There's another way to meet this niggling "paid directly" requirement. Under the IRS guidelines, you will be treated as paying directly from your separate funds if you pay at the closing, from funds *not* borrowed, an amount at least equal to the points. Such payment from you would include your down payment, the application of earnest money at the closing, and other funds paid directly by you at the closing.

> **Example**
>
> You purchase a principal residence for $150,000, paying $7,500 in closing costs, including $3,000 in points. You provide $4,500 in unborrowed funds to pay closing costs other than points and finance the payment of the $3,000 in points by increasing the mortgage loan by $3,000. You will be deemed to have met the "paid directly" requirement because you have provided unborrowed funds ($4,500) at least equal to the amount of points.

A cap is placed on the amount of points deductible under the IRS guidelines. Points allocable to a home mortgage loan in excess of $1 million are not protected by the guidelines. Moreover, the guidelines do not apply to points paid on a refinancing loan, a home equity loan, or a line of credit.

> **Caution**
>
> *Nondeductible Points.* There is only a small tax consolation prize if the points are not currently deductible. Nondeductible points on a home mortgage must be "amortized" on a straight-line basis over the life of the mortgage loan. This means that only a ratable portion of the total points paid is deducted each year. For example, if you pay $1,500 in points to obtain a 15-year mortgage, you can deduct only $100 yearly for 15 years ($1,500/15 = $100).

Probably aware of the annoying complexity of its rules, the IRS has provided a flowchart simplifying understanding of the requirements for the deduction of points. The chart is reproduced in Figure 1.1.

Home Improvement Loans. According to the chart and contrary to its own guidelines, points may be deducted even if the loan is for the improvement of your principal residence, not just its purchase. If your loan is for the improvement of your principal residence rather than its purchase and you meet the other requirement of the guidelines, deduct the points. Few IRS agents would be willing to challenge the chart.

1.4 Moving Expenses: Does Your Move Qualify for Deduction?

If you move to a new principal place of work, the tax law may give you an indirect subsidy for your moving expenses. The subsidy comes in the form of a moving expense deduction that can reduce your after-tax cost for the move. It doesn't matter whether you move for your present employer or for a new employer.

The Deductible Expenses. The moving expense deduction is allowed for moving expenses you pay in connection with beginning work at a new principal place of work. The deductible expenses are the reasonable expenses of moving your household goods and personal effects from your former residence to your new residence. You can also deduct the costs of traveling, including lodging, from your former residence to your new residence. For your spouse and children, these expenses are allowed only if your spouse and children have both your former residence and your new residence as their principal place of abode and are members of your household. The expense of meals is not deductible for either you or your family.

Distance and Time Rules. To prevent the deduction of moving expenses for either short-distance moves or short-duration moves, a distance rule and a time rule must be met to get the deduction.

- ***Distance Rule.*** The distance rule is a mileage requirement. Your new principal place of work must be at least 50 miles farther from your former residence than was your former principal place of work. Thus, if your former job was 20 miles from your former residence and your new job is more than 70 miles from your former residence, you qualify.
- ***Time Rule.*** The time rule is a duration requirement. During the 12-month period immediately following your arrival in the general location

DEDUCTIONS IN YEAR YOU BUY YOUR HOME

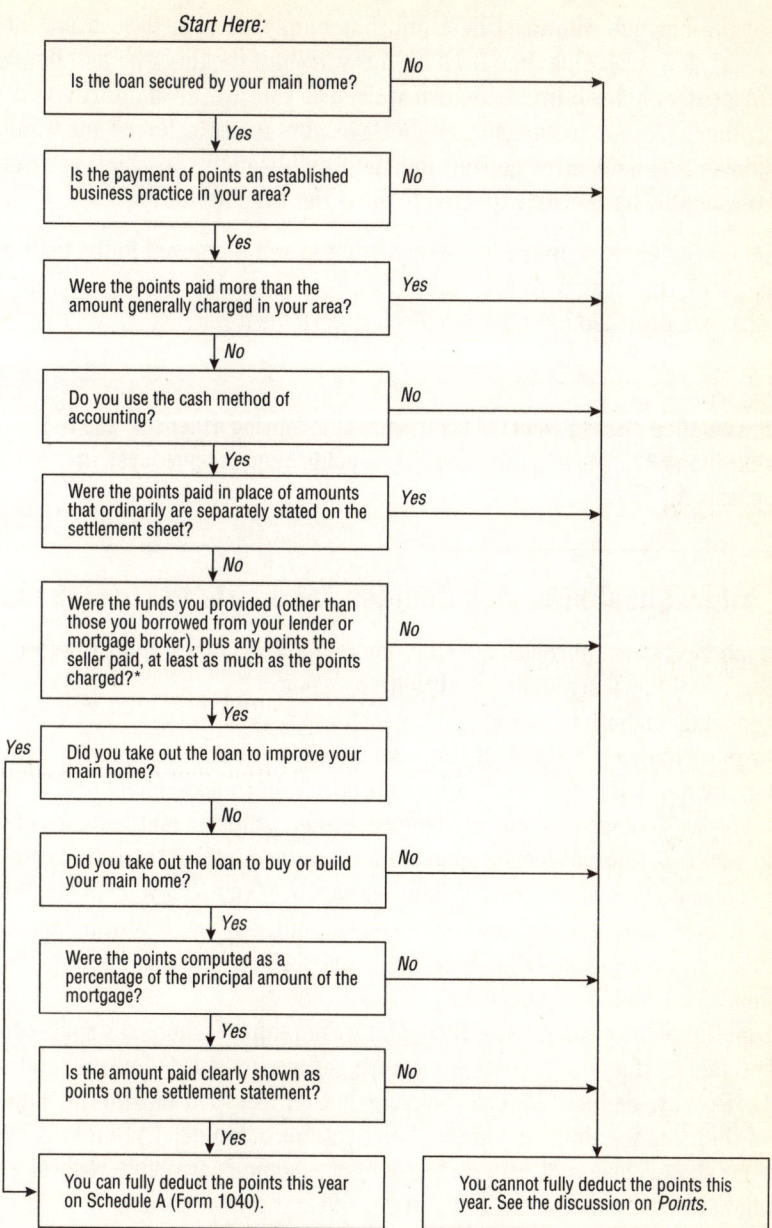

FIGURE 1.1 Are My Points Fully Deductible This Year?
*The funds you provided do not have to have been applied to the points. They can include a down payment, an escrow deposit, earnest money, and other funds you paid at or before closing for any purpose.

of the new job, you must be a full-time employee at such location for at least 39 weeks. This time limitation is waived if it cannot be met because of death or disability. It is also waived if you are involuntarily laid off (other than for willful misconduct), or you are transferred for the employer's benefit after getting full-time employment in which you could reasonably have been expected to meet the time limitation.

The moving expense break is also available to self-employed individuals and members of the armed forces, subject to special rules. More generous allowances are provided for moves to foreign work locations.

> **For a detailed discussion of the tax treatment of moving expenses, see IRS Publication 521, "Moving Expenses." This publication is reproduced in Appendix B.**

1.5 How Should Married Couples Take Title to Their Home?

For a married home purchaser, a title question often comes up just before the closing: Shall I own my home jointly with my spouse?

It depends on both personal and tax factors.

For most married couples, if the marriage is good and expected to remain so, joint ownership of the home is appropriate from the personal point of view. This is because of what happens to jointly owned property on the death of one of the spouses. It assures each spouse that, on the death of the other, the surviving spouse will own the home. In other words, if you own your home jointly (legally, as a "joint tenant" or "tenant by the entirety" with your spouse), on the death of your spouse full title to the home vests in you immediately. This is automatic, no deed being necessary.

From the income tax perspective, joint ownership of a home by spouses is a neutral factor. If a joint income tax return is filed, mortgage interest and real estate taxes are deductible regardless of whether the spouses own the home in one of their names alone or jointly. (See Sections 2.3 and 2.4.) Similarly, eligibility for the exclusion of gain on the sale of a home is available regardless of whether the spouses own the home in one of their names alone or jointly. (See Sections 4.5 through 4.9.)

Estate taxes may or may not play a role in determining how the home is owned. At least for couples with combined assets below the federal estate tax "exemption" level, joint ownership of the home has no adverse tax implications. Such may not be the case for wealthier spouses. (See Section 10.2.)

1.6 Purchase Expenses: The Importance of Records

You can't purchase a home without incurring substantial "incidental" closing costs. Few buyers walk out of a closing without having paid more in closing costs than they thought they would.

Except for the real estate taxes and points discussed earlier, these expenses are not deductible. However, they may provide you with a tax benefit later. Expenses in this nondeductible but potentially valuable category include:

- Legal fees, including the cost of preparing and reviewing the contract of sale and deed, title search charges, and abstract fees
- Inspection fees, survey costs, and title insurance premiums
- Any amounts owed by the seller that you agree to pay, including recording or transfer taxes, broker's sales commission, back taxes or interest, and the cost of repairs or improvements

The Later Benefit. While you can't deduct these types of closing costs, you can add them to the purchase price of your home for purposes of determining the tax cost of your home, known as your "tax basis" in legalese. Since these expenses are added to the tax basis for your home, they may provide you with a tax benefit on a later taxable sale of your home if you sell for an amount in excess of the allowable $250,000/$500,000 exclusion (discussed in Sections 4.3 through 4.9). To the extent the tax basis of your home is increased by these costs, the sales price is offset, reducing the gain subject to tax.

Reducing Taxable Gain on Future Sale. Baseball player Satchel Paige advised, "Don't look back. Something may be gaining on you." But homeowners whose gain on a future sale of their home exceeds the available $250,000/$500,000 exclusion will have to look back to the time they purchased their homes if they are to reduce their taxable gain by adding closing costs to their tax basis.

Example

Say you purchased your home for $350,000, incurring closing costs of $13,000. You sell the home five years later for $625,000, and under the exclusion rules discussed in Sections 4.3 through 4.9 you are permitted to exclude $250,000 of your gain. If you kept good records that permit you to prove the amount of your closing costs, you can reduce your taxable gain from $25,000 to $12,000.

(Continued)

Example

Selling price	$625,000
Tax basis without closing costs	350,000
Gain	$275,000
Exclusion	250,000
Taxable gain before closing costs	25,000
Closing costs	13,000
Taxable gain after deduction of closing costs	$ 12,000

Closing costs may be used to offset gain on a partially taxable sale only if they can be substantiated. If you are purchasing a home with the happy anticipation of future gain on a sale in excess of the exclusion, your closing statement, other closing documents, and canceled checks should be preserved. Preserving this evidence of costs will help you prove the amount of your closing costs.

Keeping Records of Improvement Costs. Like closing costs, the cost of improvements to your home also is added to the tax basis for your home. Accordingly, you should keep records of improvements to your home. For a discussion of how to keep tax records, including how long to keep tax records, see IRS Publication 530, reproduced in Appendix C. Publication 530 also contains a useful chart that can be used to keep a record of improvement costs, listing the type of improvement made, the date it was made, and its cost.

1.7 Helping with the Down Payment: First-Time Homebuyer's IRA Break

It may seem like giving ice away in the winter, but if you own a regular individual retirement account (IRA) you can catch a small break if you are a first-time homebuyer. You can withdraw up to $10,000 from your IRA to help with the down payment on your new home without incurring the 10 percent premature withdrawal penalty usually otherwise applicable to withdrawals before age $59\frac{1}{2}$.

The break is a mixed blessing: You still have to pay regular income tax on the amount of the withdrawal.

To get this tax door to open, you have to meet the following requirements.

- **First-Time Homebuyer.** To be a "first-time homebuyer" technically doesn't mean quite what it says. It means that you, or you and your spouse if you're married, must not have had an ownership interest in a principal residence during the two-year period ending on the date of acquisition of your new home. For this purpose the date of acquisition of your new home is the date on which a binding contract to purchase the home is entered into or the date on which construction or reconstruction of the home is commenced.

- **Qualified First-Time Homebuyer Distribution.** The payment from your IRA must be a qualified first-time homebuyer distribution. This is a payment to you from your IRA if it is used within 120 days to pay qualified acquisition costs for your new principal residence. Qualified acquisition costs are the costs of acquiring, constructing, or reconstructing a residence and any usual or reasonable settlement, financing, or other closing costs. Your "principal residence" basically is where you live on a full-time basis, as explained in Section 4.7.
- **Dollar Limitation.** The payment to you from your IRA, when added to any other first-time homebuyer payments to you from your IRA, cannot exceed $10,000.

Oddly, despite the "first-time homebuyer" name given to these rules, they don't require that you actually be a first-time homebuyer. As indicated earlier, all that is required is that you, or you and your spouse if you're married, must not have had an ownership interest in a principal residence during the two years before the date you acquire your new home.

Example

In 2000 Thelma and Louise sold their Baltimore home, then moved to Boston and lived in an apartment until 2005 when they purchase a new home. Thelma takes a $10,000 distribution from her IRA to help with the down payment on the new home. Because Thelma has not had an ownership interest in a principal residence within the preceding two years, Thelma will not have to pay the additional 10 percent premature withdrawal penalty tax on her IRA distribution. However, the amount of the distribution will be includible in Thelma's income under the usual IRA rules.

Tax Tip

Deduct Your Mortgage Points. You may get clipped for several thousand dollars in "points" to get your lender to give you a mortgage. While points are not added to your tax basis, they may be even better taxwise: They may be currently deductible *interest*. (See Section 1.3.)

1.8 Purchaser's Tax-Planning Checklist

- **Exclusion Qualification.** If you are purchasing a new principal residence as a replacement of your old principal residence, you should first make sure that any gain on the sale of your old residence qualifies for the $250,00/$500,000 exclusion of gain from taxation. (See Sections 4.3 through 4.9.)
- **Form of Ownership.** If you are married, the practical as well as the income and estate tax aspects of the form of ownership of your home should be checked. (See Sections 1.5 and 10.2.)
- **Deduction of Real Estate Taxes.** The deduction for real estate taxes for the year you purchase your home is based on a formula that splits the taxes between you and the seller according to the number of days in the year each of you owns the property. (See Section 1.2.)
- **Points.** If you pay points to your lender, the points are not deductible if they are a charge for services. But if they are additional interest, they *may* be currently deductible as home mortgage interest. Advance planning often may permit a deduction for the purchaser that otherwise might be lost. (See Section 1.3.)
- **Purchasing Expenses.** While the fees and closing costs you pay at the closing are nondeductible, they normally can be added to the cost or "tax basis" of your home to reduce any future taxable gain on its sale. (See Section 1.6.)
- **Moving Expenses.** If you are buying your new home as a result of a job change, job-related moving expenses may be deductible. But specified requirements must be met. (See Section 1.4.)
- **Tax-Free Cash from Trading Up.** If gain on the sale of your former home is shielded from tax by the exclusion provisions, and the sale price of your former home exceeds both the mortgage on the former residence and the cash required to purchase your new residence, the mortgage on the new residence can provide you with tax-free cash, even though you are trading up. (See Section 7.5.)
- **Delinquent Real Estate Taxes.** Verify that there are no delinquent real estate taxes not paid by the seller. Delinquent taxes paid by the seller prior to the closing are deductible by the seller. But if they are paid by you, they are treated as part of your purchase price for the home and are not deductible by you.
- **Transfer and Recording Taxes.** Any transfer and recording taxes you pay are not deductible. They are treated as part of the acquisition cost of the property and are added to the tax basis of the property.

- **Interest on Mortgage.** In the unusual situation in which you purchase property subject to an existing mortgage, you may deduct interest on the mortgage only to the extent it accrues *after* the date of your purchase.
- **Information Reporting.** The person responsible for closing your sale may have to report information to the IRS, including the identity of the seller, the property sold, the date of the sale, and the sale price. (See Section 4.13.)
- **Nonforeign Affidavit.** When a foreigner sells real estate, the purchaser usually has to withhold tax. For you to get assurance that you are not required to withhold, you normally should obtain a nonforeign affidavit from the seller.

CHAPTER 2

Recurring Deductions Every Year You Own Your Home

> It takes more effort to make out the income tax form than to make the income.
> — Alfred Newman

2.1 Overview

The tax code sternly prohibits you from taking deductions for "personal, living or family expenses." As examples of these nondeductible expenses, the IRS lists the cost of maintaining a household and the cost of homeowners' insurance.

The Big Breaks. But Congress has winked at this prohibition for two of the heaviest expenses of home ownership: home mortgage interest and real estate taxes. Despite their obviously personal nature when associated with home ownership, interest and taxes generally are fully deductible. Subject to limitations, so is the amount of loss from damage to your home from fires, storms, and other so-called "casualties."

The tax revenue cost of homeowners' deductions for interest and taxes is immense, so it's not surprising that these deductions have been eyed greedily by congressional budget balancers. Indeed, they have started to limit these deductions. Their first nibble at the deductions came when a not-so-serious (for most of us) $1 million ceiling was placed on the amount of a home mortgage loan on which interest deductions are allowed.

Watch That Camel! The nose of the congressional camel reappeared under the homeowners' tent in legislation cutting down further on the deduction of taxes and interest for higher-income homeowners. It provided that deductions you itemize on your return, including homeowners' interest and taxes, are to be reduced by 3 percent of adjusted gross income if you are a high-income individual. But then the Bush tax-cutting Congress pushed back on the camel's nose. The limitation on itemized deductions was phased out, reduced by one-third for taxable years beginning in 2006 and 2007, by two-thirds for taxable years beginning in 2008 and 2009, and entirely for taxable years after 2009. Stay tuned: The pushing will continue.

Tax Watch

What can be done to keep the camel away? You may want to let your congressperson know you are watching.

2.2 Planning to Maximize Deductions

The Plain Vanilla Deductions. Tax planning normally involves setting up the mechanics of a transaction to reduce taxes. But the "mechanics" of home ownership are usually inflexible, with mortgage interest and real estate tax payments virtually inevitable and occasional casualty losses only a little less certain. So tax planning for the period during which you own your home primarily requires a working knowledge of the rules concerning the deductibility of these home ownership expenses and a careful saving of canceled checks and other records to substantiate the deductions. This chapter will first show you how to take advantage of these routine deductions and, in some cases, possibly increase their amount. Subsequent chapters will give you a collection of money-saving tax-planning ideas for your home in special situations.

The Home Office. If you have a home office, significant tax-planning opportunities may exist. To take advantage of them, you not only have to be aware of the requirements for the deduction of home office expenses, but you also have to make arrangements necessary to qualify for the deductions. This chapter explains how to make such arrangements. It also explains how you may be able to deduct otherwise nondeductible commuting expenses if your home is your principal place of business.

Tax Tip

More Hidden Gold. While the deductions for mortgage interest and real estate taxes are the biggest routine homeowner tax breaks, there are other, less well-known opportunities. These tax breaks, including using your home to get tax-free rent and tax-free mortgage proceeds, are discussed in Chapter 3 and Chapter 7, respectively.

2.3 Deduct All Your Real Estate Taxes

As a homeowner, you get a special break when it comes to real estate taxes on your home. You can't deduct most taxes, such as sales taxes or your federal income taxes. But when you put on your homeowner's hat, you get special treatment.

As a homeowner, you can deduct state and local real property taxes on your home. These taxes are a so-called "itemized deduction" that you can claim only if you itemize your deductions on Schedule A of Form 1040. If you use the standard deduction rather than itemizing your deductions to figure your tax, you can't claim the itemized deduction for real estate taxes.

> **Tax Tip**
>
> If you're a homeowner, you'll probably pay less income tax by itemizing your deductions than by using the tax table. But check it out both ways to make sure.

What If Taxes Are Included in Your Mortgage Payment? You can claim a deduction for taxes only in the tax year you actually pay the taxes. This rule can present some uncertainty if your mortgage payments include installment payments of taxes along with periodic interest and principal payments. Do you "pay" the tax when it is deposited with your lender or only when your lender turns it over to the local tax collector? Technically, the tax is deductible only in the year when the lender pays the tax, since the lender is acting as your agent.

Taxes Paid? As a practical matter, you can assume the lender paid your taxes to the local tax collector the same year you paid the taxes to the lender. To be safe, you can verify this by checking the year-end statement sent to you by the lender, which normally shows the amount of tax paid.

Boosting Your Deduction. Can you boost your deduction for real estate taxes this year by prepaying real estate taxes due next year? Such prepayment is a standard year-end tax-planning move. It's an especially good tax-planning strategy if you will be in a higher tax bracket this year than you will be next year, because the deduction will save more taxes this year than next year.

> **Caution**
>
> In rare cases, real estate tax prepayment might be regarded as a nondeductible deposit rather than a payment. If you want to make sure that a prepayment will not be treated as a deposit, call your local real estate assessor's office and inquire.

RECURRING DEDUCTIONS EVERY YEAR YOU OWN YOUR HOME

> **Caution**
>
> This advance payment technique is a one-year break. You either get a smaller deduction next year when you pay less real estate taxes or you have to keep prepaying your real estate taxes in future years to get a full deduction in the future years. Note, also, that increasing your real estate tax deduction won't help you if you are subject to the alternative minimum tax.

2.4 Tax Magic of Home Mortgages: Your Interest Deductions

Tax magic? Almost

Like a magician turning water into wine, a Congress friendly to homeowners has turned nondeductible personal interest into deductible homeowner interest. While so-called "personal" interest usually is not deductible, all of the interest you pay on a mortgage to purchase your home is deductible. On top of that, while personal interest on your credit card debt and car loan is not deductible, you can magically transform such nondeductible interest into deductible interest if you use a "home equity" mortgage loan to pay off these debts. (Home equity loans are discussed in Section 3.3.)

Of course, as with any deduction, there are certain requirements you have to meet. But the circumstances under which most home mortgage loans are made assure that the requirements will be met.

> **Caution**
>
> The type of mortgage loans discussed here are for the purchase, construction, or improvement of your home. A mortgage you take out after you own your home for some other purpose, so-called "home equity mortgages," are discussed in Section 3.3.

> **Tax Tip**
>
> As with real estate taxes, you can deduct home mortgage interest only if you itemize your deductions on Schedule A of Form 1040, instead of using the standard deduction. If you're paying mortgage interest and real estate taxes, you'll probably pay less income tax if you itemize your deductions rather than taking the standard deduction. To make sure, compare your total itemized deductions to the allowable standard deduction.

Mortgage Requirements. Interest paid on a loan to purchase, construct, or substantially improve your home is deductible if it is so-called "acquisition indebtedness." Acquisition indebtedness is a loan that meets three requirements:

1. The home purchased, constructed, or substantially improved must be either your principal residence or a second home, such as a vacation home.
2. The mortgage must be secured by the residence. This means the mortgage has to be recorded in your local land records office and has to create a lien on your home (which will be insisted on by your lender, anyway).
3. The total amount that may qualify as acquisition indebtedness cannot exceed $1 million, or $500,000 if you are married and file a separate return. This ceiling is for both your principal residence and any second home combined.

That's it. For most homeowners, these conditions are met without any tax-planning action on their part.

> **Caution**
>
> When you get a mortgage loan to finance the purchase of your home, your monthly payment to the lender usually will include amounts applied to both the payment of your mortgage interest and your real estate taxes. While these amounts are deductible, other portions of your total monthly payment to the lender may not be deductible. For example, portions of your monthly payment applied toward reduction of the amount of your mortgage (called amortization) and toward insurance premiums are not deductible. You should check the statement you receive from your lender after the close of the year to ascertain the amount of your total payments that is for deductible real estate taxes and interest.

Late Payment Charge. If you are late in making a mortgage payment, the lender may charge you a late payment fee. A late payment fee is deductible if it is additional interest charged for the late payment, not a charge for some specific service of the lender.

2.5 Refinanced Home Mortgage— Watch Out for Interest Deduction and Points

If you refinance your home mortgage, the interest you pay on the refinanced mortgage is usually deductible. But there are limits.

RECURRING DEDUCTIONS EVERY YEAR YOU OWN YOUR HOME

Here's how it works:

In general, if you refinance your original mortgage for an amount larger than its current balance, you can't deduct interest allocable to the new mortgage in excess of the current balance of your original mortgage. In other words, the amount of interest deductible on the new mortgage cannot exceed the portion of such mortgage equal to the current balance on your original mortgage. Interest on the excess is not deductible.

An example will show how this works.

> **Example**
>
> Suppose you obtained a $185,000 mortgage to purchase your principal residence. This is your original acquisition indebtedness. After a number of years of payments, your original mortgage has been paid down to $160,000. You can't deduct interest on a new mortgage on your home above the paid-down amount of $160,000 by refinancing for a larger amount. If the mortgage is increased above $160,000, say to $200,000, interest on the $40,000 excess ($200,000 − $160,000) can't be deducted as interest on acquisition indebtedness.

As the example shows, acquisition indebtedness is reduced by principal payments on your original mortgage and generally can't be increased by refinancing.

Is there a way around this limitation?

Maybe. Your refinancing proceeds—the amount you receive from the lender over what is used to pay off the balance of your original mortgage—may still qualify.

Tax Break. Unlike acquisition indebtedness, "home equity indebtedness" up to $100,000 need not be "incurred" for any particular purpose. So if your refinancing proceeds will exceed your acquisition indebtedness limit, you may be able to treat the balance as a home equity loan on which the interest will be fully deductible. You can check out the home equity loan requirements in Section 3.3.

Another Tax Break. Acquisition indebtedness includes refinancing proceeds used to make a substantial improvement to your home. So if you use the excess refinancing proceeds to substantially improve your home, interest on the excess is deductible.

What about Points? Mortgage points paid to the lender when you refinance your home mortgage are not currently deductible. Instead, the points must be "amortized" over the life of the refinanced loan—that is, a ratable portion of the total points paid is deducted each year.

> **Example**
>
> You pay $1,000 in points up front to refinance your mortgage. The refinanced mortgage has a 10-year term. You can deduct or "amortize" the $1,000 in points at the rate of $100 each year for 10 years.

Break on Second Refinancing. We have to go around the barn to explain this one.

The IRS acknowledges that if you spread your deduction for points over the life of the mortgage you can deduct any remaining balance of spread points in the year the mortgage ends, by prepayment, refinancing, or otherwise. But the IRS goes on to say that if you refinance the mortgage with the same lender, you cannot deduct any remaining balance of spread points. Instead, you deduct the balance of spread points over the remaining term of the new loan.

But what if you refinance with a *different* lender? The IRS doesn't say, but you should be able to deduct the remaining balance of spread points on the first refinancing because the new loan then can't be considered just a continuation of the original loan. And even if the refinancing is with the same lender, the remaining balance of the spread points on the original loan should be deductible if you sign a new note with different terms, such as a changed interest rate and maturity.

2.6 Home Damaged? Let the IRS Help Pay!

Every homeowner occasionally gets hit with damage from a storm or some other unexpected major or minor disaster. If it's a heavy uninsured loss, you don't have to suffer alone. The IRS will provide indirect help by allowing you a tax deduction.

You can deduct losses from an uninsured "casualty" to your home, such as damage from a fire or storm. But there are limits. Losses from casualties are deductible only to the extent that your *total* casualty losses during the taxable year exceed 10 percent of your adjusted gross income as figured on your Form 1040. (Your adjusted gross income is essentially all your income minus specified deductions, such as alimony payments, capital loss deductions, the deduction for IRA contributions, and moving expense deductions.) Also, no casualty loss is deductible unless it exceeds $100. The way you figure the deduction is illustrated on page 25.

> **Observation**
>
> ***Husband and Wife.*** If you're married, then for purposes of the 10 percent and $100 rules, you and your spouse are treated as one individual if you file a joint return. If you and your spouse own your home jointly, each of you may deduct half the casualty loss if you file separate returns, even though one of you pays the entire cost of repairs.

Many Kinds of Home Casualties. In addition to fire and storm damage, a wide variety of other home disasters can be claimed as casualty losses. To qualify for the deduction, the loss generally must be occasioned by a sudden and destructive force. For example, deductions are permitted for losses caused by events such as earthquakes, floods, vandalism, or bursting pipes. On the other hand, losses do not qualify as casualty losses when they result from gradual deterioration from processes such as rusting, corrosion, or contamination.

> **Observation**
>
> ***Termite Cases.*** Borderline cases arise, and occasionally the bickering between the IRS and taxpayers over what qualifies as a casualty approaches the bizarre. In over a dozen cases, the judiciary has wrestled with the question of whether a loss from termite infestation is sufficiently "sudden" to be a casualty. A deduction has been denied for damage occurring over a three-year period, but permitted for damage occurring and discovered within one year.

If a drought produces a loss from the progressive and gradual deterioration of property, the loss may not be sufficiently sudden to be considered a casualty. But the withering of plants and shrubs over a three- to four-month period directly resulting from an extraordinary and calamitous drought has been held sufficiently sudden to qualify.

So how do you tell if unusual damage will qualify?

IRS Guidelines. In a ruling concerning flood and storm damage, the IRS says the term *casualty* refers to an identifiable event of a sudden, unexpected, or unusual nature, and that damage from progressive deterioration through a "steadily operating cause" is not a casualty. The following examples help show the rules of the game:

- Losses from physical damage as a result of wave action or wind during a storm are deductible, as are losses due to flooding of buildings and basements as a result of a storm.
- Damage due to gradual erosion, gradual subsidence of land, and collapse of a patio roof caused by dry rot rather than wind are not sufficiently sudden.
- Damage from a series of closely timed storms, which would individually constitute casualties, is not damage in the nature of progressive deterioration caused by a steadily operating force. It's sufficiently sudden.
- Damage from gradual settlement of a house resulting from faulty construction is not sufficiently sudden to qualify as a casualty.
- Damage caused by vandalism qualifies as a casualty. But the casualty loss deduction may be denied if the homeowner fails to prove the year in which the vandalism occurred or the amount of loss attributable to specific acts of vandalism.
- Loss of a home and furnishings from a lawful eviction does not qualify as a casualty, because it is not caused by a sudden, unexpected, external event.
- A casualty loss deduction may be allowed for the death of trees from infestation by beetles.
- A roof leak resulting from gradual deterioration is not sudden enough to qualify as a casualty. But if the contractor repairing the leak causes damage to the roof, such damage may qualify. The amount of the casualty loss from damage caused by a contractor's negligent workmanship normally would be measured by the cost of repairing it.

What about Insurance? If your damage is completely covered by insurance, you don't really have a loss. It follows that no deduction is allowed to the extent your loss is compensated for by insurance. Of course, you're not compensated by insurance to the extent you have to pay a "deductible" before the insurance kicks in. If you have a claim for insurance reimbursement for which there is a reasonable prospect of recovery, your loss is not "sustained" until it can be ascertained with reasonable certainty that such reimbursement will not be received.

> **Tax Tip**
>
> *Afraid to Make a Claim?* What if you have a deductible loss that is covered by your insurance, but you don't make an insurance claim because you think the claim may result in a policy cancellation or an increase in your premiums. Can you still deduct your loss, even though you don't file a claim?
>
> The answer is no. No deduction for an insured casualty loss is allowed unless you file a timely insurance claim for the loss and the claim is rejected or your loss exceeds the insurance.

Now that you know what kind of loss qualifies as a casualty loss, the next question is how much you can deduct when you have a casualty loss.

How Much Can You Deduct? Figuring the amount you can claim on your tax return as a casualty loss deduction is a two-step process.

- **Step 1.** Figure the amount of the loss that is *eligible* for the deduction.
- **Step 2.** Subtract the 10 percent of adjusted gross income and $100 per casualty *limitations* from the eligible loss.

The two-step process for figuring the deduction is illustrated below.

The Eligible Loss. The eligible loss is the lesser of two amounts. Specifically, the eligible loss is the lesser of the loss in value of your property or the so-called "adjusted basis" of your property at the time of the casualty. The loss in value of your property is the difference in the value of your property before and after the casualty. The adjusted basis of your property generally is its purchase price plus the cost of any improvements to the property, less any prior deductible casualty losses and any depreciation deductions. The example below illustrates how these amounts are figured.

You can show the fair market value of your property before and after the casualty by getting an appraisal, but there's a simpler way. The reasonable cost of repairs essential to restore the property to its prior condition is good evidence of the amount of loss in value.

Here's an example that shows how you figure the amount of a casualty loss deduction.

Example

Suppose a house that originally cost $200,000 exclusive of land is completely destroyed by fire. Based on an appraisal, immediately before the fire the house and land had a fair market value of $300,000, and the house had an adjusted basis of $200,000 (its cost). Fire insurance proceeds amount to $120,000. In the year of the casualty, the homeowner's adjusted gross income is $100,000. After the fire the value of the property is the value of the land, $70,000. The deductible loss would be figured as follows.

Step 1. Determination of Loss Eligible for Deduction

Value of property immediately before casualty		$300,000
Less: value of property immediately after casualty (land)		70,000
Loss in value		230,000
Loss eligible for deduction before insurance recovery (lesser of amount of loss in value [$230,000] or basis [$200,000])		200,000
Less insurance recovery		120,000
Loss eligible for deduction		$ 80,000

Step 2. Application of 10 Percent and $100 Limitations

Loss eligible for deduction		$80,000
Less: 10 percent of adjusted gross income	10,000	
$100 floor	100	
		10,100
Deductible casualty loss ($80,000 − $10,100)		$ 69,900

Quick Reference Table. Figuring the deduction isn't particularly complicated, but there are many possible fact variations. The IRS has provided a table (Table 2.1) that shows you the tax consequences of casualty losses under just about any set of circumstances you might have. The table disregards the 10 percent of adjusted gross income limitation and the $100 floor. The values shown are imaginary, used to simplify the illustrations.

To check out your situation using the table, find the line in the table with values and other amounts analogous to your circumstances in columns (a) through (e), then check the results in columns (f), (g), and (h).

TABLE 2.1 Figuring Your Casualty Loss Deduction

	(A) Value before Disaster	(B) Value after Disaster	(C) Loss in Value, (a) Minus (b)	(D) Cost or Other Basis	(E) Insurance or Other Compensation Received or Recoverable	(F) Allowable Casualty Loss Deduction, Lesser of (c) or (d) Minus (e)	(G) Taxable Gain, (e) Minus (d)	(H) Remaining Tax Basis, (d) Plus (g) Minus Sum of (e) and (f)
(1)	$15,000	$11,000	$ 4,000	$10,000	$ 3,000	$ 1,000		$6,000
(2)	$15,000	$ 3,000	$12,000	$10,000		$10,000		
(3)	$ 5,000	$ 2,000	$ 3,000	$10,000	$ 3,000			$7,000
(4)	$15,000	$ 1,000	$14,000	$10,000	$ 3,000	$ 7,000		
(5)	$19,000	$10,000	$ 9,000	$5,000	$ 8,000		$3,000	
(6)	$18,000		$18,000	$10,000	$12,000		$2,000	

2.7 How to Boost Your Damage Loss Deduction

How you figure your casualty loss deduction is explained above. Now you are ready for the advanced course: How can you boost your deduction?

Short Answer. The short answer is to get an appraisal that shows a decrease in value from the damage that is *more* than you pay for repairs.

You may be able to deduct this larger amount.

Here's the story:

When a storm or other casualty damages your home, you should consider what repairs to make with an awareness of both the cash outlay required and the tax consequences. Minimizing repairs will reduce your cash outlay, but it won't necessarily reduce your casualty loss deduction. A full casualty loss deduction is permitted even though you choose not to restore the property to its prior value.

Value of Appraisal. As explained previously, if your home is damaged by a casualty, the amount deductible is the difference between the value of your home immediately before and immediately after the casualty (not to exceed your adjusted basis for the home), reduced by the amount of insurance, subject to the $100 floor and 10 percent of adjusted gross income limitation. Most homeowners take repair costs as the measure of the decrease in value. But the tax law says the decrease in value may be determined by appraisal, and this is the better approach if you want to maximize your casualty loss deduction while saving cash by minimizing repairs.

A court case based on values some years ago illustrates how an appraisal can boost the casualty loss deduction above repair costs that do not fully restore value. The principles of the case are equally applicable today.

The Hagertys' Fire. A fire severely damaged the Hagertys' $78,000 house. Immediately after the fire, Mr. Hagerty retained a contracting firm to inspect the house and determine the cost of repairs to restore it to its former condition. Based on the contracting firm's estimate of $53,000 to restore the house, it appeared to Mr. Hagerty that the value of the house immediately after the fire was $25,000 ($78,000 − $53,000 = $25,000), and that the decrease in value was $53,000. However, the Hagertys' house was insured, and the insurance company obtained a separate repair bid of $33,000. Mr. Hagerty accepted this bid, and the house was repaired for this amount. Since he believed the less expensive repairs did not restore the house to its former condition or value, Mr. Hagerty claimed a casualty loss deduction of $20,000 (value before fire, $78,000, less value after fire, $25,000, equals $53,000, less insurance recovery, $33,000, equals $20,000).

The IRS said the repairs fully restored the house to its prefire condition, so that the loss was fully compensated by insurance. The court disagreed and, based on the evidence of the decrease in value, allowed a $10,000 deduction. (Hagerty's $20,000 figure was rejected as too high.)

The higher repair estimate obtained by Mr. Hagerty served as the "appraisal" in this case. But you probably can do better with an actual professional appraisal. If a well-documented opinion of a real estate appraiser had been obtained, an even larger deduction probably would have been allowed.

Tax Tip

The Dog's Tail. **The tail shouldn't wag the dog. If lifestyle considerations and your pocketbook warrant full repair, forget about this tax-savings idea and do what you have to do.**

Full Repairs Done? Suppose you do a full repair job that you think restores your home to its former value. Maybe you should you get an appraisal anyway. It may be that the decrease in value of your home exceeded your cost of repairs. This might occur, for example, if prospective buyers would add an amount to the repair costs for the hassle they would have in arranging for and supervising repair work. It might not hurt just to talk with an appraiser to check it out.

Bottom Line. Your cash position or other factors may discourage full restoration of your damaged home. If you undertake only a partial restoration, you should consider claiming a casualty loss deduction equal to the full decrease in value, subject to the limitations discussed above. The best way to show the full decrease in value is to obtain a reliable appraisal of the value of your home before and after the casualty.

2.8 When Your Damage Is from a Presidentially Declared Disaster

California has been much in the news in recent years, having suffered a series of major natural disasters from fires, earthquakes, and storms. News reports of the Mississippi and other rivers running wild are commonplace. Every year, major natural disasters seem to strike somewhere.

If you live in an area hit by this type of catastrophe and the president declares it a disaster area, the IRS lightens up on the tax rules. Help comes in the form of generous special rules that apply to insurance proceeds you receive for damages to your residence and its contents that you otherwise would have to include in your income.

The Tax Break.   If you meet some easy requirements, you don't have to worry about property insurance proceeds being included in your income and being taxed. Insurance proceeds you receive for unscheduled personal property—that is, property such as clothing and furniture that is not listed on a schedule in your insurance policy—escapes tax altogether. In addition, insurance proceeds for damage to your home and your scheduled property—that is, property such as expensive jewelry that *is* listed on a schedule in your insurance policy—escapes tax if, as is usual, there is a qualifying replacement.

Here's how it works:

If your principal residence or any of its contents are destroyed and you get an insurance recovery, you don't pay tax on the insurance for lost unscheduled personal property. If you get insurance proceeds for scheduled property and the residence itself lumped together, that amount also is not subject to tax if you use it to acquire a new residence and contents.

The IRS has provided an illustration showing how insurance proceeds received on the destruction of a home and its contents may be reinvested so that you don't have to report any income. The example makes it clear that recognition of income can be entirely avoided in most cases.

> **Example**
>
> Smith's principal residence and its contents were completely destroyed in a presidentially declared disaster. The destroyed contents included furniture, appliances, clothing, and other household furnishings that were not separately listed on Smith's insurance policy. In addition, the destroyed contents included scheduled jewelry and silverware. Smith's cost or "basis" of the property for tax purposes was $250,000 for the residence, $5,000 for the jewelry, and $2,000 for the silverware.
>
> Later in the year, Smith received insurance proceeds as follows: $300,000 for the loss of the residence, $35,000 for the loss of the unscheduled household contents, $7,000 for the loss of the jewelry, and $3,000 for the loss of the silverware. In the following year, Smith spent $300,000 to construct a new residence on the site of the destroyed residence, $40,000 to purchase assorted home furnishings and clothing as replacements for those destroyed in the disaster, and $10,000 to purchase a painting to display in the new residence. Smith did not replace either the jewelry or the silverware.
>
> Under these facts, the insurance proceeds are treated as follows:
>
> *Unscheduled Property.* The $35,000 received for the destruction of unscheduled contents is not taxable, regardless of the use to which Smith puts the $35,000.
>
> *Dwelling and Scheduled Property.* The $310,000 received for the destruction of the house and its scheduled contents ($300,000 for the residence, $7,000 for the jewelry, and $3,000 for the silverware) is lumped together as a "common fund." Tax is avoided on this amount to the extent Smith spends an amount equal to this common fund to purchase a new principal residence and its contents. Smith spent $300,000 to replace the destroyed residence and $50,000 to furnish the new home ($40,000 for general furnishings and clothing, and $10,000 for the painting). Since Smith spent $350,000 to purchase a replacement dwelling and its contents, which is in excess of the $310,000 common fund received, he pays no tax on receipt of the insurance proceeds.

As the example illustrates, you don't have income from the receipt of insurance proceeds for unscheduled contents, regardless of the use to which the proceeds are put. Moreover, as to insurance proceeds for the destroyed residence and scheduled contents, you don't have income to the extent of reinvestment in any combination of replacement residence and contents of any type, whether scheduled or unscheduled.

Bottom Line. As illustrated in the example, insurance proceeds from the disaster may entirely escape tax.

2.9 How to Deduct Your Home Office Expenses

Deduct part of your household expenses?

It's possible, if you have a home office or otherwise conduct business from your home.

It's reported that millions of Americans have some sort of office in their homes. If you are one of this group and meet a fairly stiff set of eligibility requirements, you can take deductions for home ownership expenses attributable to maintenance of the office.

Yogi Berra is said to have made an observation that is relevant to understanding whether you are eligible for home office deductions. "If you don't know where you're going, when you get there you'll be lost." To avoid getting lost when you're trying to sift through all the rules to determine if you are eligible for home office deductions, you need a road map. The IRS has provided a road map in the form of the chart in Figure 2.1. We'll link our eligibility discussion to the qualification questions in the boxes on the chart.

First, we'll discuss the rules for employees, who generally will have difficulty in qualifying. (See Section 2.10.) Then we'll discuss individuals who have their own businesses, including employees who may have a sideline business. These individuals and employees usually either will be eligible for deductions for the business use of their homes or can do some tax planning to enable them to make arrangements that will permit them to become eligible. (See Section 2.11.) After the discussion of eligibility, we'll get into how you figure the amount of deductions for the business use of a home—usually as a home office. (See Section 2.12.)

2.10 Eligibility of Employees

If you're one of the many employees who lug office work home for catch up in the evening or over the weekend, you would be justified in expecting that you could deduct expenses for a home office. But employees have to meet tough eligibility standards. As indicated in the chart, in addition to the requirements discussed below for owners of their own businesses, employees must use their home office for the convenience of their employers. An employee will not be deemed to use a home office for the convenience of the employer if the employer supplies the employee with a suitable office and does not require or expect the employee to do any work at home. As a practical matter, most employees are supplied with suitable office space at work, so this eligibility requirement prevents them from deducting home office expenses.

SHELTERING YOUR INCOME WITH HOME DEDUCTIONS

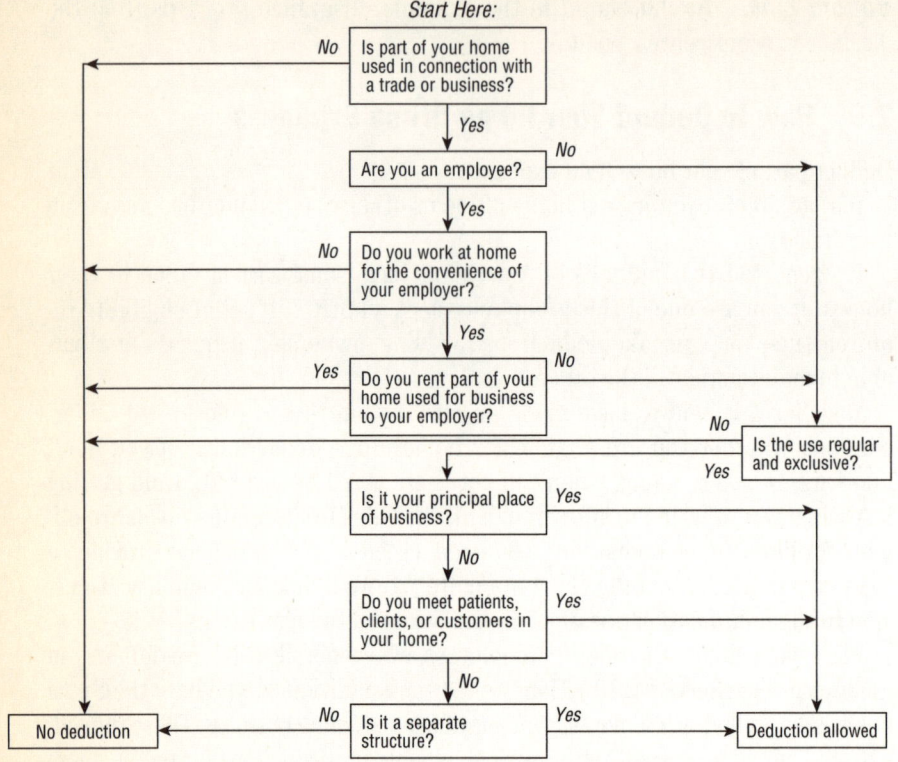

FIGURE 2.1 Can You Deduct Business Use of the Home Expenses?

Tax Tip

Sideline Business. If you have a business that you operate from home, you may be able to get home office deductions even though you have a regular job. (See Section 3.6.)

Tax Tip

If your employer doesn't provide you with suitable office space and requires you to do work at home, it would be helpful for you to obtain a written statement from your employer saying so, and that your home office is "for the convenience of the employer." Keep the written statement with your permanent records.

The Miscellaneous Deduction Floor. Adding insult to injury, the rules provide that even if an employee is eligible to deduct home office expenses, the amount deductible is more restricted than the deductions allowed to individuals with their own businesses. Specifically, home office deductions of employees are limited by the floor on miscellaneous itemized deductions that can be claimed on Schedule A of Form 1040. Unreimbursed employee expenses, including home office expenses, are part of miscellaneous itemized deductions that are deductible only to the extent they exceed 2 percent of adjusted gross income. Thus, disregarding any other miscellaneous itemized deductions, if adjusted gross income is $100,000, the employee's home office expenses are deductible only to the extent they exceed $2,000.

> **Observation**
>
> ***The Rental Limitation.*** A question in the chart directed to employees is, "Do you rent part of your home used for business to your employer?" This seemingly odd question is prompted by a provision in the law designed to discourage overly ingenious planning that would permit employees to circumvent the limitations on home office deductions by renting portions of their homes to their employers. Home office deductions are not allowed if the employee rents a portion of the employee's home to his or her employer and uses the rented portion in the performance of services for the employer.

If you are an employee and you pass the employee eligibility tests, further testing remains. You then must run the gauntlet of the eligibility tests imposed on individuals with their own businesses.

We discuss these requirements next.

2.11 Eligibility of Business Owners

Revisiting the IRS chart, you will see that regardless of whether you are an employee, a critical question is, "Is the use regular and exclusive?" This question is prompted by the so-called "exclusive use" test.

Exclusive Use Test. You can deduct expenses for the business use of your home only if the expenses are for a portion of your home that you use both *exclusively and on a regular basis* for a qualifying business purpose. There are three qualifying business purposes.

1. Use of your home as your principal place of business
2. Use of your home as a place of business used by patients, clients, or customers in meeting or dealing with you in the normal course of your business

3. If your property has a separate structure not attached to the house, such as an artist's studio, use in connection with your business

Mixed Use. You don't meet the exclusive use requirement where a portion of your home, such as a den, is used for both personal and business purposes. The portion of your home used for business must be used *exclusively* for business. On the other hand, it is not essential for the home office or other business area to be in a separate room or partitioned-off area, provided that the exclusive use requirement is met for specific space used. But when only part of a room is used for business, it normally will be difficult to show that business and personal use were not intermingled.

Tax Tip

If possible, you should set aside an entire room or rooms exclusively for business use. The IRS is inclined to be skeptical when it is claimed that part of a room is used exclusively for business purposes.

Trade or Business Requirement. The activity you carry on at home must be a "trade or business." Whether your activity amounts to a trade or business is a question of fact. Generally, you are carrying on a trade or business if you are attempting to make a profit from your activities and you carry out your activities in a sufficiently regular, systematic, and continuous manner. The busier you are, the better.

Examples

Ownership and management of real property for the production of income generally will qualify as a business if the ownership and management activities are sufficiently extensive. But full-time management of securities portfolios for your own account, whether or not providing your principal source of income, is not a trade or business.

Stretched Principal Place of Business Rule. As indicated above, exclusive use of part of your home as your "principal place of business" may entitle you to home office deductions. Your principal place of business is self-evident if your business is carried on exclusively from your home.

But what if it's not?

In many businesses the owner's activities are carried out at more than one location, raising the question of whether the home office is the *principal* place of business. In general, if there is more than one place of business, the principal place of business is the place of business with the greatest importance based on the functions performed and the time spent at the location.

But regardless of where the most important location is, a home office that is the *only* location where administrative or management activities are conducted may qualify as a principal place of business. (See Section 2.13.)

As indicated in the IRS chart, if you meet the exclusive use test you get to the prize box: "Deduction allowed." The next question is, "How much?"

Tax Tip

Off the Chart. The IRS chart and the discussion here does not deal with the special rules involved when you use your home for the storage of inventory or product samples or operate a day-care facility. For the rules in these special situations, see IRS Publication 587, "Business Use of Your Home (Including Use by Day-Care Providers"). See also Gary Carter, *J.K. Lasser's Taxes Made Easy for Your Home-Based Business.*

2.12 Figuring the Deduction

The simplest way to figure your home office deductions is to use the IRS form that walks you through the process. The process is designed to carve home business expenses out of total home expenses and involves three steps.

1. Determine the business percentage—the portion of your home used for business.
2. Determine the percentage of home maintenance expenses allocable to business use.
3. Determine the amount of depreciation allocable to the portion of your home used for business.

The form to be used is IRS Form 8829, which we'll go through, step by step. But before we discuss that form, it will be useful to show the relationship of Form 8829 to your Schedule C.

Tax Tip

Form 8829. You're required to figure deductible expenses for the business use of your home on Form 8829. Part I of the form is used to figure the amount of space in your home allocable to business use, Part II to figure the deductible portion of your expenses, Part III to figure your allowable depreciation, and Part IV to show the carryover to next year of disallowed expenses.

Starting with Schedule C. If you're using your home for business, you usually will be reporting your profit or loss from the business on Schedule C of your Form 1040. A sample filled in Schedule C appears in Figure 2.2. It shows the business income and deductions of John Stephens, who runs a tax preparation service out of his home as a sole proprietor.

Mr. Stephens has gross income from his business of $34,280, recorded on line 7. He has a collection of business expenses recorded on lines 8 through 27, totaling $8,728, recorded on line 28. When the business deductions are subtracted from the business income, his tentative profit recorded on line 29 is $25,552. The profit is a "tentative profit" because it is figured *before* his deduction for home office expenses. To determine his home office expenses, he is directed to Form 8829.

Don't be put off by the number of steps. As Mark Twain once observed about the music of Wagner, "It's not as bad as it sounds." The steps aren't as complicated as they first appear.

Filling in Form 8829. A sample, filled in Form 8829 appears in Figure 2.3 and is based on the facts of the following example. The first step in using Form 8829 is to figure the business percentage using Part I of the form, which determines the percentage of the home used for business.

> **Example**
>
> John Stephens operates a tax preparation service out of his 2,000-square-foot home as a sole proprietor, using a single 200-square-foot room for his work. Thus, the percentage of his home used for business purposes is 10 percent, which amount is recorded on line 7 of Form 8829. This is his business percentage. (Lines 4 through 6, applicable to day-care facilities not used exclusively for business, are left blank.)

> **Caution**
>
> Err on the side of conservatism in your estimate of your business percentage. It's not smart to create a blip on the IRS radar screen.

After entering the business percentage, the tentative profit from the business from Schedule C, $25,552, is entered on line 8.

The second step is to determine the amount of deductible expenses. To make this determination, it is necessary to segregate personal from business expenses.

RECURRING DEDUCTIONS EVERY YEAR YOU OWN YOUR HOME

SCHEDULE C (Form 1040)
Department of the Treasury
Internal Revenue Service (99)

Profit or Loss From Business
(Sole Proprietorship)
▶ Partnerships, joint ventures, etc., must file Form 1065 or 1065-B.
▶ Attach to Form 1040 or 1041. ▶ See Instructions for Schedule C (Form 1040).

OMB No. 1545-0074
2003
Attachment Sequence No. **09**

Name of proprietor: John Stephens
Social security number (SSN): 465 00 0001

A Principal business or profession, including product or service (see page C-1 of the instructions)
Tax Preparation Services
B Enter code from pages C-7, 8, & 9 ▶ 5|4|1|2|1|3

C Business name. If no separate business name, leave blank.
Stephens Tax Service
D Employer ID number (EIN), if any

E Business address (including suite or room no.) ▶ 821 Union Street
City, town or post office, state, and ZIP code   Hometown, IA 52761

F Accounting method: (1) ☒ Cash (2) ☐ Accrual (3) ☐ Other (specify) ▶
G Did you "materially participate" in the operation of this business during 2003? If "No," see page C-3 for limit on losses . ☒ Yes ☐ No
H If you started or acquired this business during 2003, check here . . . . ▶ ☐

Part I Income

1	Gross receipts or sales. **Caution.** If this income was reported to you on Form W-2 and the "Statutory employee" box on that form was checked, see page C-3 and check here ▶ ☐	1	34,280
2	Returns and allowances	2	– 0 –
3	Subtract line 2 from line 1	3	34,280
4	Cost of goods sold (from line 42 on page 2)	4	– 0 –
5	**Gross profit.** Subtract line 4 from line 3	5	34,280
6	Other income, including Federal and state gasoline or fuel tax credit or refund (see page C-3)	6	– 0 –
7	**Gross income.** Add lines 5 and 6 ▶	7	34,280

Part II Expenses. Enter expenses for business use of your home **only** on line 30.

8	Advertising	8	250	19	Pension and profit-sharing plans	19	
9	Car and truck expenses (see page C-3)	9		20	Rent or lease (see page C-5):		
				a	Vehicles, machinery, and equipment	20a	
10	Commissions and fees	10	1,266	b	Other business property	20b	
11	Contract labor (see page C-4)	11		21	Repairs and maintenance	21	
				22	Supplies (not included in Part III)	22	253
12	Depletion	12		23	Taxes and licenses	23	
13	Depreciation and section 179 expense deduction (not included in Part III) (see page C-4)	13	3,879	24	Travel, meals and entertainment:		
				a	Travel	24a	310
14	Employee benefit programs (other than on line 19)	14		b	Meals and entertainment 512		
15	Insurance (other than health)	15	750	c	Enter nondeductible amount included on line 24b (see page C-5) 256		
16	Interest:						
a	Mortgage (paid to banks, etc.)	16a		d	Subtract line 24c from line 24b	24d	256
b	Other	16b	200	25	Utilities	25	347
17	Legal and professional services	17	350	26	Wages (less employment credits)	26	
				27	Other expenses (from line 48 on page 2)	27	267
18	Office expense	18	600				
28	**Total expenses** before expenses for business use of home. Add lines 8 through 27 in columns ▶					28	8,728
29	Tentative profit (loss). Subtract line 28 from line 7					29	25,552
30	Expenses for business use of your home. Attach **Form 8829**					30	1,481
31	**Net profit or (loss).** Subtract line 30 from line 29.						
	• If a profit, enter on **Form 1040, line 12,** and **also** on **Schedule SE, line 2** (statutory employees, see page C-6). Estates and trusts, enter on Form 1041, line 3.					31	24,071
	• If a loss, you **must** go to line 32.						
32	If you have a loss, check the box that describes your investment in this activity (see page C-6).						
	• If you checked 32a, enter the loss on **Form 1040, line 12,** and **also** on **Schedule SE, line 2** (statutory employees, see page C-6). Estates and trusts, enter on Form 1041, line 3.					32a ☐ All investment is at risk. 32b ☐ Some investment is not at risk.	
	• If you checked 32b, you **must** attach **Form 6198.**						

For Paperwork Reduction Act Notice, see Form 1040 instructions.   Cat. No. 11334P   Schedule C (Form 1040) 2003

FIGURE 2.2 Schedule C: Profit or Loss from Business

40 SHELTERING YOUR INCOME WITH HOME DEDUCTIONS

Form 8829 — Expenses for Business Use of Your Home
OMB No. 1545-1266

▶ File only with Schedule C (Form 1040). Use a separate Form 8829 for each home you used for business during the year.
▶ See separate instructions.

Department of the Treasury
Internal Revenue Service (99)

2003
Attachment Sequence No. **66**

Name(s) of proprietor(s): John Stephens
Your social security number: 465 00 0001

Part I — Part of Your Home Used for Business

#	Description		Value
1	Area used regularly and exclusively for business, regularly for day care, or for storage of inventory or product samples (see instructions)	1	200
2	Total area of home	2	2,000
3	Divide line 1 by line 2. Enter the result as a percentage	3	10 %

- For day-care facilities not used exclusively for business, also complete lines 4–6.
- All others, skip lines 4–6 and enter the amount from line 3 on line 7.

#	Description		Value
4	Multiply days used for day care during year by hours used per day	4	hr.
5	Total hours available for use during the year (365 days × 24 hours) (see instructions)	5	8,760 hr.
6	Divide line 4 by line 5. Enter the result as a decimal amount	6	
7	Business percentage. For day-care facilities not used exclusively for business, multiply line 6 by line 3 (enter the result as a percentage). All others, enter the amount from line 3 ▶	7	10 %

Part II — Figure Your Allowable Deduction

#	Description	(a) Direct expenses	(b) Indirect expenses		Total
8	Enter the amount from Schedule C, line 29, **plus** any net gain or (loss) derived from the business use of your home and shown on Schedule D or Form 4797. If more than one place of business, see instructions			8	25,552
	See instructions for columns (a) and (b) before completing lines 9–20.				
9	Casualty losses (see instructions)				
10	Deductible mortgage interest (see instructions)		4,500		
11	Real estate taxes (see instructions)		1,000		
12	Add lines 9, 10, and 11		5,500		
13	Multiply line 12, column (b) by line 7		550		
14	Add line 12, column (a) and line 13			14	550
15	Subtract line 14 from line 8. If zero or less, enter -0-			15	25,002
16	Excess mortgage interest (see instructions)				
17	Insurance				
18	Repairs and maintenance	300	400		
19	Utilities		1,400		
20	Other expenses (see instructions)		1,800		
21	Add lines 16 through 20	300	3,600		
22	Multiply line 21, column (b) by line 7		360		
23	Carryover of operating expenses from 2002 Form 8829, line 41	−0−			
24	Add line 21 in column (a), line 22, and line 23			24	660
25	Allowable operating expenses. Enter the **smaller** of line 15 or line 24			25	660
26	Limit on excess casualty losses and depreciation. Subtract line 25 from line 15			26	24,342
27	Excess casualty losses (see instructions)				
28	Depreciation of your home from Part III below		271		
29	Carryover of excess casualty losses and depreciation from 2002 Form 8829, line 42				
30	Add lines 27 through 29			30	271
31	Allowable excess casualty losses and depreciation. Enter the **smaller** of line 26 or line 30			31	271
32	Add lines 25 and 31			32	1,481
33	Casualty loss portion, if any, from lines 14 and 31. Carry amount to **Form 4684**, Section B			33	
34	Allowable expenses for business use of your home. Subtract line 33 from line 32. Enter here and on Schedule C, line 30. If your home was used for more than one business, see instructions ▶			34	1,481

Part III — Depreciation of Your Home

#	Description		Value
35	Enter the **smaller** of your home's adjusted basis or its fair market value (see instructions)	35	130,000
36	Value of land included on line 35	36	20,000
37	Basis of building. Subtract line 36 from line 35	37	110,000
38	Business basis of building. Multiply line 37 by line 7	38	11,000
39	Depreciation percentage (see instructions)	39	2.461 %
40	Depreciation allowable (see instructions). Multiply line 38 by line 39. Enter here and on line 28 above	40	271

Part IV — Carryover of Unallowed Expenses to 2004

41	Operating expenses. Subtract line 25 from line 24. If less than zero, enter -0-	41	
42	Excess casualty losses and depreciation. Subtract line 31 from line 30. If less than zero, enter -0-	42	

For Paperwork Reduction Act Notice, see page 4 of separate instructions.   Cat. No. 13232M   Form **8829** (2003)

FIGURE 2.3   Form 8829: Expenses for Business Use of Your Home

Personal vs. Business Expenses. Some of your home maintenance expenses are directly related to the business use of your home, some are indirectly related, and some are completely unrelated. You generally can deduct all your directly related expenses and a portion of your indirectly related expenses, but none of the unrelated expenses. The unrelated expenses are those expenses that concern only the part of your home you do not use for business, such as repairs of personal areas.

Direct expenses are those expenses that relate only to the business part of your home. They include painting, repairs, and other maintenance for the room or rooms used for business. Indirect expenses are those expenses that relate to the overall upkeep and running of your entire home and that benefit both the business and personal parts of your home. Examples of indirect expenses include:

- Utilities, including electricity and trash removal
- Insurance
- Security systems
- Repairs to heating, plumbing, and air-conditioning systems
- Real estate taxes
- Home mortgage interest
- Depreciation

You generally can deduct the "business percentage" of your indirect expenses.

Casualty Losses. Casualty losses, discussed in Section 2.6, are treated as a direct, indirect, or unrelated expense, depending on where they hit. If the loss affects only the portion of your property that you use for business, the entire loss is used to figure your business use deduction. If the loss is on property you use for both business and personal purposes, such as a furnace, only the business percentage is used to figure your business deduction. If the loss is on property you do not use in your business, such as landscaping, none of the loss is deductible as a business expense, though it may be deductible as a casualty loss, as explained in Section 2.6.

Observation

The Telephone. The IRS is a tightwad when it comes to the phone. Your basic local telephone service charge for the first telephone line into your home is completely nondeductible. However, charges for business long-distance calls on that line, as well as the cost of a second line into your home used exclusively for business, are deductible as business expenses.

Example

Assume Mr. Stephens has repairs costing $300 made to the room he uses for business. He can deduct this business expense in full because it is not a general home maintenance expense. Assume also that he has the following general home maintenance expenses for the year that have to be allocated between business and personal use.

Home mortgage interest	$4,500
Real estate taxes	1,000
Insurance	400
Repairs and maintenance	1,400
Utilities	1,800

Observation

The mechanics of the computation process on Form 8829 prevent you from using your household expenses to create a tax loss, as explained later.

First, Mr. Stephens determines the amount of mortgage interest and taxes that he can deduct as business expenses. The interest and taxes aggregate $5,500 ($4,500 + $1,000). Multiplying this amount, $5,500, by the business percentage, 10 percent, produces the interest and taxes that are deductible as business expenses, $550, which is entered on line 14. The balance of interest and taxes is deducted by Mr. Stephens as a personal expense on Schedule A of his Form 1040.

Next, Mr. Stephens determines the amount of insurance, $400, repairs and maintenance, $1,400, and utilities, $1,800, totaling $3,600, allocable to the business use of his home. Multiplying the total of $3,600 by the business percentage, 10 percent, produces the home maintenance expenses that are deductible as business expenses, $360. This amount of deductible indirect home expenses, $360, is added to the wholly deductible direct business expenses for

Observation

A Parallel Universe: Renting Vacation Home. The procedure for figuring the amount of deductions for the business use of your home closely parallels the procedure for figuring the amount of deductions when you rent out a vacation home for 15 or more days during the year and also use it for personal purposes. (See Section 8.4.)

repair to the room used for business, $300, providing a total of $660 deductible expenses, entered on line 24.

The third and final step is to determine the amount of depreciation allocable to the portion of the home used for business. To make this determination, you first have to determine the amount of the basis of your home allocable to the business use of your home.

Figuring the Basis for Depreciation Deduction. To figure your depreciation deduction, you multiply the portion of the basis for your home allocable to business use by a depreciation percentage. Before you can do this, you have to determine the basis for your entire home, and multiply this by the business percentage. So the starting point for figuring depreciation for the business use of your home is the basis for depreciation for your entire home, its so-called *adjusted basis*.

The adjusted basis for your home generally is the cost of your home plus the cost of permanent improvements, minus the part of your cost attributable to land and any casualty losses and depreciation you deducted in prior years. If you start using a home office as soon as you purchase your home, before you have any improvements or casualty loss or depreciation deductions, your adjusted basis for the entire home will be your cost for the home, less the part of your cost attributable to land. If you start using a home office at a later date, the adjusted basis for depreciation is figured differently. When you switch part of your home from personal to business use, your basis for depreciation is the lesser of the following:

- The adjusted basis of your home on the date of the change, excluding the part of your cost attributable to land
- The fair market value of your home on the date of the change, excluding the part of value attributable to land

These figures are reflected in lines 35 through 38 of Form 8829.

The only remaining step for figuring the amount of depreciation is to multiply the portion of basis allocable to business use by the depreciation percentage. The depreciation percentage is found on page 3 of the Instructions for Form 8829, reproduced in Appendix A. The percentage, assuming use of the office commenced in January of the year, is 2.461 percent. The portion of total basis allocable to business use, $11,000, is multiplied by 2.461 percent, producing a depreciation deduction of $270.71, which, when rounded off, provides a depreciation deduction of $271. This depreciation deduction is entered on line 40 of Form 8829 and added to the previous deductions of $550 and $660, pro-

Example

Mr. Stephens purchased his property for $110,000, $20,000 of which was attributable to the value of the land. He subsequently made improvements to the house costing $20,000, so that his adjusted basis for the entire property is $130,000 ($110,000 + $20,000). On the date he started his business in his home, the entire property had a fair market value of $165,000, $20,000 of which was attributable to the land. Mr. Stephens's basis for figuring depreciation is $11,000, figured as follows:

Original basis (purchase price)	$110,000
Improvements	+20,000
Adjusted basis of entire property	$130,000
Basis allocable to land	−20,000
Adjusted basis of house	$110,000
Fair market value of entire property	$165,000
Portion of fair market value allocable to land	−20,000
Fair market value of house	$145,000
Lesser of adjusted basis of house or fair market value of house	$110,000
Business percentage	×.10
Basis of house allocable to business use	$ 11,000

Caution

While the cost of permanent improvements increases the tax basis of your home, the cost of repairs does not. Determining whether an expenditure is for a permanent improvement or a repair is not always a slam dunk. In general, a permanent improvement materially adds to the value of your home or considerably prolongs its useful life. Capital improvements would include adding a recreation or other room, replacing plumbing, heating, or air-conditioning systems, installing a new roof, or paving a driveway. Repairs in contrast, merely keep your home in ordinary operating condition. Repairs would include repainting the outside or inside of your home and fixing gutters, a roof leak, a damaged floor, or broken windows.

Tax Tip

The cost of repairs that you make as part of a planned extensive renovation or remodeling of your home, taken together, can qualify as the cost of an improvement that you can add to the tax basis of your home.

ducing total home office deductions of $1,481. This total is carried to line 30 of Schedule C, where it is subtracted from the tentative profit of $25,552, leaving a final profit for Mr. Stephens of $24,071.

There's one more twist to figuring home business deductions.

> **Tax Tip**
>
> Will Rogers quipped, "The income tax has made more liars out of the American people than golf has." Don't be tempted to join this dubious group by exaggerating the space used in your home or other deductions for the business use of your home. As with any improper deduction, penalties could apply.

Ceiling on Business Expense Deductions and Carryover. To prevent the deduction of expenses for the business use of a home from creating a tax loss, a ceiling is placed on the deduction of such expenses. The steps for figuring the ceiling are exasperatingly complicated, but condensed to fit in a nutshell the limitation boils down to this: Deductions for the business portion of insurance, repairs, maintenance, utilities, and depreciation cannot exceed net business income, *after* reduction of net business income by the allocable share of mortgage interest, real estate taxes, and any casualty loss. The mechanics of the instructions on the face Form 8829 automatically implement this rule by preventing the allowable deductions from exceeding business income.

> **Example**
>
> Suppose in the preceding example that John Stephens was a freelance photographer who had a bad year, having failed to earn any income, but he met all the requirements for the deduction of $1,481 of expenses for the business use of a portion of his home. Since he has zero net income, he can deduct no expenses for the business use of his home. Form 8829 automatically implements this rule because the entry on line 15 will be zero, making the deductible amount on line 25 (allowable operating expenses) and line 26 (limit on depreciation) also zero. (Home mortgage interest and real estate taxes aggregating $550 remain fully deductible.)

But all is not lost if you have a bad year. If otherwise allowable expenses and depreciation do exceed net income so as to be disallowed, as in the example, such deductions may be carried over to the following year. In the following year they will be deductible as expenses for the business use of your home, subject again to the net income limitation. The amount carried over is recorded in Part IV of Form 8829.

So much for how you figure the amount of home office deductions. We now turn to the question of whether you can claim home office deductions when you have a home office but work outside your home.

2.13 If You Work outside Your Home: How to Get Home Office Deductions

If you do essentially all your work in your home, then your home meets the "principal place of business" requirement for the deduction of home business costs, discussed above. For example, if you operate a mail-order business from home or are a freelance writer, your home should easily qualify as your principal place of business.

But suppose you run the administrative part of your business from your home and do your most important work outside your home. You could be in this situation, for example, if you operated from your home as a plumber or were in the home improvement business. In these situations, is your "principal place of business" your home or the location where you perform your work?

Grinch Rules. It used to be that you couldn't get business deductions for your home if you worked out of a home office but the most important part of your work was performed at another location. This was because your home office had to be your "principal" place of business and your principal place of business was where you performed the "essence" of your work. For example, home office deductions were denied to an anesthesiologist who worked from his home because the "essence" of his work was performed at hospitals.

This test unfairly denied home office deductions to homeowners who managed their businesses from their homes but had to perform their most important work outside. The rules were changed so that now, regardless of where the most important part of your work may be performed, a home office used to conduct administrative or management activities may qualify as a principal place of business. This liberalized rule affords home office deductions to many homeowners who formerly were disqualified.

Liberalized Rules. The liberalized rules provide that a "principal place of business" includes a place of business that you use for administrative or management activities of your business if you have no other fixed location of the business where you conduct substantial administrative or management activities. The other requirements discussed above continue to apply, such as the requirement that the office be used exclusively and on a regular basis as a place of business and, in the case of an employee, the exclusive use must be for the convenience of the employer.

If you use your home only for administrative or management activities, you must meet a two-part test:

1. You must perform administrative or management services in your home office.
2. You must not have another fixed location of your business where you conduct substantial administrative or management activities of your business.

Is there another location where you conduct substantial administrative or management activities? It may be okay. The IRS says you can disregard the following:

- Administrative or management work at sites that are not fixed locations of your business, such as your car or a hotel room
- Administrative or management work at a fixed location other than your home office if such activities are not substantial, such as occasional minimal paperwork at another fixed location of your business
- Substantial nonadministrative or nonmanagement business activities at a fixed location of your business outside your home, such as meeting with or providing services to customers, clients, or patients at a fixed location of your business away from home
- Administrative or management activities elsewhere by others, such as billings

Bottom Line. Based on the liberalized rules, you should have no problem qualifying your home as your principal place of business if you work outside your home, as long as you perform substantial administrative or management work for the business in your home.

We now turn to another possible tax advantage of having a home office: It may make commuting expenses deductible.

2.14 How Home Office Makes Commuting Costs Deductible

Commuting costs are usually nondeductible. For example, if you live in the suburbs and drive or take the bus or train to your job in the city, no deduction is allowed for your transportation costs. This is because these commuting costs are considered nondeductible "personal expenses."

Tax Break. Homeowners who have a qualifying home office may be the beneficiaries of a little-known tax break. Their transportation costs to visit clients or customers and other work-related trips may be fully deductible.

The general rule is that the costs of commuting from your home to your place of business or employment are nondeductible. The regulations are explicit. "The taxpayer's costs of commuting to his place of business or employment are personal expenses and do not qualify as deductible expenses." On the other hand, the IRS has ruled that the costs of going from one business location to another business location generally are deductible as business expenses.

Now suppose your business is run from your home and you drive from home to a customer's store on business. Is the trip a commute between your home and a business location or a business trip between one business location and another? The answer is obvious: It's both. The real question is whether the IRS will permit the deduction of transportation costs despite this duality.

Court Case. The issue was presented in a significant court case in which the taxpayer incurred daily transportation expenses in traveling between an office in the taxpayer's residence and other work locations. The travel was in connection with the taxpayer's rental real estate management business. The court held the transportation expenses to be deductible because the home office was the taxpayer's principal place of business for the business conducted by the taxpayer at the other work locations. The court put it plainly:

> We see no reason why the rule that local transportation expenses incurred in travel between one business location and another are deductible should not be equally applicable where the taxpayer's principal place of business with respect to the activities involved is his residence.

The IRS Position. The IRS has essentially adopted this position. Its view is that "great weight" must be given to the inherently personal character of a taxpayer's residence and trips to and from that residence in determining whether daily transportation expenses incurred in going to and from a place of business located in a taxpayer's home are more properly treated as nondeductible personal commuting expenses on the one hand, or deductible business expenses on the other. Nevertheless, if the office in the taxpayer's residence satisfies the principal place of business requirement for the deduction of home office expenses, then the business activity there is so central to the taxpayer's business as to overcome the inherently personal nature of the residence. Thus, if an office in the taxpayer's residence satisfies the principal place of business test discussed above, "commuting" expenses become deductible.

Your Deductions. If your home office meets the principal place of business test, you may deduct daily transportation expenses incurred in going between your residence and another work location in the same trade or business, regardless of whether the other work location is regular or temporary and regardless of the distance.

Expanded Benefit from Liberalized Home Office Rules. As discussed previously, Congress liberalized the home office rules by expanding the definition of "principal place of business." This expansion greatly increases the number of taxpayers who will be eligible to deduct "commuting" expenses. Now a principal place of business includes a place of business used by you for administrative or management activities of any trade or business you operate if there is no other fixed location for your business where you conduct substantial administrative or management activities for the business. Thus, whether you are a physician traveling to hospitals, a contractor, or other tradesperson traveling to job sites or a salesperson traveling to customers' offices, as long as you manage your business exclusively from your home, transportation costs to such work sites can be deductible.

Observation

Bottom Line. For many individuals who work out of their homes, the liberalized "principal place of business" rules will, in effect, allow the deduction of commuting expenses. For a discussion of the deduction of automobile expenses, see *J.K. Lasser's Your Income Tax 2004*, Chapter 43.

There's still more good tax news for homeowners who have an office at home: They can get a full deduction for the cost of their office equipment. We discuss this next.

2.15 Deduct Your Home Office Equipment Cost—Up Front

The purchase of equipment for your home office can provide you with a tax subsidy. It's like getting an extra discount on the purchase.

If you're buying new equipment for your home office, you may be able to write off the *entire cost* of the equipment in the year you buy it. No gradual, stretched-out, yearly depreciation—just a 100 percent deduction for its cost, up front.

The versatility and productivity afforded by home office equipment is going up just as its price is coming down. This tax subsidy makes it even better.

Here's the story:

To eliminate the nuisance of keeping records of depreciation for equipment of relatively low cost, you can elect to deduct the entire cost of such equipment in the year you buy it. The ceiling on the amount you can deduct is currently $100,000. The types of equipment that you can elect to expense include computers, printers, photocopiers, and office furniture and furnishings. It doesn't include either air-conditioning or heating units. The equipment has to be used in the active conduct of your trade or business.

The election to expense must be made in the original income tax return for the year the property is placed in service. A statement on the return must specify the items to which the election applies and the portion of the cost to be deducted currently. For home office equipment, the portion typically will be 100 percent.

There's a phase-out of the deduction when large amounts of equipment are purchased, but it won't affect home offices except maybe in mansions and palaces. Also, while the amount you can deduct can't exceed the amount of your taxable income from your business for the taxable year, you can carry over any unused amount to next year.

What Is It Worth? It's been estimated that up to half of American households have home offices. It's also estimated that equipment for outfitting new home offices costs between $3,000 and $5,000, and that about $1,000 is spent annually on upgrades for home office equipment. Obviously, then, over a period of years, deductions for home office equipment can save homeowners thousands of dollars in taxes.

CHAPTER 3

Special-Situation Deductions for Homeowners

> Sign in store window: "Tax Returns Prepared—Honest Mistakes Are Our Specialty."

3.1 Overview

In Chapter 2 we covered the bread-and-butter deductions for homeowners—real estate taxes, interest, casualty losses, and the home office deduction. These routine deductions can provide you with welcome relief at tax time. There is genuine delight in entering these deductions on your Form 1040 and watching your tax bill shrink.

But there may be other tax shelter opportunities in your home beyond these deductions. For example, you can pocket tax-free income from a short-term rental of your home or get medical expense deductions for improvements you make to your home on doctor's orders. These and other, more unusual homeowners' tax breaks are discussed in this chapter.

3.2 How to Get Tax-Free Income from Short-Term Rental

Rent is always taxable income. Right?

Not quite. While everybody else pays tax on all the rent they receive, there's a special break for homeowners who rent their homes for short periods. Congress created this break to prevent occasional short-term rentals by homeowners from becoming subject to a complicated set of deduction-limiting rules. These rules, discussed in Section 8.4, become applicable when a home is used extensively for both personal and rental purposes.

SHELTERING YOUR INCOME WITH HOME DEDUCTIONS

The Tax Break. If you rent your home for less than 15 days during the taxable year, the rental income you receive is *not subject to tax*. This special break does not prevent the deduction of your regular homeowner deductions, including real estate taxes and home mortgage interest. It's like temporarily turning your home into a tax-free municipal bond.

Practical Use for You. This homeowner's break can help any homeowner, but it's especially useful if you live where housing is in strong demand for short periods, such as south Florida or near a ski resort in Vermont or Colorado. In these areas the two-week period from just before Christmas to New Year's is a prime time for the rental of your property—possibly at rates of $2,500 to $3,500 a week. You can rent your home for less than 15 days during the year, taking advantage of temporary high rents, yet entirely avoid tax on the rental income. This type of opportunity also arises in special-event locations, such as Indianapolis for the Memorial Day races, Louisville during Derby Week, and New Orleans during Mardi Gras, and when cities like Atlanta or Los Angles host the Olympics.

Tax Watch

Break Survives Attack. Tax reformers hate this tax break and have tried to kill it. But legislators from states with big resort area constituencies linked up with the National Association of Realtors to beat back the attack. Other supporters of the break are congressional representatives from localities hosting mega-events, such as the big furniture shows in North Carolina, where short-term rentals of homes to event attendees can put windfall-like dollars in local homeowners' pockets.

While you don't have to report your rental income from the short-term rental, there is a restriction: You can't deduct any rental expenses. For example, if you have expenses for advertising your Florida condo or pay extra cleanup expenses after your guests depart, these expenses are not deductible.

Second Homes. This break also applies to second homes, such as a cabin retreat in the mountains or a condo in Manhattan.

3.3 How to Make Your Credit Card and Car Loan Interest Deductible

"I have to get out from under my monthly credit card payments. They're eating me alive."

Sound familiar?

If you are paying heavy interest charges on credit card, car loan, and other consumer credit, a home equity loan can be a financial lifeline. Home equity loans carry interest rates far below most consumer loans, especially credit card debt that can run 18 percent a year or higher. With the proceeds of a home equity loan, you can pay off all your consumer and credit card debt, substantially lowering your monthly payments on the consolidated debt as a result of lower interest charges.

The Tax Break. In addition to lower interest rates, home equity loans can provide a valuable tax break. Interest on credit card and other consumer debt is "personal" interest that is not deductible. But when you consolidate these loans into a home equity loan, the interest you pay is transformed into deductible home mortgage interest. This means that in addition to reducing your monthly payment burden, the home equity loan reduces the real *after-tax* cost of your borrowing because your interest on the home equity loan becomes a tax deduction. For example, if your home equity loan carries interest at 8.5 percent, the value of the tax deduction for interest may make your real, *after-tax* cost just over 5.5 percent.

With a home equity loan, the roof over your head can take the financial weight off your shoulders.

What Is a Home Equity Loan? A home equity loan is simply a loan keyed to the equity in your home. The equity in your home is the value of your home less the balance of the mortgage you used to purchase the home and any other debt secured by the home, such as a tax lien, judgment lien, or second mortgage. Lenders generally set the credit limit on a home equity loan by taking a percentage, say 75 percent, of the appraised value of the home, reduced by the balance owed on the mortgage. For example, if your home is worth $100,000 and the balance of the mortgage on your home is $45,000, you might be able to get a $30,000 home equity mortgage, figured as follows:

Appraised value of home	$100,000
Credit limit percentage	× 75%
Adjusted appraised value	$ 75,000
Less mortgage debt	45,000
Potential home equity loan	$ 30,000

Two Kinds of Equity Loans. There are basically two kinds of home equity loans: a home equity line of credit and a second mortgage. A home equity line of credit is a form of revolving credit (like a credit card) secured by your home, with a set maximum credit limit. You can usually borrow any amount up to your limit, any time the home equity loan is in effect, such as five years. These plans typically involve interest rates that change from time to time, so-called "variable" interest rates, rather than fixed interest rates that stay the same over the entire duration of the loan. Terms for repayment and other features, such as the minimum amount that you can borrow, vary from plan to plan.

A traditional second mortgage loan also is a loan secured by your home, but provides you with a fixed sum immediately, repayable over a fixed period, usually in equal monthly installments. You usually would consider using a second mortgage if you need a specific sum immediately for a specific purpose, such as making an addition to your home. For example, you might use a second mortgage to obtain funds to build a lap pool required for medical reasons for which you could get a medical deduction, as explained later in this chapter. You can use either a home equity line or a second mortgage to consolidate your debts.

Check the Loan Costs. Costs for either type of loan can vary substantially from lender to lender. You need to be a Black Belt shopper to get the best deal. Be sure that the fees and other costs of the home equity loan are reasonable. You want to make sure you are in a *much* better financial position after the loan consolidation than before.

> **Observation**
>
> **It's important not to run up substantial credit card debt after the consolidation if you want a permanent improvement in your financial position.**

There's an important financial feature of home equity loans you should consider. Debt on your home is different than unsecured consumer debt, such as credit card debt. While unsecured creditors can make life unpleasant for you, they can't take your home without a lot of hassle. They would have to sue you in court to get a judgment against you, record a lien on your home, then get the judgment lien enforced by selling the home. This is an expensive and time-consuming procedure that unsecured creditors rarely undertake. A home equity lender, however, *can* take your home if you fall behind in payments simply by foreclosing on the home equity mortgage. Be sure you can make the loan payments before you consider home equity financing. If your employment history is

SPECIAL-SITUATION DEDUCTIONS FOR HOMEOWNERS 55

shaky or you anticipate incurring other heavy expenses soon, *don't* put your home at risk by turning your credit card debt into a home equity loan.

How to Make Your Interest Deductible. It's important that you qualify to get tax deductions for the interest you pay on your home equity loan. To do so, the loan has to be "home equity indebtedness." This is a mortgage that meets two requirements.

1. The home equity loan must be secured by a mortgage on either your principal residence or a second home you select for purposes of getting the interest deduction. As explained in Section 4.7, your "principal residence" generally is where you live on a full-time basis. Your second home generally qualifies if you use it for vacation or other personal purposes for a number of days during the year that exceeds the greater of 14 days or 10 percent of the number of days the residence is rented out at a fair rental.

2. The total amount that may qualify as home equity indebtedness, on a principal residence and second home combined, cannot exceed $100,000, or $50,000 in the case of a married individual filing a separate return.

Ceiling Rule. There's a ceiling rule on home equity indebtedness you should look out for if you are obtaining a so-called "high-loan-to-value" loan. Qualifying home equity indebtedness can't exceed the difference between the present balance on the mortgage you obtained when you acquired your home and the present fair market value of your home. This rule can clip your deduction if you borrow too heavily against your home.

An example will show how the ceiling rule works.

Example

You purchased your home for $200,000, paying $50,000 in cash and using a $150,000 mortgage to finance the balance. If you obtain a home equity loan of $30,000 while the value of your home remains $200,000, you have not exceeded the permissible ceiling.

Original mortgage	$150,000
Home equity loan	30,000
Total mortgage debt	180,000
Permissible ceiling	200,000
Excess (total mortgage debt over ceiling)	-0-

Now suppose, instead, that you obtain a $60,000 home equity loan. You then will have exceeded the ceiling by $10,000.

Original mortgage	$150,000
Home equity loan	60,000
Total mortgage debt	210,000
Permissible ceiling	200,000
Excess (total mortgage debt over ceiling)	10,000

Because the total mortgage debt exceeds the permissible ceiling by $10,000, interest on the $10,000 portion of the loan is not deductible.

The Bottom Line. Often, there's more than one route for implementing a transaction. While the pretax results may be substantially the same regardless of which route is chosen, the after-tax results can be strikingly different if the tax-saving route is taken. Taking the tax-saving route by capitalizing on the tax

Caution

There are unscrupulous home equity lenders out there who push serial refinancings to the point where home equity is wiped out. The elderly are particularly vulnerable to these predators because they often have substantial equity in their homes but live on fixed incomes.

There are three practices by these lenders that alone or in combination with each other can be particularly harmful.

1. *Equity Stripping.* The lender makes a loan to the borrower based on the amount of equity the borrower has in the home, not on the borrower's ability to repay. When a lender makes a loan to a borrower and the lender knows the borrower does not have the ability to repay, the loan is designed to go into default so that the lender can foreclose on the borrower's home.

2. *Packing.* This is the practice of selling credit insurance and other products and services to the borrower together with the loan. The cost of these extras may be wrapped into the loan package and not adequately disclosed.

3. *Flipping.* After the borrower has taken the initial home equity loan, the lender attempts to get the borrower to refinance at regular intervals, providing the lender with the opportunity to charge more points and fees.

Regulators and consumer groups are well aware of these abusive lender practices but have limited means to stop them.

benefits of home ownership through use of a home equity mortgage to borrow funds instead of using credit card borrowing and auto loans is a prime example of taking the smart tax-planning route. And it's yet another example of why your home is a tax shelter.

3.4 How to Deduct Cost of Medical Home Improvements

You usually can't deduct any part of the cost of improvements to your home. These are so-called nondeductible "personal expenses."

But what about medically mandated home improvements?

The Tax Break. An expenditure that qualifies as a medical expense doesn't become nondeductible just because it improves your home. Such expenditures may qualify as deductible medical expenses if their primary purpose is medical care. If an expenditure for the permanent improvement of your home directly relates to medical care, it can qualify as a medical expense deduction to the extent it exceeds the increase in value of your home resulting from the expenditure.

Here's how the deduction is figured.

Example

You are advised by a physician to install an elevator in your residence so that your spouse, who has a heart problem, will not be required to climb stairs. The cost of installing the elevator is $10,000 and the increase in the value of your residence from the improvement is only $7,000. The difference of $3,000, which is the cost of the medical improvement in excess of the increase in value of your home, is deductible by you as a medical expense. If the installation of the elevator produced *no* increase in the value of your home, the *entire* $10,000 cost would be deductible as a medical expense. Moreover, the cost of operating the elevator, including repairs and maintenance, also would be deductible as a medical expense.

Like other medical expenses, medical improvement deductions are allowed only to the extent that they are part of unreimbursed medical expenses that exceed 7.5 percent of your adjusted gross income for the year. Adjusted gross income is all your salary and other income, minus specified deductions, principally individual retirement account (IRA) deductions, moving expenses, one half of self-employment tax and alimony.

Example

Assume, in the above example, that you have adjusted gross income for the year of $87,000 and that your general unreimbursed medical expenses for the year are $4,300. Assume also that you have obtained a written real estate broker's opinion that, because of the nature of your neighborhood, the installation of the elevator did not increase the value of your home. This will qualify the entire cost of the elevator, $10,000, as a deductible medical expense. Accordingly, your aggregate unreimbursed medical expenses for the year are $14,300 ($4,300 + $10,000 = $14,300). You are entitled to claim a medical expense deduction of $7,775, figured as follows.

Unreimbursed medical expenses		$14,300
Adjust gross income	$87,000	
Percentage limitation	×.075	
	$ 6,525	6,525
Allowable medical deduction		$7,775

As the example illustrates, the amount of your medical deduction, $7,775, is the amount by which your medical expenses exceed 7.5 percent of your adjusted gross income.

Tax Tip

Note that, due to the adjusted gross income limitation, the timing of the payment of medical expenses can have tax significance. If you anticipate relatively large medical expenses, you generally should, if practical, attempt to "bunch" them into one tax year, either this year or next year. By doing so, the adverse effect of the 7.5 percent of adjusted gross income limitation will be reduced because it will tend to limit deductions in only one year rather than two years.

How about a Swimming Pool? A court case involving the installation of a swimming pool illustrates the amount of deductions that medically mandated improvements can produce.

A homeowner had a severe back problem. Her physician recommended that she install an indoor swimming pool in her home and swim in it twice daily for the rest of her life to prevent permanent paralysis. She built an addition to her home, including a pool, at a cost of $195,000. Part of this high cost was attributable to having the addition made architecturally and aesthetically compatible with the residence. She deducted $86,000 of the cost as a medical expense. This figure was arrived at by reducing the total cost of the addition by the cost of items not related to medical care, such as cooking equipment and entertainment facilities, and by the amount by which the value of the residence was increased by the medically essential part of the addition.

The IRS did *not* challenge the propriety of the deduction. Instead, it just claimed that the cost was too high. It asserted that a medically sufficient pool could have been constructed for $70,000, that such pool would have added $31,000 in value to the residence, and that only the difference, $39,000, was properly deductible. The court disagreed, stating, "We are aware of no case limiting a medical expense to the cheapest form of treatment." So ruling, the court allowed $82,000 of the $86,000 claimed.

Too Good to Be True. The IRS appealed the decision and, on appeal, the lower court's generosity was reduced. The appeals court held that the substantial expense for architectural and aesthetic compatibility did not have medical care as its " primary purpose" nor was it "related directly to" medical care. "Where a taxpayer makes a capital expenditure that would qualify as being 'for medical care,' but does so in a manner creating additional costs attributable to such personal motivations as architectural or aesthetic compatibility with the related property, the additional costs incurred are not expenses for medical care." Accordingly, the allowable deduction was reduced.

Planning Is Essential. It's only natural that the IRS might be skeptical about the medical motivation for a swimming pool or other improvement that has recreational features. So before you install this or any other type of medical improvement, you need to do some homework.

- Gather evidence that the improvement is medically required. A letter from at least one physician should be obtained explaining the background and nature of the medical problem and the need for the improvement to provide for its treatment. The stronger the medical evidence, the better.
- To establish the amount of the deduction, a qualified real estate appraiser should be retained to determine the excess of the cost of the improvement over the increase, if any, in the value of your home produced by the improvement.

- In cases involving expensive facilities, evidence should be collected showing that the deduction doesn't exceed the minimum reasonable cost of a functionally adequate facility. For example, if you are building a swimming pool, have the contractor break down the cost components in the construction contract between the basic pool and "extras," such as a pool house, landscaping, tile work, or a hot tub. The maximum deduction would be an amount not exceeding the basic pool cost.

- Evidence should clearly show that medical care was the "primary purpose" of the expenditure. For example, if the improvement is a pool, you should be able to say to the IRS that the facility was used only for exercise or therapy purposes, not for parties for friends. An occasional nonmedical use won't be fatal to the deduction, but it won't help.

Check the Alternatives. You need more than medical evidence. You also should be prepared to show that installation of the improvement was warranted by the absence of nearby alternative facilities. For example, in one case the medical deduction was denied where the availability of nearby community pools indicated that the pool constructed was primarily for personal recreational convenience rather than medical care. But the courts are not always consistent. In another case a court allowed the deduction where swimming in local public pools did not fit into an emphysema sufferer's heavy work schedule. To be on the safe side, you should be prepared to show that alternative facilities were not readily available.

In view of the potential tax benefits, any time a permanent home improvement is required for health reasons, consideration should be given to whether it can qualify as a medical expense.

> **Observation**
>
> *Other Improvements.* In addition to swimming pools and elevators, humidity control and air-conditioning equipment, as well as whirlpools and similar items, could qualify.

3.5 Deductible Home Improvements for the Disabled

Suppose you or a member of your family is disabled. Can you deduct the cost of improvements to your home installed to accommodate the disability?

The answer is *yes*.

Generally, the costs of permanent improvements to a home, called *capital expenditures* in taxspeak, are not currently deductible. But the IRS has officially stated that capital expenditures eligible for the medical expense deduction include expenses incurred for a physically disabled individual for eliminating structural barriers in his or her personal residence for the purpose of accommodating the disability.

Specific types of eligible expenditures include:

- Constructing entrance or exit ramps to the residence
- Widening doorways at entrances or exits to the residence
- Widening or otherwise modifying hallways and interior doorways to accommodate wheelchairs
- Installing railings, support bars, or other modifications to bathrooms
- Lowering or other modifications to kitchen cabinets and equipment
- Adjusting electrical outlets and fixtures

Other similar expenditures also are deductible.

According to the IRS, the six categories of expenditures in the list do not add to the value of a personal residence for tax purposes. Consequently, the IRS allows the full amount of such expenditures to qualify for the medical expense deduction—limited, of course, to the extent medical expenses exceed 7.5 percent of adjusted gross income. (For more about medical deductions for improvements, see Section 3.4.)

3.6 How an Employee Gets a Tax Break for a "Sideline" Business

Do you have to supplement your day job by moonlighting to make ends meet? If so, you may be entitled to a significant homeowner's tax break.

As explained in Section 2.11, deductions are not allowed for the expenses of a home office unless the home office is used exclusively and on a regular basis for business purposes. Most executives and professionals who lug office work home for evening or weekend labors can't get home office deductions.

But moonlighting may be different.

Have a Sideline Business? If you run a business out of your home, you usually can get home office deductions. This is so even if you are a full-time employee, provided that you have some sort of "sideline" business. Qualifying part-time endeavors would include a mail-order business, real estate brokerage or management, freelance writing, antique sales, tax consulting, pet grooming, cosmetics sales, child care, fashion designing, tutoring, catering, educational consulting, dance instruction—any active business separate from your regular day job.

The possibilities are illustrated by a court case involving a professional with a sideline business.

> **Example**
>
> A doctor who was a full-time employee of a hospital also owned and managed six rental properties: three condominiums, two townhouses, and a single-family house. He lived in a two-bedroom condominium and used one bedroom exclusively and regularly as an office for bookkeeping and other activities related to the management of his rental properties. The room was furnished with a desk, bookcase, filing cabinet, calculators, and a code-a-phone answering service. There was no television, sofa, or bed in the room, and he did not allow guests to stay there. The closet in the room was used to store items related to the rental properties, such as furnishings and signs.

The doctor purchased the rental properties to provide a source of income for his retirement. In the tax year in question, he didn't do well: His gross rental income was $24,760 but he had a net loss of $23,043 and a negative cash flow of $6,242.

IRS Says No. The IRS disallowed the deduction of depreciation and other expenses for the second bedroom. It didn't question whether the bedroom met the exclusive and regular use tests or the doctor's allocation of expenses. He passed on both counts. Instead, the IRS claimed the doctor's rental activities were not a "business" and, even if they were, his place of business was the hospital, not the second bedroom of his condominium. The IRS *lost* on both points. Here's why.

Home Activity Must Be a Business. You need to be in business at home to get home office deductions. Whether activities amount to a "business" as opposed to mere investment or some other not-for-profit activity or hobby is a question of fact. Because the doctor's personal management activities were systematic and continuous, he was deemed to be in a business.

Place of Business. On the place-of-business question, the IRS said that if a taxpayer is in more than one business, as in the doctor's case, home office

SPECIAL-SITUATION DEDUCTIONS FOR HOMEOWNERS 63

expenses are deductible only if the home office is the principal place of business. Based on time spent and income earned, the IRS said the hospital was the principal office. The court knocked down this argument simply by holding that the doctor could have more than one principal place of business if he engaged in more than one business.

Tax Watch

Congress Agrees. A tax law amendment has confirmed that a taxpayer carrying on more than one business can have more than one "principal place of business."

The Tax Break. As the court case shows, if you are an employee, getting office-at-home deductions requires tax planning. Tax planning simply means that you arrange things so that you qualify for the deduction.

Here's what you should do:

- Set aside a specific portion of your home for business activities. The set-aside portion should be furnished and used in a manner consistent with exclusive use for business purposes, as in the doctor's case.

- Keep records that show that the set-aside portion of your home was used on a regular basis for business purposes—which include administrative and management work. For example, you can keep a calendar-type diary.

- Make a proper allocation of expenses, as discussed in Section 2.12. Be reasonable. The IRS does not believe in the Tooth Fairy.

- Keep records that will help you show that the income-producing endeavor was sufficiently active to constitute a business. A diary could help here too. An "active" business generally is a business that requires your personal involvement on a regular basis with customers or clients, as opposed to investment-type activities, such as running a stock portfolio. The sideline businesses mentioned above generally would be considered active-type businesses when work is done on a regular basis and a genuine effort is made to make a profit.

While home office record keeping may seem like a chore, you won't even notice it once you get going. And if you make a little error, you are not going to be sent to jail. All the IRS will want is money.

3.7 Deduction of Fees for Home Tax Advice

You can deduct the cost of this book even though it's about your home. Why? Because just as long as the cost is for tax advice, its deductible.

You can deduct ordinary and necessary expenses in connection with the determination, collection, or refund of any tax. This includes not just tax books, but also accountant's and attorney's fees for tax advice and the cost of tax return preparation.

There's a Catch. So-called miscellaneous itemized deductions are deductions for unreimbursed employee expenses, such as job travel, union dues, and job education, and also include the cost of tax advice. Your total miscellaneous itemized deductions, including the cost of tax advice, can be deducted only to the extent they exceed 2 percent of the adjusted gross income shown on your tax return. Adjusted gross income is all your salary and other income, minus specified deductions, principally IRA deductions, moving expenses, one half of self-employment tax, and alimony. You figure the limitation on Schedule A of Form 1040.

If your miscellaneous itemized deductions, other than the cost of tax advice, at least exceed 2 percent of your adjusted gross income, then the cost of your tax advice is fully deductible. However, if your other miscellaneous itemized deductions do not exceed 2 percent of your adjusted gross income, then the cost of tax advice is deductible only to the extent such cost, when added to the other miscellaneous itemized deductions, exceeds 2 percent of your adjusted gross income. An example will illustrate the point.

Example

Assume your adjusted gross income is $100,000, so that 2 percent of your adjusted gross income is $2,000. Assume also that you have miscellaneous itemized deductions of $2,100, other than the fee for tax advice. If you pay $500 for tax advice concerning the sale of your home, you may deduct the entire $500 because your other itemized deductions, $2,100, exceed 2 percent of your adjusted gross income, $2,000. However, if your other miscellaneous itemized deductions were $1,800 instead of $2,100, you could deduct only $300 of the cost of tax advice. This is because after adding $200 of the $500 tax advice cost to the $1,800 in miscellaneous itemized deductions to reach the $2,000 floor, the amount of the cost of tax advice left over is only $300 ($500 − $200 = $300).

> **Caution**
>
> ***Need to Itemize.*** The deduction for tax advice isn't allowable if you use the standard deduction instead of itemizing your deductions.

Break for Rental Property. If you own rental property and get tax advice about your rental property, you should escape the miscellaneous itemized deduction limitation. For example, the IRS has ruled that a certified public accountant's (CPA's) fee for advice to the owners of rental properties concerning a tax deduction was not subject to the 2 percent floor. The fee was deductible because it was a fee for tax advice that didn't fall into the category of a miscellaneous itemized deduction that reduces adjusted gross income. Instead, it was an "above-the-line" *business* deduction from gross income used to arrive at adjusted gross income.

3.8   Tax-Wise Borrowing against Your Home for Business

If you borrow against your home to get funds for a business you run yourself, you want to be careful how you do it. By doing it the tax-smart way, you can deduct the interest on the business loan without using up any part of your $100,000 allowance on home equity indebtedness.

Here's the story:

Say you need to borrow to put money into your business. You can deduct interest on funds borrowed for use in your business without limit, but suppose the best loan deal you can find is from a bank that will provide you with a home equity loan. As explained in Section 3.3, you can deduct interest on home equity loans up to $100,000, but no more. It doesn't make tax sense to use up any part of your $100,000 home equity allowance on a business borrowing on which you can deduct the interest anyway.

Since the best loan deal you can get is by putting a second mortgage on your home and you want to take advantage of its favorable terms, you want to go for it. But how do you get around wasting any part of the $100,000 home equity loan ceiling? Can you take out a home equity loan without decreasing the amount of the $100,000 ceiling for home equity indebtedness and still deduct the interest on the loan?

Now You See It, Now You Don't. The answer may lie in a rule that lets you elect to treat debt secured by a qualified residence as not secured by a qualified residence. When you make this election, the amount you borrow doesn't count toward your home equity allowance of $100,000.

While on first blush an "election out" would seem counterproductive, it may be a sound tax-planning technique. An example will illustrate how it can work to your advantage.

> **Example**
>
> You take out a first mortgage to purchase your principal residence. Three years later you have an important business opportunity and you take out a second mortgage on your home in the amount of $100,000 that you immediately use in your business. In the following year you decide to install a swimming pool on your property and you take out a third mortgage on your home of $30,000. You use the third mortgage proceeds to install the pool.

How the Election Helps. If you didn't elect out on the $100,000 mortgage debt, the $100,000 debt limit on home equity indebtedness would be entirely used up by the $100,000 you borrowed for your business. Consequently, the interest on the $30,000 debt for the pool would be nondeductible personal interest. If you made the election out, however, the interest on the $30,000 debt will be deductible as qualified residence interest. At the same time, the interest on the $100,000 debt will be deductible as trade or business interest if you use the proceeds in a business you run personally.

The election out is made by attaching a statement to your income tax return for the year you borrow the amount with respect to which you want to elect out.

Bottom line: The election out has saved the deductibility of interest on the $30,000 debt.

> **Caution**
>
> As pointed out above, qualifying home equity indebtedness can't exceed the difference between the current balance of the mortgage you obtained to purchase your home and the current fair market value of your home. Also, for a married individual, the ceiling for home equity indebtedness on a separate return is $50,000, not $100,000.

3.9 Renting a Part of Your Home

To help pay the cost of home ownership, many homeowners rent out a part of their homes. Rental of a single room is common, as is rental of a top floor or basement apartment.

When you rent out a part of your home, you get a double benefit. First, of course, you get the benefit of rental income to help you defray the cost of home ownership. Second, you get the tax benefit of being able to deduct a portion of your home ownership expenses that you otherwise would not be entitled to deduct. The portion of home maintenance expenses you can deduct is the portion of such expenses allocable to the part of your home that is rented. By reducing your taxes, these deductions increase your after-tax income from the rental.

Three Categories of Expenses. When you rent part of your home, there are three categories of expenses you can deduct when you file your tax return on Form 1040.

- *Category 1.* The first category is real estate taxes and mortgage interest (discussed in Sections 2.3 and 2.4). You can deduct your real estate taxes and mortgage interest regardless of whether you rent any part of your home. But when you rent part of your home, you have to split taxes and interest between the part allocable to the rental portion of your home and the part allocable to your personal use of your home. In figuring your rental income or loss on Schedule E of Form 1040, you deduct the portion of taxes and interest allocable to the rental portion of your home. The balance of your taxes and interest is deducted on Schedule A of Form 1040. (Thus, while split, all your taxes and interest are deductible.)
- *Category 2.* The second category of expenses you can deduct is the portion of general home maintenance expenses that is allocable to the rental portion of your home. While general home maintenance expenses usually are wholly nondeductible "personal" expenses, they become partially deductible when part of your home is rented. Such general home maintenance expenses would include heating and electricity, as well as repairs to equipment that serves the entire home, such as a furnace or water heater. The cost of painting the outside of your house also would qualify.
- *Category 3.* The third category of expenses you can deduct when you rent out part of your home is expenses related directly to the rental portion of

your home. You do not have to split up these expenses. For example, if you paint a rented room, or if you pay premiums for liability insurance only in connection with the rented room, your entire cost is a deductible rental expense. While the cost of the first phone line in your home is not deductible, even if the tenant can use the phone, the cost of a second phone line installed strictly for your tenant's use is fully deductible. You can deduct depreciation (discussed in Section 2.12) on the part of your property used for rental purposes, as well as on the furniture and equipment you use for rental purposes.

How to Allocate Expenses. If an expense is for both rental use and personal use, such as mortgage interest or heat for the entire house, you have to allocate the expense between rental use and personal use. You are allowed to use any reasonable method for dividing the expense. For example, it may be reasonable to divide the cost of some items, such as heat and hot water costs, based on the number of people living in the home. However, the two most frequently used ways to divide expenses are based either on the number of rooms in the home or the square footage of the home devoted to rental use.

Example

Suppose you rent out a single room in your house that is 12 × 15 feet, or 180 square feet. The entire house has 1,800 square feet of floor space. Since the rental space is 10 percent of the total floor space, you can deduct as a rental expense 10 percent of any expense that must be split between rental and personal use. For example, if your heating bill for the year for the entire house was $900, $90 ($900 × 10 percent) is deductible as a rental expense. The balance, $810, is a nondeductible personal expense.

In effect, the splitting of expenses treats you as if you owned two separate properties, one held for personal purposes and the other for rental purposes.

3.10 Renting Your Entire Home

In the preceding discussion the tax features of renting part of your home are covered. The following discussion shows the tax consequences of renting your

SPECIAL-SITUATION DEDUCTIONS FOR HOMEOWNERS

entire home. You might rent your entire home, for example, if you bought a new home but decided to hold on to your prior home as a rental property.

The IRS has provided an example in its Publication 527 illustrating this scenario, and we adapt it here to explain the tax consequences.

The Facts. In January, Eileen Johnson moved to a condominium apartment and, instead of selling the house she has been living in, decides to change it to a rental property. She obtains a tenant who starts renting the house on February 1 at $750 a month after paying a $750 security deposit. Since the security deposit is to be returned to the tenant at the end of the lease, it is not included in Eileen's rental income for tax purposes.

The expenses of the house for the year are:

Mortgage interest	$1,800
Fire insurance (one-year policy)	100
Miscellaneous repairs (after renting)	297
Real estate taxes imposed and paid	1,200

Since Eileen started renting out the house in February, she must divide the real estate taxes, mortgage interest, and fire insurance between the personal use of the property and the rental use of the property. She can deduct eleven-twelfths of these expenses as rental expenses, and can deduct the balance of the taxes and interest on Schedule A of Form 1040 if she itemizes. The balance of the fire insurance is not deductible because it is a personal expense.

Note: The tax rules that apply when you rent your entire home are essentially the same as the tax rules that apply when you rent your vacation home year-round. Because the vacation home rules, discussed at Sections 8.7 to 8.12, deal with some rental rules not covered in the following discussion, Sections 8.7 to 8.12 should be consulted for additional rules applicable when renting your entire home.

Tax Basis for Depreciation Deduction. As explained in Section 8.11, you have to determine the adjusted tax basis for rental property before you can figure the amount of depreciation you are allowed to claim as a deduction. This is because the annual depreciation deduction is a percentage of tax basis. For your home, adjusted tax basis generally is the cost of the home exclusive of land, plus the cost of permanent improvements.

Eileen bought the house in 1979 for $35,000. She can determine the portion of the cost of the entire property allocable to the land by looking at her real property tax assessment. Her property tax is based on assessed values of $10,000 for the land and $25,000 for the house, so that the portion of the entire cost allocable to the house is $25,000.

Before changing it to rental use, Eileen added the following improvements to the house.

Remodeled kitchen	$ 4,200
Recreation room	5,800
New roof	1,600
Patio and deck	2,400
Total improvements	$14,000
Cost allocable to house	25,000
Adjusted basis	$39,000

Accordingly, Eileen's adjusted tax basis for purposes of figuring depreciation on the house is $39,000.

When property is changed from personal to rental use, as in Eileen's case, the tax basis is the *lower* of its adjusted basis or its fair market value on the date of the conversion. On February 1, when Eileen changed her house to rental property, it had a fair market value of $152,000. Of this amount, $35,000 was allocable to the land and $117,000 was allocable to the house. Since Eileen's adjusted basis is less than the fair market value on the date of the conversion, Eileen uses $39,000 as her adjusted tax basis for depreciation.

To figure the amount of the depreciation deduction, you can use a depreciation table provided by the IRS, reproduced in Section 8.11 at Table 8.2. When you use the table you look across the row for the month in which the house became rental property, in this case, February. Then, look down the column for the year representing how long the property has been rental property, in this case Year 1. The box at the intersection of the month row and year column shows the depreciation rate for the year, in this case 3.182 percent. This percentage is multiplied by the adjusted basis of the house, $39,000, producing a depreciation deduction of $1,241.

Eileen paid $4,000 on May 1 to have a new furnace installed in the house. Because the furnace is a permanent improvement, its cost can't be currently deducted as a repair. However, as a permanent improvement the cost of the furnace can be recovered through depreciation. For purposes of figuring the amount of depreciation, the furnace is considered residential rental property and the real property depreciation table is used to figure the depreciation deduction. Since the furnace was placed in service in May, the percentage is

2.273 percent. Accordingly, Eileen's depreciation deduction for the year for the furnace is $91 (.02273 × $4,000).

Personal Property Depreciation. Eileen also bought a new dishwasher for the rental property for $425 on April 1. Personal property, such as the dishwasher, has a much shorter useful life than real property, such as a building and its fixtures. Thus, the rules for depreciating personal property allow a much faster write-off. Under IRS rules for the depreciation of personal property such as the dishwasher, a five-year recovery period is used, as shown in Table 8.3 in Section 8.11 entitled "Depreciation Recovery Periods for Property Used in Rental Activities." Accordingly, Eileen's depreciation deduction for the year for the dishwasher is $85, one-fifth or 20 percent of her $425 cost. (A complicated but expiring temporary additional allowance for depreciation would make the deduction $187, which is the amount used in the following computation.)

Figuring Net Rental Income. Eileen figures her net rental income or loss for the house:

Total rental income received ($750 x 11)		$8,250
Minus: Expenses		
Mortgage interest ($1,800 x 11/12)	$1,650	
Fire insurance ($100 x 11/12)	92	
Miscellaneous repairs	297	
Real estate taxes ($1,200 x 11/12)	1,100	3,139
Balance		$5,111
Minus: Depreciation:		
House ($39,000 × 3.182%)	$1,241	
Dishwasher, including expiring allowance	187	
Furnace ($4,000 × 2.273%)	91	
Total Depreciation		1,519
Net rental income for house		$3,592

Eileen enters her income, expenses, and depreciation for the house on Schedule E of Form 1040, as shown on the illustrative Schedule E in Figure 3.1. She figures and reports her depreciation using Form 4562. Form 4562 and Publication 946 that explains how to prepare Form 4562 can be viewed and printed from the IRS web site at *www.irs.gov*.

SHELTERING YOUR INCOME WITH HOME DEDUCTIONS

SCHEDULE E (Form 1040)
Department of the Treasury
Internal Revenue Service

Supplemental Income and Loss
(From rental real estate, royalties, partnerships, S corporations, estates, trusts, REMICs, etc.)
▶ Attach to Form 1040 or Form 1041.   ▶ See Instructions for Schedule E (Form 1040).

OMB No. 1545-0074
2003
Attachment Sequence No. **13**

Name(s) shown on return: Eileen Johnson
Your social security number: 123 00 4567

Part I Income or Loss From Rental Real Estate and Royalties Note. If you are in the business of renting personal property, use Schedule C or C-EZ (see page E-2). Report farm rental income or loss from **Form 4835** on page 2, line 40.

1	Show the kind and location of each **rental real estate property**:	2	For each rental real estate property listed on line 1, did you or your family use it during the tax year for personal purposes for more than the greater of: • 14 days **or** • 10% of the total days rented at fair rental value? (See page E-3.)	Yes	No
A	Brick House 123 Main Street, Hometown, MN 56200	A			✓
B		B			
C		C			

			Properties			Totals
Income:			A	B	C	(Add columns A, B, and C.)
3	Rents received.	3	8,250			3 8,250
4	Royalties received	4				4
Expenses:						
5	Advertising	5				
6	Auto and travel (see page E-4)	6				
7	Cleaning and maintenance. . .	7				
8	Commissions	8				
9	Insurance	9	92			
10	Legal and other professional fees	10				
11	Management fees.	11				
12	Mortgage interest paid to banks, etc. (see page E-4) . . .	12	1,650			12 1,650
13	Other interest	13				
14	Repairs	14	297			
15	Supplies	15				
16	Taxes	16	1,100			
17	Utilities	17				
18	Other (list) ▶	18				
19	Add lines 5 through 18 . . .	19	3,139			19 3,139
20	Depreciation expense or depletion (see page E-4)	20	1,519			20 1,519
21	Total expenses. Add lines 19 and 20	21	4,658			
22	Income or (loss) from rental real estate or royalty properties. Subtract line 21 from line 3 (rents) or line 4 (royalties). If the result is a (loss), see page E-4 to find out if you must file **Form 6198**. . .	22	3,592			
23	Deductible rental real estate loss. **Caution.** Your rental real estate loss on line 22 may be limited. See page E-4 to find out if you must file **Form 8582**. Real estate professionals must complete line 43 on page 2	23	( )	( )	( )	
24	**Income.** Add positive amounts shown on line 22. **Do not** include any losses.					24 3,592
25	**Losses.** Add royalty losses from line 22 and rental real estate losses from line 23. Enter total losses here					25 ( )
26	**Total rental real estate and royalty income or (loss).** Combine lines 24 and 25. Enter the result here. If Parts II, III, IV, and line 40 on page 2 do not apply to you, also enter this amount on Form 1040, line 17. Otherwise, include this amount in the total on line 41 on page 2					26 3,592

For Paperwork Reduction Act Notice, see Form 1040 Instructions.   Cat. No. 11344L   Schedule E (Form 1040) 2003

FIGURE 3.1 Schedule E: Supplemental Income and Loss

3.11 Your Home as a Retirement Nest Egg

It may be surprising, but your home can be a tax-sheltered retirement nest egg. If by the time you retire you have substantially paid down your home mortgage or paid it off, the equity in your home can be an important source of retirement funds. This source of retirement funds can be tapped either by trading down or using a reverse mortgage.

Trading down tax free to increase the size of your retirement nest egg and the use of reverse mortgages to create tax-free retirement cash flow are discussed in Sections 9.2 and 9.6, respectively.

3.12 Battling Condo or Co-op Board

Virtue may be on your side if you have a disagreement with a condo or co-op board and hire a lawyer to vindicate your position. But Uncle Sam generally won't subsidize your battle by giving you a deduction for your legal fees. Such fees usually are considered nondeductible personal expenses. The expenses are considered personal in the usual case because the origin of your claim relates to the management, conservation, or maintenance of property held for personal use—namely, the condo or co-op unit where you live.

But this disallowance rule generally won't apply if the legal fee is incurred in connection with a condo or co-op that you rent to a tenant year-round. Then, if the fee is an "ordinary and necessary" business expense incurred in renting the unit, it would be currently deductible. See Section 8.7. Likewise, if you have a home office in your condo or co-op that qualifies for the home office deduction (see Section 2.9), an allocable share of the fee would be currently deductible if the fee qualifies as an "ordinary and necessary" business expense.

3.13 Suing the Builder: Tax-Free Proceeds

Suits between homeowners and their builders are commonplace, usually over issues such as alleged defective construction or failure to complete construction in accordance with plans and specifications. What are the tax consequences when you receive a settlement payment from the builder, or win the suit and receive damages awarded in a judgment?

An IRS ruling involving a suit by a condominium management association against a developer provides guidance. The association recovered damages from the developer for defective construction of common elements. The IRS ruled that the damages were not taxable to either the association or the unit owners. Instead, the amount of the damages was applied proportionately among unit owners to reduce the basis of their interests in their units and their shares of the common elements. Proceeds of the suit used later for repairs, replacements, or improvements were added to the unit owners' bases.

Analogous rules should be applicable to the owner of a single-family house. Settlement proceeds or damages received should not be included in income. Instead, the amount received should reduce the basis of the house and amounts expended to fix defective or incomplete construction should be added to the basis of the house.

PART II

Tax Shelter When You Sell Your Home

Chapter 4

Tax Shelter When You Sell Your Home

CHAPTER 4

How to Sell Your Home with No Tax on Gain

> The income tax has made more liars out of Americans than golf has.
>
> Will Rogers

4.1 Overview

Before we get into the nuts and bolts of the rules for excluding gain on the sale of your home, a short background detour will be useful. It's said that a page of history is worth a volume of logic.

How did it happen that a revenue-hungry Congress exempted gain on the sale of principal residences? With most other types of property, when a sale produces gain, a tax is payable. Exceptions are made for certain exchanges of property, such as exchanges of investment properties, but the general principal is clear that a payment to the tax collector is due when property is sold at a profit. An exception to the general rule was made long ago for homeowners. Why?

The Inflation Theory. On the theory that a homeowner's gain in an inflationary period was largely illusory, Congress created a "relief" measure that exempted gain on the sale of a principal residence from tax if an equally expensive or a more expensive residence was purchased. This tax forgiveness for so-called "rollovers" was enacted because it was thought that the entire selling price of the old residence would have to be used to purchase a replacement residence of no greater size than the residence sold.

This homeowner's tax break was unique. No asset other than personal residences has ever been shielded from inflationary gains.

Why was Congress so generous?

Could It Be Politics? Cynics would suggest that the congressional generosity was prompted by a simple fact: The homeowner constituency in the United States is by far the largest national special-interest group. There are *67 million* Americans who own their own homes, and close to 4 million homeowners sell their homes each year. Moreover, the average holding period for a home is only a little over 12 years, so that the number of potential homeowner sellers at any given time is always large.

The "inflation protection" rationale for exempting rolled over gain, a suspect rationale at best, was dropped in the Taxpayer Relief Act of 1997. This new law eliminated the rollover provisions entirely and replaced them with generous exclusion provisions, permitting the exclusion of gain of up to $250,000 for single individuals and up to $500,000 for spouses on the sale of a principal residence. Unlike the old law, the new provisions apply regardless of whether there is a replacement of the residence.

This book is about how homeowners can save taxes. But a pause for an observation on this background of the homeowner's tax break is warranted.

An Observation. The seductive congressional rationale for the original tax break on the sale of principal residences was right as far it went but, let's face it, it went only to help homeowners. Individuals and families who rent apartments also suffer from inflation. But if they move from an apartment to a house or condominium and must sell securities or other property to swing the purchase, their gain is fully taxed. That seems unfair. But it's not surprising, considering the size of the homeowner lobby. It's been noted that taxes reflect a continuing struggle among contending interests for the privilege of paying the least.

Enough of politics and philosophy. Now let's turn to what is involved in planning for the sale of a principal residence.

4.2   How to Plan for the Sale

If there will be gain on the sale of your home, your tax planning should focus with laser-like intensity on making sure the gain will qualify for exclusion from tax. This requires comparing the facts of your housing situation with the requirements for the exclusion (see Sections 4.3 through 4.9), principally the two-year ownership and use requirements and the once-in-two-years rule. If you are married and want to qualify for the larger exclusion of up to $500,000, you also should check the special qualification rules for spouses. (See Section 4.6.)

HOW TO SELL YOUR HOME WITH NO TAX ON GAIN

> **Tax Tip**
>
> *If You Will have a Loss.* In the unhappy situation in which you will be selling your home at a loss, tax planning may be a dead-end process. Usually, there is no tax benefit to be obtained from the loss. In certain special situations, however, there may be some light at the end of the tunnel. (See Section 7.8.)

4.3 Exclusion of Up to $250,000 or More of Gain

In a major overhaul in 1997, Congress both simplified and liberalized how you treat gain on the sale of your home. It enacted a large and relatively simple exclusion to replace the old rules for the tax-free rollover of gain into a replacement residence, and also replaced the old rules permitting the one-time exclusion of gain up to $125,000 for taxpayers age 55 or over.

The New Rules. Under the present rules, if you are single or if you are married and filing a separate return, you can exclude up to $250,000 of gain on the sale of your principal residence. If you are married and file jointly with your spouse, you can exclude up to $500,000. Provided you meet the eligibility rules discussed later, the exclusion is allowed *each time* you sell your principal residence.

It's Not Just the Money. We previously discussed the politics of Congress's generosity to homeowners. But in addition to politics, there are practical reasons for the new exclusion. The new exclusion puts an end to a collection of hassles created by the old rules.

Less Record-Keeping Hassle. One of the old headaches was record keeping. Many homeowners bought and sold a number of homes over the years, often making capital improvements to one or more of them. Under the old rules, detailed records concerning purchase and sale prices and the cost of improvements had to be maintained, perhaps for decades, to figure out whether gain on the ultimate sale of a home without a rollover would be protected from tax by the old $125,000 exclusion. Absent such protection from tax, many older taxpayers were discouraged from selling houses too large for their needs. The new rules, by excluding gains below the $250,000 (or $500,000) ceiling, will free all but a relatively few taxpayers from the burden of retaining records for determining the income tax consequences from home sales.

> **Caution**
>
> *High Price Homeowners.* If you are one of the few homeowners whose residence is likely to be sold at a gain in excess of the maximum exclusion amount, the nuisance of extended record keeping continues. This is because for purposes of determining the amount of gain on a sale, you will have to know the adjusted basis of your home. The adjusted basis generally is the cost of your home plus the cost of all improvements to your home, less amounts allowed as deductions for casualty losses and depreciation, if any. You will need records to prove these amounts. (See Section 4.11.)

No Replacement Home Hassle. Under the old rollover provisions, you could postpone the entire gain from the sale of your home only if you purchased another principal residence and the amount you paid for it was equal to or more than the sale price of your old home. This requirement often pushed homeowners to purchase larger or more expensive homes than they otherwise would, merely to avoid a tax liability. This difficulty was particularly tough for people who moved from areas where housing costs were high to lower-cost areas.

The new exclusion eliminates this problem. Now you can trade down to a less expensive home without paying tax.

Now let's turn to the rules you have to follow to get this large tax break.

4.4 How to Qualify for the Exclusion

In general, to qualify for the exclusion you must meet only two basic requirements.

1. *Two-Year Ownership and Use Requirement.* During the five-year period ending on the date you sell your home, you must have owned and used the home as your principal residence for periods aggregating two years or more.
2. *Two-Year Waiting Period Requirement.* During the two-year period ending on the date you sell your home, you must *not* have used the exclusion. In other words, you won't qualify if, during the two-year period ending on the date of the sale, you made another sale to which the exclusion applied.

Example

You purchased your home June 1, 2001, and occupy it as your principal residence from that date until September 15, 2004, when you sell it. You have not previously used the exclusion. You will qualify for the exclusion of gain on the sale because you will have owned and used your home as your principal residence for at least two years during the five-year period preceding the date of the sale and have not used the exclusion during the two-year period preceding the date of the sale.

Tax Tip

Multiple Exclusions Allowed. If you meet the basic eligibility requirements, you can use the exclusion *each time* you sell your principal residence.

Beyond the Basic Rules. Nobody ever said tax rules were simple. There are, of course, some variations on the basic requirements as well as some rules for special situations.

We'll start with a discussion of whether the ownership and use of your home have to be concurrent and the effect of short absences from your home. Then we'll move on to the relief you can get from the holding-period requirements if the sale of your home is caused by a job move, health needs, or other unforeseen circumstances; the special rules for the $500,000 exclusion for married couples; what makes a residence a "principal residence"; and the limitation on the exclusion where part of your property is used for nonresidential purposes.

You Don't Have to Own and Use at the Same Time. Ownership and use need not be concurrent, so long as both the ownership and use requirements are met during the five-year period ending on the date of sale. In other words, as long as there are two years of ownership and two years of use during the five years ending on the date of sale, such ownership and use may have occurred during different periods.

The IRS has illustrated this rule with an example.

Example

Taxpayer C lives in a townhouse that he rents from 1993 through 1996. On January 18, 1997, he purchases the townhouse. On February 1, 1998, C moves into his daughter's home. On May 25, 2000, while still living in his daughter's home, C sells his townhouse. The exclusion will apply to gain from the sale because C owned the townhouse for at least 2 years out of the 5 years preceding the sale (from January 19, 1997, until May 25, 2000) and he used the townhouse as his principal residence for at least 2 years during the 5-year period preceding the sale (from May 25, 1995, until February 1, 1998).

Short Absences. While occupancy of the residence is required for the "use" requirement to be met, short temporary absences, such as for vacation, are counted as periods of use. This is so even though the absence is accompanied by rental of the residence. Under these rules, a year-long sabbatical is not considered a short temporary absence, but a two-month vacation is treated as a short period of absence.

The IRS has illustrated these rules with two examples.

Example 1

Taxpayer D, a college professor, purchases and moves into a house on May 1, 1997. He uses the house as his principal residence continuously until September 1, 1998, when he goes abroad for a one-year sabbatical leave. On October 1, 1999, one month after returning from the leave, D sells the house. Because his leave is not considered to be a short temporary absence, the period of the sabbatical leave may not be included in determining whether D used the house for periods aggregating two years during the five-year period ending on the date of the sale. Consequently, D is not entitled to exclude gain because he did not use the residence for the requisite period.

Example 2

Taxpayer E purchases a house on February 1, 1998, that he uses as his principal residence. During 1998 and 1999, E leaves his residence for a two-month summer vacation. E sells the house on March 1, 2000. Although, in the five-year period preceding the date of sale, the total time E used his residence

> **Example 2** *(Continued)*
>
> is less than two years (21 months), the exclusion will apply to gain from the sale of the residence because the two-month vacations are short temporary absences and are counted as periods of use in determining whether E used the residence for the requisite period.

Don't Get Trapped by Two-Year Waiting Period Rule. You have to be careful not to get trapped by the two-year waiting period rule. An IRS example shows how easy it is to run afoul of this rule.

> **Example**
>
> Taxpayer A owns a townhouse that he uses as his principal residence for two full years, 1998 and 1999. A buys a house in 2000 that he owns and uses as his principal residence. A sells the townhouse in 2002 and excludes the gain. A sells the house in 2003. Although A meets the two-year ownership and use requirements, A is not eligible to exclude gain from the sale of the house because A excluded gain within the last two years from the sale of the townhouse.

> **Condos and Co-ops**
>
> The exclusion is available to owners of condos and co-op apartments to the same extent it applies to owners of single-family houses.
>
> For co-ops, the ownership requirement applies to the stock that tenant-stockholders own in their cooperative housing corporations rather than to a house or condo, and the use requirement applies to their apartment in the co-op.

4.5 Exceptions to the Two-Year Rule: Job Change, Health Problems, or Unforeseen Circumstances

Suppose you can't meet the two-year ownership and use requirements or the two-year waiting period requirement because of a job change, health problems, or other unforeseen circumstances. You still may be able to get the benefit of part of the exclusion if you qualify for special "hardship relief."

TAX SHELTER WHEN YOU SELL YOUR HOME

If you miss meeting either the two-year ownership and use requirements or the two-year waiting period requirement because of a change in place of employment, for health reasons, or for certain other unforeseen circumstances, you can use a fraction of the $250,000 (or $500,000) exclusion otherwise allowable. The amount of the reduced exclusion allowed generally is based on the portion or fraction of two years you meet the requirements. Specifically, the reduced exclusion is figured by multiplying the maximum dollar limitation of $250,000 (or $500,000) by a fraction. The numerator of the fraction is the shortest of:

- The period you owned the property as your principal residence during the five-year period ending on the date of the sale
- The period you used the property as your principal residence during the five-year period ending on the date of the sale
- The period between the date of a prior sale of property for which you excluded gain and the date of the current sale

The numerator may be expressed in days or months. The denominator of the fraction is 730 days or 24 months, depending on the measure of time used in the numerator.

Example

Suppose you are single and have owned and occupied your principal residence for 18 months. You get a great job offer in another state that you decide to take. You sell your house and move to the new job location, realizing a $50,000 gain on the sale. Since you met 75 percent of the two-year ownership and use requirements (18 ÷ 24), you are entitled to exclude up to $187,500 of gain (75 percent × $250,000). Thus, your full gain of $50,000 is excludable.

Tax Tip

Physically or Mentally Infirm. A separate hardship break may be available for the physically or mentally infirm. The two-year use requirement is reduced for individuals who require out-of-residence care as a result of being physically or mentally incapable of caring for themselves. In such cases, if the individual owns the residence and uses it as a principal residence for at least one year during the five-year period prior to sale, the time the individual is in a licensed nursing home or other licensed facility is counted as time the residence is used as the individual's principal residence.

This "relief" rule can cut two ways. Where you do not meet the two-year requirements, proration applies to the $250,000 or $500,000 *exclusion*, not the realized gain. As the preceding example illustrates, this treatment usually will be beneficial. But not always.

> **Example**
>
> An unmarried taxpayer owns and uses a principal residence for one year, then sells it because of a job change at a realized gain of $500,000. Only $125,000 of the gain may be excluded (one half of the $250,000 exclusion), not $250,000 of gain (one half of the $500,000 realized gain).

The exceptions to the two-year requirements are made for sales caused by a change in place of employment, health reasons, or other unforeseen circumstances. We now discuss how to qualify under these exceptions.

The Change in Place of Employment Exception. The IRS has given generally generous guidelines as to when a sale qualifies as being because of a change in place of employment, so as to permit you to avoid the two-year requirement. The IRS says the sale is by reason of a change in place of employment if the primary reason for the sale is a change in the location of a "qualified individual's" place of employment. Qualified individuals are you, your spouse, a co-owner of your residence, and a person whose principal place of abode is your home.

But there's a catch: The new place of employment has to meet a distance test. The new place of employment must be at least 50 miles farther from the residence sold than was the former place of employment. If there was no former place of employment, the distance between the individual's new place of employment and the residence sold must be at least 50 miles.

If you don't meet these "safe-harbor" rules, all is not lost. You can still qualify under the change in place of employment exception if the "facts and circumstances" show the primary reason for your move was a change in place of employment. For example, even though you fail to meet the distance test, you may qualify if you sell your home to be closer to work because at your new job you can be called to work at unscheduled hours.

The Health Problem Exception. You can qualify for the health problem exception to the two-year rules if the sale of your home meets either of two requirements:

1. You qualify for the exception if the primary reason for the sale is to obtain, provide, or facilitate the diagnosis, cure, mitigation, or treatment of disease, illness, or injury of a qualified individual.
2. You qualify for the exception if the primary reason for the sale is to obtain or provide medical or personal care for a qualified individual suffering from a disease, illness, or injury.

For purposes of the health problem exception, qualified individuals are you, your spouse, a co-owner of your residence, a person whose principal place of abode is your home, and family members of any of these individuals. You will be deemed to meet the health problem exception if you obtain a physician's recommendation for a change in residence for reasons of health.

> **Tax Tip**
>
> *Get Doctor's Orders in Writing.* If the sale is for a move that just benefits your general health or well-being, it doesn't qualify. You should get a doctor's letter saying a change of residence is required for reasons of health. The more specific the doctor's letter as to the nature of the problem and the need for a change in location, the better.

If you don't meet the physician's recommendation "safe harbor," all is not lost. You can still qualify under the health problem exception to the two-year rules if the facts and circumstances show the primary reason for the move was a health reason. For example, if you have to move out of your home and into a relative's home because you cannot care for yourself, the sale of your home will qualify. Likewise, if a relative sells his or her home to move into your home to be able to care for you, the relative's sale will qualify.

The Unforeseen Circumstances Exception. You can qualify for the unforeseen circumstances exception to the two-year rules if the primary reason for the sale is the occurrence of an event that you did not anticipate before purchasing and occupying your residence. Such events would include destruction or substantial damage to your home by fire, natural or man-made disasters, or acts of war or terrorism. In addition, as to you, your spouse, a co-owner of your residence, and a person whose principal place of abode is your home, the following events would be deemed unforeseen circumstances:

- Death
- Termination of employment, resulting in eligibility for unemployment compensation

- A change in employment or self-employment status, resulting in inability to pay housing costs and reasonable basic living expenses for the household
- Divorce or legal separation under a decree of divorce or separate maintenance
- Multiple births resulting from the same pregnancy, such as twins

Again, if you don't qualify for the unforeseen circumstances exception under these guidelines, you may still qualify if, under the facts and circumstances, the reason for the sale was an unforeseen event. For example, if you buy and move into a house with your significant other in anticipation of marriage but subsequently break up and sell the house, the sale will qualify as produced by unforeseen circumstances.

Odd events can cause the unforeseen circumstances requirement to be met. Thus, the unanticipated sale of a house was deemed caused by unforeseen circumstances where it resulted from the protests of neighbors who objected to the occupancy of the house by a family member under house arrest. Neighborhood hostility became so intense that it made living in the house intolerable.

4.6 Married Couples: How to Get the $500,000 Exclusion

Matrimony has tax virtues: While single individuals can exclude up to $250,000 of gain, married couples are eligible for a higher ceiling, up to $500,000 of gain.

But being married is not the only requirement for eligibility. There are four other requirements:

1. You must file a joint return for the year in which the sale occurs.
2. Either you or your spouse must meet the two-year ownership requirement.
3. *Both* you and your spouse must meet the two-year use requirement.
4. Neither you nor your spouse may have used the exclusion within the preceding two years.

What if You Flunk the $500,000 Requirements? What are the rules if spouses file jointly but fail to qualify for the $500,000 exclusion as a result of not meeting the two-year ownership requirement, the two-year use requirement, or the prohibition against any sale of a principal residence within the preceding two years? The consequences often may not be so serious because if spouses fail to meet these requirements, the limit on the amount of excludable gain is figured separately for each spouse.

> **Example**
>
> A couple married in June 1998 and filed a joint return for 1998. Prior to their marriage, each of them owned and used separate condominiums as principal residences for more than two years. Both condominiums were sold at a gain in the summer of 1998. The couple does not qualify for the $500,000 exclusion because they did not use the same condominium as their joint principal residence for the requisite two-year period. Nevertheless, each may exclude up to $250,000 of gain on the sale of their separate condominiums—the same exclusion they would have been entitled to if they were not married.

Since each spouse can exclude up to $250,000 of gain on the sale of residences each owned separately before marriage, can one spouse use any part of the other's unused exclusion? Unfortunately, no.

> **Example**
>
> During 1999, married Taxpayers H and W each sell a residence that each had separately owned and used as a principal residence before their marriage. Each spouse meets the ownership and use tests for his or her respective residence. Neither spouse meets the use requirement for the other spouse's residence. H and W file a joint return for the year of the sales. The gain realized from the sale of H's residence is $200,000. The gain realized from the sale of W's residence is $300,000. Because the ownership and use requirements are met for each residence by each respective spouse, H and W are each eligible to exclude up to $250,000 of gain from the sale of their individual residences. However, W may not use H's unused exclusion to exclude gain in excess of her limitation amount. Therefore, H and W must recognize $50,000 of the gain realized on the sale of W's residence.

What is the rule if spouses filing jointly fail to meet the requirements for the $500,000 exclusion for the residence they currently live in? Again, the rule is that the maximum amount that can be claimed by the couple is the sum of each spouse's exclusion amount determined on a separate return basis as if they were unmarried. The IRS has illustrated the application of this rule.

Example

Married Taxpayers H and W sell their residence and file a joint return for the year of the sale. W, but not H, satisfies the requirements for the exclusion. They are eligible to exclude up to $250,000 of the gain from the sale of the residence because that is the sum of each spouse's dollar limitation amount determined on a separate basis as if they had not been married ($0 for H, $250,000 for W).

Observation

What about Separation and Divorce? If you acquire a principal residence incident to a divorce, the period your former spouse owned the property can be added to your ownership period to figure the two-year ownership period. In addition, a separated individual owning a residence who has moved out of the residence is nevertheless treated as *using* the residence as a principal residence while such individual's spouse or former spouse is granted actual use of the residence under a divorce or separation agreement. This rule can help a spouse owning the residence who leaves the residence (typically, the husband) meet the two-year use requirement.

Married couples usually can qualify to exclude up to $500,000 of gain on the sale of a principal residence because both of them will meet the two-year use requirements. But suppose one of them meets the two-year use requirements but the other doesn't because of a change of job location that qualifies for the exception to the two-year requirement, discussed above. Can the couple get both a full $250,000 exclusion and a partial $250,000 exclusion?

An IRS example shows the results.

Example

Taxpayer H owns a house that he has used as his principal residence since 1996. On January 15, 1999, H and W marry, and W begins to use H's house as her principal residence. On January 15, 2000, H sells the house due to a change in W's place of employment. Neither H nor W has excluded gain on a prior sale or exchange of property within the last two years.

(Continued)

> **Example** *(Continued)*
>
> Because H and W have not each used the house as their principal residence for at least two years during the five-year period preceding its sale, the maximum dollar limitation amount that may be claimed by H and W will not be $500,000, but the sum of each spouse's limitation amount determined on a separate basis as if they had not been married. H is eligible to exclude up to $250,000 of gain because he meets the ownership and use requirements. W is not eligible to exclude the maximum dollar limitation amount because she does not meet the use requirement. Instead, because the sale of the house is due to a change in place of employment, W is eligible to claim a reduced maximum exclusion of up to $125,000 of the gain (365/730 × $250,000). Therefore, H and W are eligible to exclude up to $375,000 of gain ($250,000 + $125,000) from the sale of the house.

Death of Spouse. If your spouse has died, special rules may make it easier for you to qualify. To prevent hardship for surviving spouses, so-called "tacking" of holding periods is permitted. This means you can add your holding period for the home to the holding period of your former spouse for purposes of figuring the two-year holding period.

Specifically, in the case of the death of a spouse, for purposes of satisfying the ownership and use requirements, you are treated as owning and using property as your principal residence during any period that your deceased spouse owned and used the property as a principal residence, provided two conditions are met. First, your spouse must be deceased on the date of the sale. Second, you must not have remarried at the time of the sale.

The IRS has illustrated these rules with an example.

> **Example**
>
> Taxpayer H has owned and used a house as his principal residence since 1987. H and W marry on July 1, 1999, and from that date they use H's house as their principal residence. H dies on August 15, 2000, and W inherits the property. W sells the property on September 1, 2000, at which time she has not remarried. Although W has owned and used the house for less than 2 years, W will be considered to have satisfied the ownership and use requirements because W's period of ownership and use includes the period that H owned and used the property before death.

Marriages of Convenience? Is it possible for a single individual owning a principal residence with potential gain in excess of $250,000 to marry to take advantage of the $500,000 exclusion? It's been suggested that such marriages of convenience are possible. But quite apart from the propriety and practicality of such action, as well as the potential difficulty of unwinding it, the procedure presents a technical difficulty. As indicated previously, *both* spouses must meet the two-year use requirement, a requirement forcing an intimacy that should persuade even the most ardently tax adverse from embracing the stratagem. Nevertheless, if an unmarried individual contemplating the sale of a principal residence with gain substantially in excess of $250,000 is also contemplating marriage, deferring the sale until two years after the marriage may make sense.

4.7 Is Your Home Your "Principal Residence"?

You can use the exclusion only if the home you sell is your "principal residence." The law doesn't say what a principal residence is, but for most people it's obvious: It's the home where you live.

What If You Have Two Homes? Where do you live when you have more than one home? The IRS says that when you alternate between two properties, using each as a residence for successive periods, the property you use a majority of the time during the year "ordinarily" is considered your principal residence.

IRS illustrates the application of the "majority of time" rule when an individual alternates between northern and southern residences.

Example 1

Taxpayer A owns two residences, one in New York and one in Florida. From 1999 through 2004, he lives in the New York residence for 7 months and the Florida residence for 5 months of each year. In the absence of facts and circumstances indicating otherwise, the New York residence is A's principal residence. A would be eligible for the exclusion of gain from the sale or exchange of the New York residence, but not the Florida residence.

> **Example 2**
>
> Taxpayer B owns two residences, one in Virginia and one in Maine. During 1999 and 2000, she lives in the Virginia residence. During 2001 and 2002, she lives in the Maine residence. During 2003, she lives in the Virginia residence. B's principal residence during 1999, 2000, and 2003 is the Virginia residence. B's principal residence during 2001 and 2002 is the Maine residence. B would be eligible for the exclusion of gain from the sale of either residence (but not both) during 2003.

For purposes of meeting the principal residence requirement, splitting time among three homes may be more likely to produce a tax headache than splitting time between two homes. For example, a couple owning residences in three states failed to prove that their Wisconsin residence was their principal residence where more time was spent in the other two residences combined.

Must Home Be Principal Residence at Time of Sale? Not necessarily. The fact that property is not your principal residence at the time it is sold doesn't matter if it was your principal residence for at least two out of the five years preceding its sale. But occupancy by a relative does not count as occupancy by you.

> **Example 1**
>
> Taxpayer A has owned and used his house as his principal residence since 1986. On January 31, 1998, A moves to another state. A rents his house to tenants from that date until April 18, 2000, when he sells it. A is eligible for the exclusion because he has owned and used the house as his principal residence for at least 2 of the 5 years preceding the sale.

> **Example 2**
>
> Taxpayer B owns and uses a house as her principal residence from 1986 to the end of 1997. On January 4, 1998, B moves to another state and ceases to use the house. B's son moves into the house in March 1999 and uses the residence until it is sold on July 1, 2001. B may not exclude gain from the sale because she did not use the property as her principal residence for at least two years out of the five years preceding the sale.

> **Condo and Co-ops**
>
> Both condos and co-op apartments can qualify as principal residences, the same as a single-family house.

4.8 Your Home Office: Does It Qualify?

Suppose you use part of your home for business purposes, say for a home office. Are you entitled to exclude all the gain on the sale of the residence, even though part of the residence was used for your office, a nonresidential use?

Under prior rules, partial use of a residence for a home office or other business use produced a ratable reduction in the exclusion, and only the gain allocable to the residential portion of the dwelling could be excluded. In other words, the exclusion didn't apply to gain allocable to the office portion of your home.

Responding to criticism, the IRS has reversed this rule.

The IRS now says the exclusion rules don't apply to the home office or other business portion of your residence only if the nonresidential portion of your residence is *separate* from the dwelling unit. In other words, there is what might be called a "four walls" test: If the home office or other business use of your residence occurs within the dwelling itself, no allocation is required. However, to prevent a double benefit, you have to include in income any depreciation you deducted previously for the business use of your residence.

> **Example 1**
>
> Taxpayer D, an attorney, buys a house in 2003. The house constitutes a single-dwelling unit but D uses a portion of the house as a law office. D claims depreciation deductions of $2,000 during the period that she owns the house. D sells the house in 2006, realizing a gain of $13,000. D must recognize $2,000 of the gain because of the depreciation she claimed, but she may exclude the remaining $11,000 of the gain from the sale of her house because she is not required to allocate gain to the business use within the dwelling unit. If D was not entitled to any depreciation deductions with respect to her business use of the house, she could exclude the entire $13,000 of gain from the sale of her house.

4.9 Vacant Land Can Qualify

Your principal residence normally includes all the land on which it is situated. But suppose your house is on a large tract of land. Is the entire tract part of your "principal residence," so that appreciation in its value is covered by the exclusion?

The IRS gives you a big break on vacant land, even if you don't sell it at the same time you sell your home. It says that the exclusion applies to vacant land that you have owned and used as part of your principal residence if you make a qualifying sale of your residence within two years before or two years after the sale of the land. To get this break, the vacant land must be adjacent to land containing your residence, and the sale of the vacant land must otherwise satisfy the two-year ownership and use rule and the once-in-two-years rule.

Observation

Your Lot. The lot on which your house is located would be considered part of your residence, not vacant land.

The IRS has illustrated the application of the vacant land rules.

Example

In 1991, Taxpayer C buys property consisting of a house and 10 acres that she uses as her principal residence. In May 2005, C sells eight acres of the land and realizes a gain of $110,000. C does not sell the dwelling unit before the due date for filing C's 2005 return, so she is not eligible to exclude the $110,000 of gain. In March 2007, C sells the house and remaining two acres, realizing a gain of $180,000 from the sale of the house. C may exclude the $180,000 of gain. Because the sale of the eight acres occurred within two years from the date of the sale of the dwelling unit, the sale of the eight acres is included as a sale of the taxpayer's principal residence. To get a partial refund of the tax she paid on the sale of the land, C may file an amended return for 2005 to claim an exclusion for $70,000 ($250,000 exclusion – $180,000 gain previously excluded) of the $110,000 gain from the sale of the eight acres.

4.10 Snowbirds: How to Deal with the Southern Home Trap

Are you one of the thousands of retirees who will migrate from your chilly northern roost and fly south or southwest in search of warm weather after the fall foliage season?

If so, you may be one of the so-called "Snowbirds" who technically are residents of Florida, Arizona, or southern California but who return north to their old principal residences shortly after the spring crocuses peep through the winter snow. For you, the Snowbird's back-and-forth flight pattern can create a tax problem.

To illustrate, suppose you are one of the Snowbirds who owns homes both in the north and in Florida. You claim residency in Florida because Florida—unlike New York, for example—imposes no income tax. Suppose also, as often is the case, your northern home is considerably more valuable and more highly appreciated than your Florida home.

This situation presents a potentially serious tax trap for you. If the northern home is sold, will gain on its sale qualify for the exclusion? Ironically, the danger is that the very steps you may have taken to establish Florida as your residence for state income tax purposes may knock out principal residence status for your northern home for federal income tax purposes. The loss of qualification of the northern home for the exclusion can cost you big tax dollars.

Example

You and your spouse own a northern home in a desirable suburb that you bought for $150,000 years ago. It has tripled in value to $450,000, so that you would have a gain of $300,000 on its sale. Four years ago you bought a condominium in a golf course community in Florida for $100,000. You live there seven months a year and have established Florida as your legal residence. You have returned north for the summers but now plan to sell the northern house.

The Trap. If your Florida condominium became your principal residence when you bought it four years ago so that your northern home hasn't been used as your principal residence for at least two out of the last five years, the sale of your northern home will be taxable. The federal tax hit would be $45,000 (15% × $300,000, the gain on the sale). The tax could have been completely avoided if the northern home had remained your principal residence.

Tax Tip

If you plan to sell your northern home and retire permanently in Florida or another Sunbelt state where you will have your principal residence, tax planning is important if your northern home is substantially appreciated. You should sell the northern principal residence *before* you cease to meet the requirement for having owned *and used* your northern home as your principal residence for two out of the five years preceding the date of sale.

4.11 Gain in Excess of the Exclusion

Suppose your gain will exceed the $250,000 (or $500,000) exclusion. Can you shelter the excess?

In some situations, yes. Where you have gain substantially in excess of the exclusion, you may want to look into specialized tax-planning ideas for dealing with gain in excess of the exclusion. (See Sections 5.4 through 5.7.) Some of these ideas are relatively complex, but occasionally may be worth pursuing because they can keep the tax collector at bay. In addition, you should consider the following:

- *Holding Period.* Make sure your residence has been owned by you for more than the minimum 12-month holding period required for obtaining long-term capital gain.
- *Capital Losses.* Check to see if you have an unused capital loss from a prior year that can be carried over to offset the gain this year. Also check to see if you have property that can be sold to create offsetting capital losses.
- *Don't Sell.* If you are an older owner, you may want to think about the possibility of holding the home until death, either to live in or to rent to others. When you go to your eternal reward, the basis of your home for purposes of figuring gain will be "stepped up" to its fair market value. As a result, on a subsequent sale, income tax is eluded on all predeath appreciation in value.

Observation

The step-up rule is scheduled for partial repeal in 2010 and, believe it or not, reinstatement in 2011. Congress is likely to revisit this subject before 2010. The subject of estate planning for your home is discussed in Chapter 10.

Keep Good Records. If the sale of your residence is taxable, the burden of proof is on *you* to show the amount of taxable gain. To do this, you must show how much the sales price of your home exceeds the tax cost (so-called adjusted basis) of your home. Any gain in excess of the exclusion is taxable. The adjusted basis for your home generally is the original cost of the home, plus the cost of improvements, less amounts allowed as deductions for casualty losses and depreciation, if any.

Example

You purchased your home years ago for $200,000 and plan to sell now for its current highly appreciated value, $600,000. You made improvements to your home over the years at an aggregate cost of $30,000. If you are single, your taxable gain on the sale will be $120,000, assuming you can prove both your cost, $200,000, and the amount you paid for improvements, $30,000.

Adjusted Basis	
Original cost	$200,000
Improvements	30,000
Adjusted basis	$230,000
Taxable Gain	
Sales price	$600,000
Adjusted basis	230,000
Gain	$370,000
Exclusion (single individual)	250,000
Taxable gain	$120,000

The taxable gain is reported on Schedule D of your Form 1040.

While most individuals have papers that show the original purchase price of their homes, papers proving increases in basis from capital improvements can be more difficult to come by. But if you don't have copies of bills, checks, or other papers, all is not lost. The Tax Court has said that weight will be given to your cost estimates based on recollection, "bearing heavily" against you where "inexactitude" is your own fault.

Tax Tip

Other Uses for Exclusion. As to the possibility of using the exclusion as a tax shield for gain on real estate other than your present principal residence, see Section 7.2.

4.12 How to Cope with a Depressed Market by Rental before Sale

As explained above, you usually can avoid tax when you sell your principal residence at a gain. But suppose the market is depressed when you are ready to sell. You have to move, but you don't want to sell in a depressed market.

Can you move out, rent your home, then sell it later when the market recovers—and still qualify for the exclusion of gain?

With proper attention to timing, yes.

Two-Year Rule. As explained above, you are entitled to the exclusion if you meet the two-year test. Specifically, if during the five-year period ending on the date of the sale you owned and used the residence as your principal residence for two years or more, the exclusion applies. There is no requirement that the property be your principal residence *on the date of sale*. So moving out and renting the home will not result in disqualification, provided that you owned and used the property as your principal residence for two of the five years preceding the sale.

> **Example**
>
> Suppose you have owned and used your home as your principal residence since 1992. You now get a great job offer in another city. The market for your home is currently depressed, so you rent it under a two-year lease and move to your new job location. You sell your former home two years later when the lease expires and after the real estate market has recovered. Your sale qualifies for the exclusion because you owned and used the property as your principal residence for two years during the five-year period preceding its sale.

Rental Property Deductions. If you cease using your home as your residence and hold it for rental, you then become entitled to rental property deductions. These are the ordinary and necessary expenses you pay for the management, conservation, or maintenance of the property. Such expenses are deductible even though your property was formerly used by you as your home. The deductions allowed include depreciation and your operating expenses, such as repairs. These deductions are in addition to your deductions for mortgage interest and real estate taxes.

> **Tax Tip**
>
> *Tax Benefits from Rental Deductions.* The rental deductions you get when you rent out your home may provide you with the benefit of tax sheltered cash flow and, perhaps, even a tax loss to shelter your other income. (See Section 8.7.)

Can You Wear Two Hats? Does qualification of your property as your "principal residence" for purposes of the exclusion provisions prevent the property from simultaneously qualifying for rental property deductions while the property is temporarily rented prior to its sale? Under the old rollover provisions, it was held that it does not. If your residence was converted to rental use with the requisite profit motive, its continuing qualification as a principal residence wouldn't prevent the deduction of rental expenses. The same rule should apply under the present exclusion provisions. Conversely, the rental doesn't cause your former home to lose its status as a principal residence for purposes of the exclusion.

So, yes, you can wear two hats.

Bottom Line. High interest rates, a recession, or other economic factors may temporarily cause prices to be depressed when you are ready to move. Assuming you don't need the sales proceeds of your present home to purchase a new home, the rent-before-sale idea may permit you to wait for a turnaround before you sell your present home without losing the benefit of the exclusion, getting tax sheltered rental income in the meantime.

And you may make money as a landlord!

4.13 How to Avoid Reporting to the IRS

The IRS is hardly anyone's favorite government agency. So it's not surprising that home sellers are less than thrilled when they learn that the person responsible for closing the sale of their home generally has to file a form 1099-S with the IRS, providing details about the sale, including the gross proceeds.

You probably subscribe to the philosophy that it's best to let sleeping dogs lie. So even though the sale of your principal residence is nontaxable under the exclusion rules, you wouldn't mind if you could legitimately avoid reporting the sale to the IRS.

With a little effort, it's usually possible. There's an exemption from the regular real estate reporting requirements if all of your gain qualifies for the exclusion. To qualify for the exemption you have to provide the "real estate reporting person," usually the person closing the transaction, with specified written assurances.

The IRS has prescribed the written assurances that a real estate reporting person must obtain from you to exempt your sale from the information reporting requirements. It must be a written certification from you signed under the penalties of perjury that four specified "assurances" are true.

Observation

Co-owners. If the residence has more than one owner (for example, you and your spouse), the real estate reporting person must either obtain the certification from each owner, whether married or not, or follow the regular procedure of filing an information return for any owner not making the certification.

The assurances for avoiding information reporting are:

1. You owned and used the residence as your principal residence for periods aggregating two years or more during the five-year period ending on the date of the sale.
2. You have not sold another principal residence during the two-year period ending on the date of the sale.
3. No portion of the residence has been used for business or rental purposes by you (or your spouse if you are married) after May 6, 1997.
4. At least one of the following three statements applies:

    (a) The sale is of the entire residence for $250,000 or less.

    OR

    (b) You are married, the sale is of the entire residence for $500,000 or less, and the gain on the sale of the entire residence is $250,000 or less.

    OR

    (c) You are married, the sale is of the entire residence for $500,000 or less, and (1) you intend to file a joint return for the year of the sale, (2) your spouse also used the residence as his or her principal residence for periods aggregating two years or more during the five-year period ending on the date of the sale of the residence, and (3) your spouse also has not sold another principal residence during the two-year period ending on the date of the sale of the residence.

> **Observation**
>
> *Use at Time of Sale.* **The assurance that the residence was owned and used as your principal residence for periods aggregating two years or more during the five-year period preceding the sale does *not* require that you be using the residence as your principal residence at the time of the sale.**

If you qualify to exclude *all* your gain, giving the assurances presents no problem. But what if a portion of the residence has been used for business or rental purposes by you or your spouse, so that the assurance in 3 above can't be given? This presents a conundrum. The assurance that no portion of the residence was used for business or rental purposes by you or your spouse is a requirement based on rules that the IRS has changed, as explained in Section 4.8. Since home office or other business use within the "four walls" of a dwelling unit no longer produces any reduction of the exclusion, it would seem that this assurance should no longer be necessary. The IRS will probably soon amend its rules for exemption from the reporting requirements to eliminate this glitch.

The IRS has provided a sample certification form for use by the real estate reporting person to obtain the required assurances, illustrated in Figure 4.1. The real estate reporting person may obtain the certification at any time on or before January 31 of the year following the year of sale. The certification must be retained by the real estate reporting person for four years following the year of the sale. A real estate reporting person who relies on a certification made in compliance with the IRS requirements will not be liable for the penalties applicable to a failure to file an information return, provided there is no actual knowledge that any assurance is incorrect.

TAX SHELTER WHEN YOU SELL YOUR HOME

FORM

CERTIFICATION FOR NO INFORMATION REPORTING
ON THE SALE OR EXCHANGE OF A PRINCIPAL RESIDENCE

This form may be completed by the seller of a principal residence. This information is necessary to determine whether the sale or exchange should be reported to the seller, and to the Internal Revenue Service on Form 1099-S, Proceeds From Real Estate Transactions. If the seller properly completes Part I and III, and makes a "yes" response to assurances (1) through (4) in Part II, no information is sold or exchanged. Thus, if a residence has more than one owner, a real estate reporting person must either obtain a certification from each owner (whether married or not) or file an information return and furnish a payee statement for any owner that does not make the certification.

Part I. Seller Information

1. Name _____

2. Address or legal description (including city, state, and ZIP code) of residence being sold or exchanged
   _____
   _____

3. Taxpayer Identification Number (TIN) _____

Part II. Seller Assurances

Check "yes" or "no" for assurances (1) through (4).

Yes No

☐   ☐   (1) I owned and used the residence as my principal residence for periods aggregating 2 years or more during the 5-year period ending on the date of the sale or exchange of the residence.

☐   ☐   (2) I have not sold or exchanged another principal residence during the 2-year period ending on the date of the sale or exchange of the residence (not taking into account any sale or exchange before May 7, 1997).

☐   ☐   (3) No portion of the residence has been used for business or rental purposes by me (or my spouse if I am married) after May 6, 1997.

☐   ☐   (4) At least one of the following three statements applies:

The sale or exchange is of the entire residence for $250,000 or less.

OR
I am married, the sale or exchange is of the entire residence for $500,000 or less, and the gain on the sale or exchange of the entire residence is $250,000 or less.

OR
I am married, the sale or exchange is of the entire residence for $500,000 or less, and (a) I intend to file a joint return for the year of the sale or exchange, (b) my spouse also used the residence as his or her principal residence for periods aggregating 2 years or more during the 5-year period ending on the date of the sale or exchange of the residence, and (c) my spouse also has not sold or exchanged another principal residence during the 2-year period ending on the date of the sale or exchange of the residence (not taking into account any sale or exchange before May 7, 1997).

Part III. Seller Certification

Under penalties of perjury, I certify that all the above information is true as of the end of the day of the sale or exchange.

_____   _____
Signature of Seller   Date

FIGURE 4.1   Form to Determine if the Sale or Exchange of a Residence Must Be Reported

4.14 Seller's Tax-Planning Checklist

- **Taxable Gain on Sale.** When you are selling your home at a gain, the most important tax question is whether the entire gain can be excluded from your income. If you qualify, you can exclude up to $250,000 of gain if you are single or up to $500,000 if you are married. (See Sections 4.4 through 4.9.)
- **Gain in Excess of Exclusion.** If gain on the sale of your home exceeds the applicable $250,000 or $500,000 ceiling, you still may be able to avoid or postpone tax through tax planning. (See Section 4.11.)
- **Loss on Sale of Residence.** Loss on the sale of your home usually is treated as a nondeductible "personal" loss. However, it may be possible for you to avoid this limitation by converting your home to rental property prior to the sale. (See Section 7.8.)
- **Purchase-Money Mortgage.** If you receive a purchase-money mortgage from the purchaser for part of the purchase price of your home and want to delay reporting any taxable gain on the payments you will receive in the future under the mortgage, you can use the installment method of reporting. (See Section 5.6.)
- **Deduction of Real Estate Taxes.** Your deduction for real estate taxes for the year you sell your home is based on an apportionment formula. The taxes are split between you and the purchaser according to the number of days in the year each of you owns the property. (See Section 1.2.)
- **Information Reporting.** The person responsible for closing your sale may have to report information to IRS, including the identity of the seller, the property sold, the date of the sale, and the sale price. However, it may be possible to avoid reporting to the IRS. (See Section 4.13.)
- **Personal Tax Return of Seller—Form 1040.** Taxable gain from the sale of your home must be reported on your personal Form 1040 for the year in which the sale occurs.
- **Nonforeign Affidavit.** When a foreigner sells United States real estate, the purchaser may have to withhold tax. For your purchaser to be assured that you are not a foreigner, the purchaser normally will request a nonforeign affidavit from you.

CHAPTER 5

The High-Priced Home: How to Avoid Tax When Gain Will Exceed the $250,000 or $500,000 Ceiling

> Taxation is the gentle art of plucking the goose in such a way as to secure the greatest amount of feathers with the least amount of squawking.
>
> — Anonymous

5.1 Overview

For most homeowners, gain on the sale of a principal residence in excess of the available exclusions is no problem. The $250,000 ceiling on gain exclusion for singles or the $500,000 ceiling on gain exclusion for marrieds normally will more than suffice. For the great majority of homeowners, those are big numbers.

But for owners of high-priced homes with large amounts of unrealized appreciation, the exclusion may be less valuable than the old rollover provisions. This is because the exclusion shields a maximum of $250,000 or $500,000 of gain from tax, while the old rollover rules would shield *all* gain, no matter how large, as long as a more costly replacement principal residence was purchased.

The extraordinary levels of home appreciation in the past decade have pushed

THE HIGH-PRICED HOME: HOW TO AVOID TAX

an increasing number of owners of high-priced homes into a tax bind. Indeed, according to the Joint Center for Housing Studies, up to 850,000 American homes may now be valued at $1 million or more. It's likely that the rapid real estate inflation of recent years has caused appreciation on a large proportion of these homes to outrun the $500,000 ceiling established by Congress in 1997.

This chapter illustrates how the excess gain problem can arise, then provides tax ideas for possible solutions. But first, a short diversion for a purposeful riddle.

Two travelers walk one mile due south, one mile due east, and one mile due north, arriving at the point at which they began. They see a bear. What color is it?

This riddle, like the question of how to avoid tax when gain exceeds the allowable ceilings, has a correct answer, but neither can be answered with conventional approaches. The answers in this chapter are not conventional.

(The bear is white. The travelers had to start at the north pole.)

5.2 Upper-Middle-Class Victims

The excess gain problem isn't limited to the wealthy with multimillion-dollar homes. It can hit the upper-middle-class homeowner who has held a home for many years in an upscale community or the upwardly mobile corporate executive who has deferred gain on house sales by a series of rollovers while moving from place to place climbing the corporate ladder.

Example

A fast-rising star executive and his physician wife have moved repeatedly in pursuit of promotions, purchasing a more expensive home with each move. Over the years they have moved five times, using the prior law rollover rules to shield gain on the sale of their principal residence each time they moved. Their purchases and sales were as shown in Table 5.1. (*Note:* The adjusted basis of their first home, $45,000, is increased after each sale by the cost of the next home in excess of the sale price of the preceding home. The accumulated untaxed gain rolled over is the sum of the untaxed gain on each successive sale.)

If the present value of the home is $1,100,000 and it is sold for that amount after the two-year holding period is satisfied, gain on the sale is $975,000 ($1,100,000 sales price − $125,000 adjusted basis = $975,000). In other words, the total gain is the sum of gain on the sale of the present house of $150,000 ($1,100,000 − $950,000), plus prior unreported gain of $825,000.

TAX SHELTER WHEN YOU SELL YOUR HOME

TABLE 5.1 Calculating Accumulated Untaxed Deferred Gain

		Adjusted Basis	Accumulated Gain Rolled Over
Purchase 1967	$ 45,000	$ 45,000	
Sale 1972	100,000	(original cost)	$ 55,000
Purchase 1972	105,000	50,000	
Sale 1977	195,000	(45,000 + 5,000)	145,000
Purchase 1977	200,000	55,000	
Sale 1982	380,000	(50,000 + 5,000)	325,000
Purchase 1982	400,000	75,000	
Sale 1988	680,000	(55,000 + 20,000)	605,000
Purchase 1988	700,000	95,000	
Sale 1996	920,000	(75,000 + 20,000)	825,000
Purchase 1996	950,000	125,000	
		(95,000 + 30,000)	
Accumulated untaxed deferred gain:		$825,000	

5.3 Tax Time Bomb

This unreported gain from rollovers of previous sales is a ticking tax time bomb. Despite the exclusion rules exempting up to $500,000 of gain, the couple in the example will still face taxable gain of $475,000, assuming the two-year holding period and the other requirements for qualifying for the $500,000 exclusion discussed in Sections 4.3 through 4.7 are met ($975,000 − $500,000 = $475,000). Assuming a 15 percent capital gain rate, the tax bill will be $71,250 (.15 × $475,000). Under the old rollover rules, the *entire* gain of $475,000 could have been rolled over by the purchase of a principal residence for $1,100,000 or more, with *no* tax bill.

> **Tax Tip**
>
> *Be Nice to Your Spouse.* If you have a large potential gain, your marital status is important. For example, if the husband in the example had been single, he would have been able to exclude only $250,000 of gain, not $500,000. The increased tax bill: $108,750 (.15 × $725,000).

Can you avoid this kind of tax hit? Perhaps, but not with plain vanilla sales. If you are willing to consider unconventional approaches, there are several tax-planning ideas that may help solve this problem. Whether any of them are practical depends on your personal situation.

But before we get to the potential solutions, let's take a quick look at two ways of possibly avoiding the problem in the first place.

Preemptive Sale. The tax-planning ideas discussed below require consideration only when your gain will substantially exceed the available exclusion. Before you grapple with the planning ideas, you should consider whether you can entirely avoid the excess gain problem with a preemptive sale. If you own a high-priced, substantially appreciated residence and anticipate further appreciation that will push you beyond your exclusion ceiling, you should consider selling in the near future. By selling soon while gain is still covered by your exclusion, taxable gain will be avoided. Your immediate purchase of a similarly priced replacement home *would set the gain counter back to zero!*

Increasing Basis of Residence. Your gain when you sell your residence is the excess of its selling price, less selling expenses such as commissions, over your adjusted basis for the residence. Your adjusted basis generally is your original cost, *plus* the cost of improvements you have made. If you are a longtime owner, you may find that when you add the cost of your improvements to your original cost, the prospective gain can be substantially reduced. Improvement costs you can add to basis include the costs of such permanent additions as a new or renovated kitchen or bath, an added bedroom, a tennis court or in-ground swimming pool, a new furnace or roof, an air-conditioning system, insulation, a driveway, and landscaping. If you haven't saved records of these costs you can make estimates, but estimates may not hold up if challenged by the IRS.

5.4 Tax Idea 1: Deferred Sale Approach

The easiest way to avoid the tax hit on excess gain is to do nothing. If you defer the sale of your home and continue to hold it until death, the problem goes away. This is because upon your death your home will receive a "stepped-up" basis equal to its fair market value, so that a sale shortly after your death will produce no taxable gain on its appreciated value. In other words, when your home is included in your estate for federal estate tax purposes, its cost for tax purposes is "marked up" to its value at that time, so that if it is sold shortly after your death there is no capital gain.

If you use this deferred sale approach to avoiding tax, you can live in your home until your death, but you don't have to. If you have the temperament and the financial wherewithal, you can convert your home into a rental property and rent it out until death, buying or renting another home to live in. Either way, it may be possible to mortgage the home or former home to get tax-free mortgage proceeds during your life. (Mortgage loan proceeds are not taxable.)

For some owners of high-price homes, this approach may provide a satisfactory solution. However, if you are relatively young or your desire to sell your home is strong, it may be regarded as unsatisfactory.

> **Caution**
>
> The "step-up" basis rules are scheduled for partial repeal in 2010 and, strange as it seems, reinstatement in 2011. You should keep an eye on congressional action on the step-up rules if you want to use this tax-planning idea.

5.5 Tax Idea 2: The Leasehold Carve-Out

You may be able to solve your tax problem by borrowing an idea from architecture. Architect Mies van der Rohe said good design required recognition of a seemingly contradictory concept: Less is more. If you are willing to stretch, you may be able to apply a similar concept to slash the tax on the sale of your appreciated home. If you can sell *less* of the property, you can retain *more* after taxes.

How can you sell "less" of your home?

Split Your Property. You can sell "less" of your home by legally splitting it into two pieces. First, you split the property up between the land on which the house sits and the house itself. Then, you *rent* the land and *sell* only the house to the purchaser.

When you split your property into two parts like this, you are creating what is known in legalese as *fee* and *leasehold* positions. The land you retain ownership of is the fee position, and the house you sell is known as the leasehold position. You sell the purchaser the house, and the purchaser owns the house, but since the house sits on land you "ground lease" to the purchaser, the purchaser's position is called a leasehold position. Using this approach, you pay tax only on the portion of the property you sell, namely, the house.

As a result, you have less gain to report.

It's not a new idea. For example, so-called "ground rents" have been used for real estate financing in Maryland for over a century. They serve as a kind of second mortgage financing, permitting the home purchaser to avoid paying for the land when the home is initially purchased. The ground rent is "redeemable." This means the house purchaser can later purchase the land for a specified amount when the purchaser can afford it. Such ground rents are considered desirable investments.

How to Split Your Property. Assuming it's legal in your state, you can create a counterpart of the Maryland ground rent by splitting your property into fee and leasehold positions. You would lease your land to the purchaser for a set monthly rental amount that the purchaser would be required to pay to you and, at the same time you lease your land to the purchaser, the purchaser would purchase your house alone. Since you have sold only your house and not your land, you have reduced the amount of gain subject to tax. At the same time, this arrangement reduces the amount the purchaser has to pay for the property by the value of the land. You normally would give the purchaser of the house the option to purchase the underlying land for a fixed sum, possibly with an inflation adjustment. This will give the purchaser—and presumably any lender—the ability to acquire ownership of the entire property.

The Tax Break. If the option to purchase the land is not exercisable until after your death, your land will get a stepped-up basis on your death. See Section 5.4. As a result, when the option is exercised, tax will be avoided on the gain attributable to the land.

An example will illustrate how this rather exotic idea might work.

Example

Assume in the example earlier in this chapter that the owners like the leasehold carve-out idea. They hire an appraiser who appraises the land on which their house is situated at $300,000 and their house alone at $800,000, both together equaling the total $1,100,000 value for the entire property. Then, instead of selling the entire property to the purchaser for $1 million, they lease the land to the purchaser under a 99-year lease for $18,000 yearly (6 percent of $300,000), and they simultaneously sell the house to the purchaser for $800,000.

To figure the gain on the sale of the house, the first step is to split the basis for the entire property, $125,000, between the house and the land. You do this by multiplying the value of the entire property, $1 million, by the ratio of the value of the house to the value of the entire property. Thus, of the seller's total basis of $125,000 for the house and land, $90,909 is allocated to the house (800,000/1,100,000 × $125,000), so that the gain on the sale is $709,091 ($800,000 − 90,909 = $709,091). By reducing the selling price and allocating the basis for the entire property between the land and the house in the ratio of their values, the gain on the sale is reduced to $709,091.

Result: After applying the $500,000 exclusion, taxable gain is reduced from $475,000 to $209,091 ($709,091 − $500,000), and the tax is reduced from $71,250 to $31,364 (.15 × $209,091), *or a savings of $39,886.*

Is all the complexity worth it? In some cases it may be. Let's see how the parties make out.

The Sellers. For the sellers, the obvious advantage is that they have saved a tidy $39,866 in tax. In addition, they have also created a solid, income-producing asset for themselves in the form of a valuable ground rent that they can hold for investment. It is also possible that they could swap the ground rent tax free for other investment property, such as a rental condominium, and mortgage it and receive the loan proceeds tax free.

The Purchaser. For the purchaser the deal also may be attractive. First, by helping the sellers reduce tax, the purchaser may be able to strike a better bargain in purchasing the house. Second, cost is lowered. The out-of-pocket outlay or mortgage financing needed to purchase the house is reduced by the amount attributable to the land. This makes the purchase easier for the purchaser to handle.

Practical Issues. Implementing the carve-out approach may present practical difficulties. Often, purchasers will not be comfortable with owning a house on leased land. Similarly, you may not be comfortable with being a landlord. Also, the purchaser's bank may be unwilling to finance the purchase of a home on leased land, even though you would be willing to give the purchaser and the bank an option to purchase the land at its agreed value. These or related problems may make the use of the leasehold carve-out strategy inappropriate.

> **Caution**
>
> Implementing a leasehold carve-out requires sophisticated legal know-how. Be sure to consult with an experienced real estate lawyer before using this technique.

Alternative Approach. There is a variation on the "less-is-more" theme that may be easier to implement than the leasehold carve-out. This alternative format may be available when your property consists of more than just the house and lot.

Extra Lot or Land. You can sell less than your entire property if you have a separate additional lot or acreage that can be spun off. The same is so if you have a separate cottage, studio, barn, or other building. These situations offer you the opportunity for splitting the property up between your house and its lot and the rest of the property, selling the house and lot alone and retaining the balance of the property. With this variation on the less-is-more approach, the selling price may be sufficiently reduced so that your gain either does not exceed the $250,000 or $500,000 ceiling, or is reduced to a tolerable level.

Taking the above example, suppose your property had a separate building lot worth $300,000 that you could retain while selling the house and the lot for $800,000. Using this variation on the less-is-more theme, the selling price and tax could be reduced to the same extent as in the leasehold carve-out example.

And with considerably less angst.

5.6 Tax Idea 3: The Installment Sale

If you don't want to defer the sale of your home and the less-is-more approaches discussed above are not practical for you, you should consider the alternative of an installment sale. An installment sale is a sale in which the purchase price is paid to you in installments. For example, the purchaser of your home might pay you 20 percent of the purchase price of your home as a down payment, and pay you the balance of the purchase price in installments, say five equal annual installments or 60 equal monthly installments. The installments would be paid with interest.

The installment sale technique will not eliminate tax on the amount of gain in excess of the exclusion, but it will *delay* the date when tax on such gain becomes payable. This tax deferral can last for many years and, as will be shown below, can provide you with an important financial benefit.

Observation

Retirement Planning Pointer. For some individuals, an installment sale may be a useful retirement planning strategy. The installment sale creates an income-producing asset for you—the purchaser's installment note payable to you. This note usually is a safe investment because it usually is secured by a mortgage in your favor on your former residence. In other words, you are in a position similar to a bank that can foreclose on a mortgage if the mortgage debt isn't paid. If the installment note pays interest and principal over an extended period, it can be an excellent source of secure retirement income.

The amount of monthly cash flow from a 15-year installment note is illustrated in the sample Loan Payment Calculator (Table 5.3) on page 117.

The Tax Break. With the typical all cash deal, you have to pay an immediate tax on the entire gain not covered by the exclusion. This up-front tax payment

TAX SHELTER WHEN YOU SELL YOUR HOME

reduces the after-tax proceeds you retain from the sale and, correspondingly, the funds you have to invest to produce income.

With an installment sale, however, you don't have to report taxable gain not covered by the exclusion except on the down payment and on the installments, and the installments may be spread out over many years. As a result, an installment sale substantially reduces your current tax burden. Moreover, the installment sale creates a valuable investment asset: the interest-bearing installment note you get from the purchaser representing the balance of the purchase price.

This happy tax effect can be illustrated by an example.

Example

The facts are the same as in the prior example, except the sellers are approaching retirement. They have paid off their mortgage and own the house free and clear. Since they have become empty nesters and the house is much too large for their needs, they want to sell the house and purchase a condominium in a retirement area. The value of the house represents the largest portion of their retirement nest egg, and they are anxious to avoid the current tax hit that would result from a regular sale. To lighten the tax hit, they decide to make an installment sale of the house. They will take a down payment of 25 percent of the value of the house, $275,000, so that they will have the funds to purchase their retirement condominium, and they will take the balance of the purchase price, $825,000, in the form of a 15-year installment note from the purchaser. The installment note will be self-amortizing. In other words, each installment payment to them will include both principal and interest, with the principal component in each payment increasing so that when the last installment payment is made the entire principal balance will be paid off or "amortized." Interest at the rate of 7.5 percent per year will be paid on the unpaid balance of the installment note.

Observation

Payments under a 15-year $825,000 self-amortizing installment note with interest at 7.5 percent are illustrated in the Loan Payment Calculator in Table 5.3 (page 117).

THE HIGH-PRICED HOME: HOW TO AVOID TAX

How Do the Numbers Work? By making an installment sale, the sellers have spread the tax hit over 16 years, that is, the year the down payment is received and the succeeding 15 years during which annual (or, if desired, monthly) principal payments are received under the installment note. Since in the year of sale they pay tax only on the recognized gain included in the 25 percent down-payment received, they leave 75 percent of the sale price or $825,000 working for them *without reduction by taxes*. As shown in Table 5.2, this produces an income of $74,734 per year (disregarding principal payments). Thus, the installment sale has created a relatively long-term source of income for them. The purchaser's installment note secured by a purchase-money mortgage on their former home will provide them with a secure retirement income for 15 years to supplement their pension income. By spreading the tax on this gain over 15 years, they may even get to pay the capital gains tax at a rate less than 20 percent as they receive the installment payments of principal over the years.

Comparing the Numbers. A comparison of the investment return the owners can obtain on an outright sale with the return they can obtain on an installment sale demonstrates the virtues of an installment sale. Assume the owners can invest the cash they receive on an outright sale for a safe 5 percent return but, as is likely, they can get a higher return from interest on the installment note secured by the purchase-money mortgage, say 7.5 percent.

TABLE 5.2 Comparison of Investment Returns

	Cash Deal	Installment Deal
Sale price	$1,100,000	$1,100,000
Cash payment	1,100,000	275,000
Tax at 15% after exclusion	71,250	17,813
After tax cash retained	1,028,750	257,187
Return at 5%	51,438	12,859
Interest on mortgage at 7.5%	-0-	61,875
Total return	$51,438	$74,734

Note: The 15 percent capital gain rate is applied against the gain on the sale *after* such gain is reduced by the full $500,000 exclusion and the basis for the home, $125,000 ($1,100,000 − ($500,000 + $125,000) = $475,000 x .15 = $71,250).

Using an installment sale, the investment return is *almost 50 percent higher* in the first year. Why? Because the sellers have substantially more money at work at a higher rate of return with the installment sale than with an outright sale.

The interest earned on the installment note principal will be reduced as the principal of the installment note is paid off, but the reduction is gradual.

Observation

Level Payments Possible. If the sellers want the installment payment amounts to be the same each month for the entire term of the installment note, the note can be made a so-called "level payment" self-amortizing note, illustrated in the Loan Payment Calculation in Table 5.3 (page 117). Then the reduction in the interest component in each monthly payment is accompanied by a corresponding increase in the principal component of the monthly payment, so that the amount of each payment over the 15-year payout period will remain the same each month. When the last monthly payment is made, the full amount of the principal of the debt will have been paid. The declining amount of interest received each year will be subject to tax as ordinary income and the increasing installments of principal received each year will be taxed as capital gain.

Extra Cash Needed? If the sellers need more cash on the sale, they can take a larger down payment. Alternatively, they should consider mortgaging the property *prior* to the sale to obtain the necessary funds. But if they take this approach to getting extra cash, they should mortgage the property well before it is placed on the market for sale. Otherwise, the IRS might claim the mortgage proceeds should be considered a taxable payment in the year of sale for installment reporting purposes.

Caution

Proper documentation of an installment sale with a valid purchase-money mortgage should not be a do-it-yourself undertaking. It requires the expertise of an experienced real estate attorney. It's also important for the attorney to understand the tax rules applicable to installment sales.

5.7 Tax Idea 4: Conversion to Rental and Exchange

Investment rental properties can be exchanged tax free. This fact forms the basis of still another planning approach to avoiding tax on excess gain, the conversion to rental and exchange technique. The idea is to convert the personal residence to rental property held for investment, then either continue to hold it for the production of rental income or exchange it tax free for other income-producing property. The procedure is illustrated below.

The conversion and exchange approach may be suitable for owners approaching retirement who plan to trade down to a less expensive home, or who for other reasons do not need the sales proceeds from the sale of their residence to acquire another residence. For such individuals, conversion of their residence to investment rental property may be another approach to avoiding excess taxable gain—and incidentally creating a real estate investment that will produce retirement income.

How to Do the Conversion. The first step to implement a conversion is to convert the residence to rental property. To do so, the owners would move to a new home and rent their former residence to a tenant. After they have rented the property for some respectable period of time on arm's-length terms, say for a year or so at fair rental value, the former residence will be "converted" for tax purposes from their principal residence to property held by the owners for investment. Property held for investment can qualify for a tax-free like-kind exchange for other property held for investment.

To Exchange or Not to Exchange. That may be the question. After you have converted your former home to rental property, you may decide that you like it as an investment and want to retain it. If it is a relatively trouble-free investment that produces a steady return, keeping it may be preferable to obtaining another investment in an exchange. Also, as explained in Section 8.5, the rental of the home, like the rental of other real estate, can provide tax-sheltered cash flow for you and, possibly, a tax loss with which you can shelter other income.

However, an exchange for other rental property may be desirable for a variety of reasons, such as a higher return, fewer vacancy problems, better appreciation potential, or fewer management headaches.

> **Example**
>
> Assume the home is worth $1 million, as in the prior examples. Assume also that the net income from rental of the residence is substantially less than the net income that could be derived from a small apartment building that you could acquire in a swap, using the $1 million value of the residence. To implement the swap you would find a buyer for the residence and use the buyer's money to purchase the apartment in a so-called three-way exchange. (This three-way exchange procedure is explained in Section 7.3.)

If an owner wants to avoid involvement with management of apartments or other real estate, a trade of the former residence for high-quality net leased property might be possible. A *net lease* is a lease that places part or all of the property management responsibilities on the tenant, including the responsibility for the payment of expenses.

> **Caution**
>
> Successful implementation of tax-free exchanges requires expertise in both tax law and real estate law. Be sure to get legal guidance from a lawyer experienced in both areas before you proceed.

5.8 Summing Up

After reviewing the tax-planning ideas discussed in this chapter, you know the devil is in the details. Each of the plans involves drawbacks, and none of them should be undertaken without competent professional help. Indeed, even if you own a high-priced home with potential gain substantially in excess of the available exclusion, you might prefer to pay a current tax rather than undertake any of these unconventional approaches to tax avoidance. But if tax avoidance is an important objective for you, these tax-planning strategies warrant evaluation.

THE HIGH-PRICED HOME: HOW TO AVOID TAX

TABLE 5.3 Loan Payment Calculator

Amount Borrowed	$ 825,000.00
Annual Interest Rate	7.5
Number of Payments	12
Amortization Period in Years	15
	$
Payment Amount is	7,647.85
Principal	$ 825,000.00
Interest Paid	$ 551,613.35
Total Repaid	$1,376,613.35

Payment Number	Payment	Principal	Interest	Balance
1	7,647.85	2,491.60	5,156.25	822,508.40
2	7,647.85	2,507.17	5,140.68	820,001.22
3.	7,647.85	2,522.84	5,125.01	817,478.38
4.	7,647.85	2,538.61	5,109.24	814,939.77
5	7,647.85	2,554.48	5,039.37	812,385.29
6	7,647.85	2,570.44	5,077.41	809,814.84
7	7,647.85	2,586.51	5,061.34	807,228.34
8	7,647.85	2,602.67	5,045.18	804,625.66
9	7,647.85	2,618.94	5,028.91	802,006.72
10	7,647.85	2,635.21	5,012.54	799,371.41
11	7,647.85	2,651.78	4,996.07	796,719.63
12	7,647.85	2,668.35	4,979.50	794,051.27
Totals	91,774.22	30,948.73	60,825.50	– YEAR 1
13	7,647.85	2,685.03	4,962.82	791,366.24
14	7,647.85	2,701.81	4,946.04	788,664.43
15	7,647.85	2,718.70	4,929.15	785,945.73
16	7,647.85	2,735.69	4,912.16	783,210.04
17	7,647.85	2,752.79	4,895.06	780,457.25
18	7,647.85	2,769.99	4,877.86	777,687.26
19	7,647.85	2,787.31	4,860.55	774,899.95

(Continued)

TABLE 5.3 *(Continued)*

Payment Number	Payment	Principal	Interest	Balance
20	7,647.85	2,804.73	4,843.12	772,095.22
21	7,647.85	2,822.26	4,825.60	769,272.97
22	7,647.85	2,839.90	4,807.96	766,433.07
23	7,647.85	2,857.65	4,790.21	763,575.42
24	7,647.85	2,875.51	4,772.35	760,699.92
Totals	183,548.45	64,300.08	119,248.37	– YEAR 2
25	7,647.85	2,893.48	4,754.37	757,806.44
26	7,647.85	2,911.56	4,736.29	754,894.88
27	7,647.85	2,929.76	4,718.09	751,965.12
28	7,647.85	2,948.07	4,699.78	749,017.05
29	7,647.85	2,966.50	4,681.36	746,050.55
30	7,647.85	2,985.04	4,662.82	743,065.52
31	7,647.85	3,003.69	4,644.16	740,061.83
32	7,647.85	3,022.47	4,625.39	737,039.36
33	7,647.85	3,041.36	4,606.50	733,998.00
34	7,647.85	3,060.36	4,587.49	730,937.64
35	7,647.85	3,079.49	4,568.36	727,858.15
36	7,647.85	3,098.74	4,549.11	724,759.41
Totals	275,322.67	100,240.59	175,082.08	– YEAR 3
37	7,647.85	3,118.11	4,529.75	721,641.31
38	7,647.85	3,137.59	4,510.26	718,503.71
39	7,647.85	3,157.20	4,490.65	715,346.51
40	7,647.85	3,176.94	4,470.92	712,169.57
41	7,647.85	3,196.79	4,451.06	708,972.78
42	7,647.85	3,216.77	4,431.08	705,756.01
43	7,647.85	3,236.88	4,410.98	702,519.13
44	7,647.85	3,257.11	4,390.74	699,262.02
45	7,647.85	3,277.46	4,370.39	695,984.56
46	7,647.85	3,297.95	4,349.90	692,686.61

TABLE 5.3 *(Continued)*

Payment Number	Payment	Principal	Interest	Balance
47	7,647.85	3,318.56	4,329.29	689,368.05
48	7,647.85	3,339.30	4,308.55	686,028.75
Totals	367,096.89	138,971.25	228,125.64	– YEAR 4
49	7,647.85	3,360.17	4,287.68	682,668.57
50	7,647.85	3,381.17	4,266.68	679,287.40
51	7,647.85	3,402.31	4,245.55	675,885.10
52	7,647.85	3,423.57	4,224.28	672,461.53
53	7,647.85	3,444.97	4,202.88	669,016.56
54	7,647.85	3,466.50	4,181.35	665,550.06
55	7,647.85	3,488.16	4,159.69	662,061.90
56	7,647.85	3,509.97	4,137.89	658,551.39
57	7,647.85	3,531.90	4,115.95	655,020.03
58	7,647.85	3,553.98	4,093.88	651,466.05
59	7,647.85	3,576.19	4,071.66	647,889.86
60	7,647.85	3,598.54	4,049.31	644,291.32
Totals	458,871.12	180,708.68	278,162.44	– YEAR 5
61	7,647.85	3,621.03	4,026.82	640,670.29
62	7,647.85	3,643.66	4,004.19	637,026.63
63	7,647.85	3,666.44	3,981.42	633,360.19
64	7,647.85	3,689.35	3,958.50	629,670.84
65	7,647.85	3,712.41	3,935.44	625,958.43
66	7,647.85	3,735.61	3,912.24	622,222.82
67	7,647.85	3,758.96	3,888.89	618,463.86
68	7,647.85	3,782.45	3,865.40	614,681.41
69	7,647.85	3,806.09	3,841.76	610,875.32
70	7,647.85	3,829.88	3,817.97	607,045.43
71	7,647.85	3,853.82	3,794.03	603,191.62
72	7,647.85	3,877.90	3,769.95	599,313.71
Totals	550,645.34	225,686.29	324,959.05	– YEAR 6

(Continued)

TAX SHELTER WHEN YOU SELL YOUR HOME

TABLE 5.3 *(Continued)*

Payment Number	Payment	Principal	Interest	Balance
73	7,647.85	3,902.14	3,745.71	595,411.57
74	7,647.85	3,926.53	3,721.32	591,485.04
75	7,647.85	3,951.07	3,696.78	587,533.97
76	7,647.85	3,975.76	3,672.09	583,558.21
77	7,647.85	4,000.61	3,647.24	579,557.59
78	7,647.85	4,025.62	3,622.23	575,531.98
79	7,647.85	4,050.78	3,597.07	571,481.20
80	7,647.85	4,076.09	3,571.76	567,405.10
81	7,647.85	4,101.57	3,546.28	563,303.53
82	7,647.85	4,127.20	3,520.65	559,176.33
83	7,647.85	4,153.00	3,494.85	555,023.33
84	7,647.85	4,178.96	3,468.90	550,844.37
Totals	642,419.57	274,155.63	368,263.94	– YEAR 7
85	7,647.85	4,205.07	3,442.78	546,639.30
86	7,647.85	4,231.36	3,416.50	542,407.94
87	7,647.85	4,257.80	3,390.05	538,150.14
88	7,647.85	4,284.41	3,363.44	533,865.73
89	7,647.85	4,311.19	3,336.66	529,554.53
90	7,647.85	4,338.14	3,309.72	525,216.40
91	7,647.85	4,365.25	3,282.60	520,851.15
92	7,647.85	4,392.53	3,255.32	516,458.62
93	7,647.85	4,419.99	3,227.87	512,038.63
94	7,647.85	4,447.61	3,200.24	507,591.02
95	7,647.85	4,475.41	3,172.44	503,115.61
96	7,647.85	4,503.38	3,144.47	498,612.23
Totals	734,193.79	326,387.77	407,806.02	– YEAR 8
97	7,647.85	4,531.53	3,116.33	494,080.71
98	7,647.85	4,559.85	3,088.00	489,520.86
99	7,647.85	4,588.35	3,059.51	484,932.51
100	7,647.85	4,617.02	3,030.83	480,315.49

THE HIGH-PRICED HOME: HOW TO AVOID TAX

TABLE 5.3 *(Continued)*

Payment Number	Payment	Principal	Interest	Balance
101	7,647.85	4,645.88	3,001.97	475,669.61
102	7,647.85	4,674.92	2,972.94	470,994.69
103	7,647.85	4,704.14	2,943.72	466,290.56
104	7,647.85	4,733.54	2,914.32	461,557.02
105	7,647.85	4,763.12	2,884.73	456,793.90
106	7,647.85	4,792.89	2,854.96	452,001.01
107	7,647.85	4,822.85	2,825.01	447,178.16
108	7,647.85	4,852.99	2,794.86	442,325.18
Totals	825,968.01	382,674.82	443,293.19	– YEAR 9
109	7,647.85	4,883.32	2,764.53	437,441.86
110	7,647.85	4,913.84	2,734.01	432,528.02
111	7,647.85	4,944.55	2,703.30	427,583.46
112	7,647.85	4,975.46	2,672.40	422,608.01
113	7,647.85	5,006.55	2,641.30	417,601.46
114	7,647.85	5,037.84	2,610.01	412,563.61
115	7,647.85	5,069.33	2,578.52	407,494.29
116	7,647.85	5,101.01	2,546.84	402,393.27
117	7,647.85	5,132.89	2,514.96	397,260.38
118	7,647.85	5,164.97	2,482.88	392,095.40
119	7,647.85	5,197.26	2,460.60	386,898.15
120	7,647.85	5,229.74	2,418.11	381,668.41
Totals	917,742.24	443,331.91	474,410.65	– YEAR 10
121	7,647.85	5,262.42	2,385.43	376,405.99
122	7,647.85	5,295.31	2,352.54	371,110.67
123	7,647.85	5,328.41	2,319.44	365,782.26
124	7,647.85	5,361.71	2,286.14	360,420.55
125	7,647.85	5,395.22	2,252.63	355,025.32
126	7,647.85	5,428.94	2,218.91	349,596.38
127	7,647.85	5,462.87	2,184.98	344,133.51

(Continued)

TAX SHELTER WHEN YOU SELL YOUR HOME

TABLE 5.3 *(Continued)*

Payment Number	Payment	Principal	Interest	Balance
128	7,647.85	5,497.02	2,150.83	338,636.49
129	7,647.85	5,531.37	2,116.48	333,105.11
130	7,647.85	5,565.95	2,081.91	327,539.17
131	7,647.85	5,600.73	2,047.12	321,938.44
132	7,647.85	5,635.74	2,012.12	316,302.70
Totals	1,009,516.46	508,697.30	500,819.16	– YEAR 11
133	7,647.85	5,670.96	1,976.89	310,631.74
134	7,647.85	5,706.40	1,941.45	304,925.34
135	7,647.85	5,742.07	1,905.78	299,183.27
136	7,647.85	5,777.96	1,869.90	293,405.31
137	7,647.85	5,814.07	1,833.78	287,591.24
138	7,647.85	5,850.41	1,797.45	281,740.84
139	7,647.85	5,886.97	1,760.88	275,853.86
140	7,647.85	5,923.77	1,724.09	269,930.10
141	7,647.85	5,960.79	1,687.06	263,969.31
142	7,647.85	5,998.04	1,649.81	257,971.27
143	7,647.85	6,035.53	1,612.32	251,935.73
144	7,647.85	6,073.25	1,574.60	245,862.48
Totals	1,101,290.68	579,137.52	522,153.16	– YEAR 12
145	7,647.85	6,111.21	1,536.64	239,751.27
146	7,647.85	6,149.41	1,498.45	233,601.86
147	7,647.85	6,187.84	1,460.01	227,414.02
148	7,647.85	6,226.51	1,421.34	221,187.51
149	7,647.85	6,265.43	1,382.42	214,922.08
150	7,647.85	6,304.59	1,343.26	208,617.49
151	7,647.85	6,343.99	1,303.86	202,273.50
152	7,647.85	6,383.64	1,264.21	195,889.85
153	7,647.85	6,423.54	1,224.31	189,466.31
154	7,647.85	6,463.69	1,184.16	183,002.63

THE HIGH-PRICED HOME: HOW TO AVOID TAX

TABLE 5.3 *(Continued)*

Payment Number	Payment	Principal	Interest	Balance
155	7,647.85	6,504.09	1,143.77	176,498.54
156	7,647.85	6,544.74	1,103.12	169,953.80
Totals	1,193,064.91	655,046.20	538,018.71	– YEAR 13
157	7,647.85	6,585.64	1,062.21	163,368.16
158	7,647.85	6,626.80	1,021.05	156,741.36
159	7,647.85	6,668.22	979.63	150,073.14
160	7,647.85	6,709.89	937.96	143,363.25
161	7,647.85	6,751.83	896.02	136,611.42
162	7,647.85	6,794.03	853.82	129,817.39
163	7,647.85	6,836.49	811.36	122,980.89
164	7,647.85	6,879.22	768.63	116,101.67
165	7,647.85	6,922.22	725.64	109,179.46
166	7,647.85	6,965.48	682.37	102,213.98
167	7,647.85	7,009.01	638.84	95,204.96
168	7,647.85	7,052.82	595.03	88,152.14
Totals	1,284,839.13	736,847.86	547,991.27	– YEAR 14
169	7,647.85	7,096.90	550.95	81,055.24
170	7,647.85	7,141.26	506.60	73,913.98
171	7,647.85	7,185.89	461.96	66,728.09
172	7,647.85	7,230.80	417.05	59,497.29
173	7,647.85	7,275.99	371.86	52,221.30
174	7,647.85	7,321.47	326.38	44,899.83
175	7,647.85	7,367.23	280.62	37,532.60
176	7,647.85	7,413.27	234.58	30,119.33
177	7,647.85	7,459.61	188.25	22,659.72
178	7,647.85	7,506.23	141.62	15,153.49
179	7,647.85	7,553.14	94.71	7,600.35
180	7,647.85	7,600.35	47.50	0.00
Totals	1,376,613.35	825,000.00	551,613.35	– YEAR 15

CHAPTER 6
When Spouses Split

> *The difference between a taxidermist and a tax collector is that the taxidermist leaves the hide.*
>
> **Anonymous**

6.1 Overview

For heinous offenses in ancient China, death was by "slow slicing." For couples locked in modern matrimonial combat, the financial counterpart of slow slicing is dismemberment of their marital property.

In many cases one spouse leaves the principal residence, never to return. This can create a tax problem. Also, in many split-ups it's necessary to raise cash by selling off a vacation home or investment condominium to implement the requirement for equitable distribution of marital property. This, too, can create a tax problem.

Since these actions can have significant tax consequences, planning is important. With planning, solutions may be possible.

6.2 Don't Lose the Exclusion on Principal Residence Sale!

As explained in Section 4.6, a married couple normally can avoid tax on gain up to $500,000 on the sale of their home. But in a separation or divorce, a spouse who moves out of the marital home while retaining ownership of the home may jeopardize the exclusion. This is because the departure may cause the departing owner-spouse to fail to qualify for the exclusion.

The Exclusion Rules. Under the present exclusion rules, there is an ownership and use requirement. The exclusion is available only if the owner of the home, during the five-year period ending on the date of the sale, owned and used the property as his or her principal residence for periods aggregating two years or more. A prolonged separation without any legal action may cause a departing owner-spouse to fail to meet this two-years-in-five rule.

> **Example**
>
> An owner-husband moves out of the marital home and into the home of his girlfriend. The husband and wife remain separated without any legal action and the home is sold four years later. The husband would fail to meet the two-years-in-five test. He would have *used* the property as his principal residence for only *one* year during the five-year period ending on the date of the sale.

The Cure. A separation or divorce can cure this problem. A spouse owning a home is treated for tax purposes as *using* the home as a principal residence during any period the other spouse or former spouse is granted use of the home under a divorce or separation agreement.

To illustrate, suppose in the above example that the wife was granted use of the home under a separation agreement at the time the husband left. Then the wife's use of the home would be attributed to the husband during the four-year period she alone used the home. As a result, the husband would be treated as having both owned *and used* the home for the requisite two-year period prior to the sale.

6.3 Transfer of Home to Spouse

How does the two-years-in-five rule work when a spouse owning the marital residence transfers it to the other spouse in a divorce settlement? Under the general two-years-in-five rule, if a husband owns the home and transfers the home to the wife in the divorce proceeding, the wife wouldn't qualify for the exclusion on an immediate sale because of the ownership requirement. She would have to wait until two years after the transfer to her.

Does she have to wait two years?

No. The two-year rules are relaxed when property is acquired by a spouse in a divorce. If a spouse acquires property in a transfer in a divorce, the spouse's period of ownership is treated as including the other spouse's period of ownership. This so-called "tacking" of holding periods can permit the former spouse to sell the property anytime after it is received and qualify for the exclusion, even though owned by such spouse for less than two years.

> **Example**
>
> A husband purchased a home in his own name in 2001, and he and his wife moved into the home immediately. In 2004, the couple is divorced and the residence is awarded to the wife under a written agreement signed in connection with the divorce decree. The former wife is eligible for the $250,000 exclusion *immediately* because her former husband's holding period (three years) is tacked to her holding period.

In the example, the former wife is entitled to the exclusion for $250,000, not the $500,000 exclusion allowed to married couples. In other words, since she was not married at the time of the sale, only the $250,000 exclusion was available to her.

This brings up the next question.

6.4 Is It Smart to Sell Prior to Divorce?

Many matrimonial disputes seem like the War of the Roses. But regardless of how antagonistic the parties may be toward each other, they unquestionably retain something in common. The tax collector remains the adversary of both of them. If they can work together against this common adversary when it comes to the sale of a high-priced home, both may come out ahead financially *after taxes*.

This temporary alliance can be beneficial in situations where gain on the sale of the home will exceed $250,000. In these cases it may be prudent to sell the home *prior* to divorce to take advantage of the $500,000 exclusion ceiling available only to married couples. At least where one of the spouses is not intent on continuing to live in the house indefinitely, the additional after-tax proceeds can mitigate the financial pain of the divorce.

> **Example**
>
> A divorcing couple has owned and used their jointly owned principal residence for many years. The home, originally purchased for $200,000, is now worth $650,000, so that a sale will produce a gain of $450,000. If the husband signs his interest in the home over to the wife in the divorce proceedings and she later sells the house, she will be able to shield only $250,000 of the gain from tax and will be required to pay tax on the remaining $200,000 of capital gain. But if the couple sells the house prior to the divorce when they can file a joint return, the *entire* $450,000 of gain can be excluded.

If the wife in the example intended to sell the house in the relatively near future rather than live in it indefinitely, she would be better off to sell it before the divorce becomes final. By doing so the capital gains tax would be avoided, leaving more for the parties to split up between themselves. The IRS would be the loser.

This brings to mind a little tax rhyme composed by Wilbur Mills, former Chairman of the House Ways and Means Committee:

> Don't tax me,
> Don't tax thee,
> Tax that man
> Behind the tree.

6.5 How to Avoid Gain on a Vacation Home

Many couples own valuable vacation homes or investment condominiums. If bought years ago, these properties often will have appreciated substantially in value. While gain on the sale of the couple's principal residence can be sheltered from tax by the exclusion provisions, gain on the sale of their vacation home or investment condominium is fully taxable. The tax burden imposed on the sale of such property can make a matrimonial settlement especially painful.

But if the desire to avoid tax is strong enough, there may be a way around the problem.

Double Principal Residence Plan. In some cases the financial pain of a taxable sale can be sidestepped by making the vacation home or investment condominium a principal residence.

Here's how it would work:

While one of the spouses remains in the couple's present principal residence, the other would move into the vacation home or investment condominium, making it his or her principal residence. Each would take ownership of the property in which he or she resides. Assuming the move is for real, a sale of the former vacation home or investment condominium after the two-year

> **Observation**
>
> ***Practical Problems.*** Implementing this plan often will be stymied by serious practical problems. For example, if the vacation home or investment condominium is too far away, a move by one of the spouses usually will be impractical, especially if both have jobs. But where it is just a question of inconvenience, the move may be worth it.

ownership and use requirements are met should qualify as a sale of a principal residence by the spouse who occupies the property. This would make the exclusion for gain up to $250,000 available.

What's It Worth? Where this tax strategy is feasible, the savings can be impressive. For example, if property that cost $100,000 is presently worth $250,000, the federal tax alone at 15 percent on the $150,000 gain on a sale is $22,500. Such tax savings may outweigh the inconvenience and disruption involved in the plan.

Make It for Real. This planning idea requires the spouse moving into the vacation home or investment condominium to genuinely make the property that spouse's principal residence. The property should actually be lived in on an essentially full-time basis as a principal residence for the requisite two-year period.

6.6 Splitting Up Marital Property: Beware the Tax Trap

In a matrimonial settlement, ignorance of the tax law can be financially perilous.

When you part with your spouse, you usually split up your property. While the transfer of property to a spouse usually has no immediate tax consequences, the tax basis of the property transferred can be significant to the transferee spouse in the future. The reason that tax basis is important is that any taxable gain on a future sale is figured by subtracting basis from the selling price.

> **Example**
>
> The tax basis for your vacation home is $75,000 and you sell it for $130,000. Disregarding selling expenses, your taxable gain is $55,000 ($130,000 − $75,000 = $55,000).

> **Observation**
>
> ***Figuring Basis.*** The tax basis of real estate, including a principal residence, vacation home, or rental property, generally is its purchase price plus the cost of any improvements, less any depreciation and deductible casualty losses.

When you transfer property to your spouse incident to a divorce, the transfer generally will be treated as a nontaxable gift. Because the transfer is treated as a nontaxable gift, the tax basis of the property carries over from you to your spouse and becomes the tax basis of the transferred property in your spouse's hands. This seemingly innocuous "carryover basis" rule sometimes may create a valuable tax break for one of the spouses while imposing an unexpected and unwelcome tax burden on the other.

Example

Suppose you own a vacation house that has a basis of $225,000 and a value of $325,000. Your spouse owns a rental property that has both a basis and a value of $325,000. As part of a divorce settlement, you swap the properties: You get the rental property and your spouse gets the vacation house. If you were to sell the rental property for its present value, $325,000, you would have no taxable gain (sale price, $325,000 – carryover basis, $325,000 = 0). But if your spouse were to sell the vacation house for its present value, $325,000, your spouse would have $100,000 of taxable gain (sale price, $325,000 - carryover basis, $225,000 = $100,000). Thus, an ostensibly equal division of properties based on values may result in an unequal division *after taxes*.

This potential tax liability may come as an unwelcome surprise to a spouse who was unaware of the tax consequences of the swap.

Tax Tip

The tax-planning point that the carryover basis rules suggest is that the basis characteristics of property should be taken into account in determining how to split up the ownership of property. Other things being equal, the more desirable property is the property with the smallest built-in taxable gain.

The difference between value and carryover tax basis is not the only tax trap that may await an unwary spouse when marital property is split up. A spouse who trades away the principal residence in the settlement bargaining without giving consideration to the special tax status of the principal residence may be making a mistake. Since the principal residence may be essentially "exempt" from taxation on its sale, it may be a more valuable property *after taxes* than other property with an identical market value.

> **Example**
>
> Your spouse owns the house that you use as your principal residence. You own a condo in a ski resort. As part of the property settlement in your divorce, the principal residence is transferred to you and the condo is transferred to your spouse. The principal residence has a basis of $300,000 and a fair market value of $450,000, and the condo has a basis of $100,000 and a fair market value of $250,000. If your spouse sells the condo, your spouse will realize a taxable gain of $150,000. But if you sell your principal residence and meet the requirements for the exclusion of gain discussed in Sections 4.3 through 4.9, as will be likely, your gain of $150,000 will totally escape taxation.

Here, properties with ostensibly equal amounts of built-in gain can produce dramatically different tax consequences on a subsequent sale.

> **Observation**
>
> *Tax Treatment of Transfers in Divorce.* A transfer between spouses or former spouses that is "incident to the divorce" does not produce taxable income. Instead, the transfer is treated as a nontaxable gift that is excluded from the transferee spouse's income, and the transferee spouse obtains a carryover basis for the property received. This means that the basis of the property to the transferee spouse is the same as the basis for the property in the hands of the transferor spouse. A transfer is "incident to the divorce" if it occurs within one year after the date on which the marriage ceases or is related to the cessation of the marriage.

As the examples illustrate, spouses overlook the tax aspects of property settlements at their financial peril.

PART III

Tax Shelter from Homeowner Loopholes and Vacation Homes

CHAPTER 7

Little-Known Loopholes Can Provide Big Savings

> The only people who don't have to pass the Civil Service exam to work for the government are taxpayers.
>
> **Anonymous**

7.1 Overview

This chapter provides a small collection of tax-planning ideas for homeowners that some would regard as loopholes. They might be so regarded because, at least in some cases, they appear to be unintended benefits of the law, not foreseen by the writers of the tax code.

There is another definition of a loophole, usually propounded by someone who can't use it. It is a tax break given to somebody else. Or, as former President Ronald Reagan put it when discussing tax reform, "One man's loophole is another man's noose."

Loopholes or not, these planning ideas can produce substantial tax savings. While they generally are "special situation"–type opportunities that won't apply to everyone, you should review them to see if you can take advantage of them.

7.2 The Super Loophole: How to Use Home Sale Exclusion to Shield Gain on Other Real Estate from Tax

Louis Pasteur observed that innovation is essentially "chance favoring the prepared mind." This observation applies not only to scientific work but also to tax planning. There may be a chance for you—an opportunity—that permits you to avoid tax if your mind is prepared with tax know-how. Understanding how the home sale exclusion can shield gain on the sale of other assets from tax is tax know-how that may let you take advantage of a hidden tax avoidance opportunity.

As explained in Sections 4.3 through 4.9, tax on up to $250,000 of gain on the sale of your principal residence can be avoided if you are single, or up to $500,000 if you are married. Can you use this exclusion as a tax shield for gains on real estate *other* than your home?

The answer may be yes, if you own either a vacation home or a rental house or condominium that has appreciated in value. But it's not easy. You have to move out of your present home and into your vacation home or rental unit, live there two years, then sell the former vacation home or rental unit. There are three steps for this "serial sale" strategy:

- *Step 1.* Either sell your present principal residence or rent it, then move out of it.
- *Step 2.* Move into your vacation home or rental property and make it your principal residence.
- *Step 3.* After the two-year waiting period, sell the vacation home or rental property, now your principal residence, tax free.

If you own a substantially appreciated vacation home or rental property and are willing to make the lifestyle sacrifice usually involved in the serial sale strategy, the tax reward can be large.

The example below illustrates how it's done.

Quick Refresher. Before we go further, a quick refresher about the exclusion from tax of gain on the sale of a principal residence may be helpful. As explained in Sections 4.3 through 4.9, an eligible single homeowner or a married homeowner filing a separate tax return can exclude up to $250,000 of gain on the sale of a principal residence, and eligible married homeowners filing jointly can exclude up to $500,000. Subject to the eligibility rules, you can use the exclusion each time you sell a principal residence.

Your eligibility to exclude gain from tax generally is keyed to your ownership and use of a principal residence for a minimum two-year period. Specifically, the exclusion is applicable to the sale of your principal residence if, during the five-year period ending on the date of sale, the home was owned and used by you as your principal residence for two years or more.

There is a waiting period. The exclusion generally applies to only one sale during any two-year period. So you generally can't take advantage of the exclusion if, during the two-year period ending on the date of the sale, you made another sale to which the exclusion applied.

Will the Serial Sale Technique Work for You? This tax-planning idea isn't just for the rich and famous who own several houses. It also can work for middle-class owners—for example, if you bought or inherited a vacation home years ago that has appreciated substantially in value. Likewise, if you own a substantially appreciated single-family rental property—whether a house or condominium—you can benefit from the serial sale strategy.

Practical Aspects. Of course, the strategy presents practical challenges: You must be willing either to sell or to move out of and rent your present principal residence, move into the vacation or rental property, then actually use it as your principal residence for at least two years. For many individuals this strategy will be unattractive because of the considerable personal inconvenience involved, or for other reasons. But where the move will save significant tax dollars—as it often will—overcoming the personal difficulties may be worthwhile.

> **Example**
>
> Suppose you're married and have a potential gain of $250,000 on the sale of your principal residence. You also have been fortunate with a rental condominium that you bought years ago. It now has a potential gain of $200,000 on its sale. Under the exclusion rules, tax on the entire $250,000 gain on the sale of your principal residence can be avoided. But the $200,000 gain on the sale of your rental condominium will be taxable, producing a substantial tax. The tax on the sale of the rental condominium can be reduced to *zero* if you move into the condominium and make it your principal residence for at least two years before you sell it.

For the serial home sale strategy to succeed, you must actually make the new residence your principal residence. Your move must be for real. Factors showing you have made the new residence your principal residence would include the sale or rental of your prior residence, physically moving into and residing in the new residence and switching auto and voting registrations to the new address. Also, subject to a few exceptions described in Sections 4.3 through 4.9, you must own and actually use the new residence as your principal residence for a minimum of two years, and you must not have used the principal residence exclusion provisions for at least two years before you sell the new residence.

The serial home sale strategy may be most practical for older baby boomers and prospective retirees who are ready to downsize. But anyone can use it, and, given the right numbers, it can produce important tax savings.

7.3 How to Buy a Vacation Home with Tax-Free Dollars from Sale of Rental Property

Suppose you have located a vacation home you want to purchase. You don't have the cash for the purchase, but you do own a rental property that is worth close to what the vacation home will cost. You want to sell the rental property to raise the cash to buy the vacation home, but you have a tax problem. Since the rental property has appreciated substantially in value, a sale of the rental property will force you to pay a large tax.

Is there is a way around this tax problem? If you're willing to do an exchange deal, yes. But be forewarned: It's not for the faint of heart.

Tax-Free Exchange. If you sell your appreciated rental property, you pay tax on your gain. If, instead, you *exchange* your rental property for so-called "like-kind" property, such as other rental property, you can avoid tax entirely. The rules can be complicated, but the basic point is that you may be able to swap your appreciated rental property tax-free for the vacation home, provided the vacation home is temporarily rented out after the swap. To keep the swap tax free, it is essential that you rent out the vacation home for awhile after you receive it in the swap so that it will qualify as like-kind property.

> **Observation**
>
> *The Waiting Period.* How long must the vacation home be rented before it is used by you for vacation purposes? There are no guidelines, but a year might work, and two or three years definitely would suffice.

Working out the exchange requires several transfers.

The Triangular Transfer Procedure. When you work out a tax-free exchange, you don't follow the usual straightforward real estate transfer proce-

LITTLE-KNOWN LOOPHOLES CAN PROVIDE BIG SAVINGS

dure. Instead, when you sell your appreciated rental property, you arrange to have your purchaser pay the purchase price for your rental property not to you but to the owner of the vacation home you are purchasing. The owner of the vacation home then immediately transfers the vacation home to you. This is known as a "three-way" or "triangular" exchange because there are three transfers:

1. You transfer your rental property to the purchaser.
2. Your purchaser transfers the purchase price for your rental property to the owner of the vacation property.
3. The owner of the vacation property transfers the vacation property to you.

Figure 7.1 contains a diagram illustrating the three transfers.

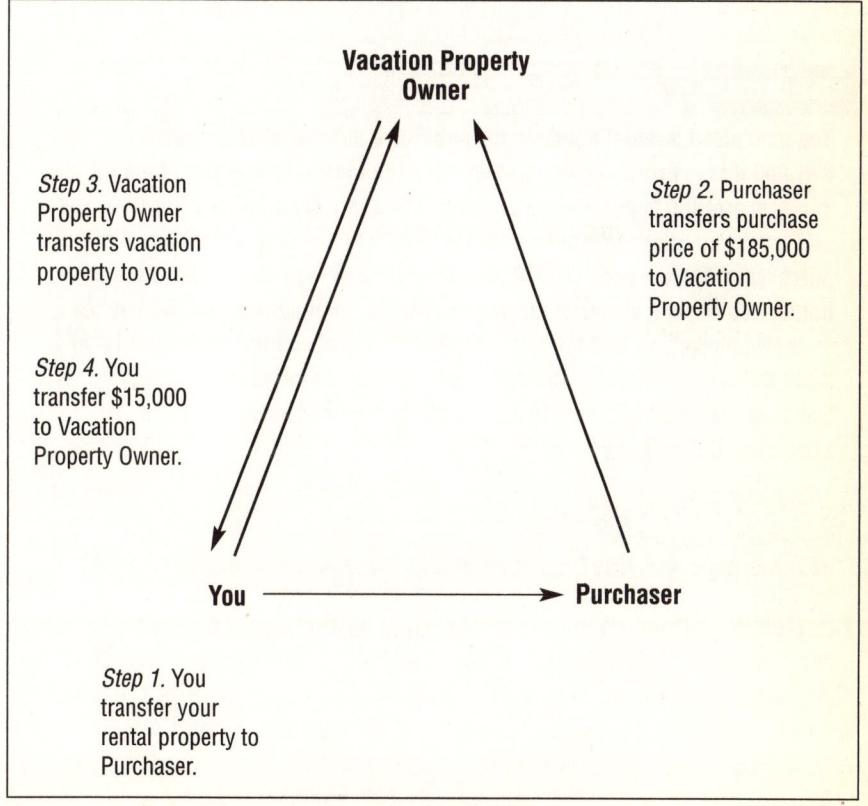

FIGURE 7.1 Closing Three Transfers Simultaneously

It's best to have all three transactions occur simultaneously at a single closing, but so-called deferred exchange arrangements are possible. Also, it's usually necessary to use some cash to adjust differing values of the properties or adjust mortgages.

> **Caution**
>
> The use of cash and the presence of mortgages can make an exchange deal taxable. Both the tax rules governing tax-free exchanges and the legal aspects of the multiple real estate transfers involved in exchanges can be complicated. Exchange transactions should be undertaken with the counsel of a lawyer with expertise in both the tax and real estate law aspects of the transaction.

Let's consider an example where all three transfers are closed simultaneously.

> **Example**
>
> You purchased a rental house in the suburbs a number of years ago for $75,000 that is presently worth $185,000. The mortgage has been paid off. You now arrange to purchase a vacation home in a ski area for $200,000. You sell the rental house to a purchaser for $185,000 and arrange to have the purchaser transfer the $185,000 purchase price to the owner of the vacation home. You pay the owner of the vacation home an additional $15,000 out of your own pocket, so that the total received by the vacation homeowner is the $200,000 purchase price. The owner of the vacation home immediately transfers the vacation home to you, which you immediately rent to an independent third party.

IRS has approved this type of exchange arrangement (see Figure 7.1).

Tax Result. Properly handled, the swap is tax free, one rental property having been exchanged by you for another, a nontaxable "like-kind" exchange. In other words, you "sell" your rental property and use the sale proceeds to purchase a vacation home, but don't pay any tax on the gain on the sale of your rental property because the transaction has been set up as a tax-free exchange.

How Much Have You Saved? If you had sold your rental property rather than exchanging it, you would have paid a tax on the gain on its sale. Assume your original $75,000 cost basis for the rental house was reduced to $45,000 by depreciation deductions. Your tax basis for figuring your taxable gain then would be $45,000, so that you would have had a taxable gain of $140,000 on the sale (sale price, $185,000 – tax basis, $45,000 = $140,000). This gain would have produced a substantial federal income tax, and possibly a state income tax as well. The tax-free exchange lets you avoid the federal tax—and usually the state tax also—and use the full proceeds of the sale of your rental property to purchase your vacation home.

Beware Personal Use. For an exchange to be tax free, both the property transferred by you *and* the property received by you must be used for rental purposes. If you immediately use the vacation home you receive in the exchange for personal purposes, the exchange won't be tax free. You have to make the vacation home rental property by renting it to an independent third party, or the exchange will be taxable.

> **Observation**
>
> *Retirement Homes.* You can adapt this exchange strategy for the purchase of a retirement home instead of a vacation home. You can even adapt it to purchase your principal residence. But in all cases, for the exchange to be tax free, you must rent out the property you receive in the exchange for at least a year—and preferably two or three years—before you use it as a residence.

What about Mortgages? You may be able to do a tax-free exchange even though mortgages are involved, either on your property or the property you receive in the exchange, or both. Sometimes you may even be able to put a mortgage on the property you transfer before you transfer it or on the property you receive after the exchange is completed and, in either case, pocket the loan proceeds tax free. The tax rules on mortgages are quite technical, and you'll need expert help to thread your way through them. Basically, to avoid tax, you should make sure any mortgage on the property you receive in the exchange is at least as large as any mortgage on the property you transfer.

The Mortgage Alternative. In the example, it was assumed that you owned the rental property free and clear. If so, or if you had a mortgage that was relatively small, it's possible that instead of exchanging the property you could mortgage it and use the tax-free mortgage proceeds to purchase the vacation home. But while a mortgage transaction is much simpler than an exchange, it may not be possible to obtain a sufficiently large mortgage, or available mortgage financing may be unattractive, or there may be other factors making a mortgage undesirable. The choice between a mortgage or an exchange for purposes of raising funds for a purchase will depend on the circumstances.

7.4 Avoiding Tax When Your Land Includes Both House and Investment Property

The tax-free exchange rules just discussed may be advantageous for you in other situations. For example, suppose you own a residence with a separate rented cottage or separate building lots held for investment, or a home with separate acreage rented for agricultural use. This separate investment property may not be part of your principal residence eligible for the exclusion of gain on its sale (discussed in Sections 4.3 through 4.9).

To illustrate, say you sell your principal residence and a nearby rental cottage on your property together. While gain on the sale of your house will qualify for the $250,000 (or $500,000, if married) principal residence sale exclusion, gain on the sale of the separate rental cottage won't qualify for the exclusion if the cottage is not part of your "principal residence." For purposes of the exclusion, if the cottage is separate property held for investment rather than part of your principal residence, the exclusion will be inapplicable.

The sale of the separate rental property could produce a large tax.

This situation involves ownership of what might be called the "divisible residence." This is a residence that can be divided into components, one of which can be sold tax free under the home sale exclusion rules and the other of which is property held for investment that can be swapped tax free under the tax-free exchange provisions.

Since the rules permitting the exclusion of gain on the sale of a personal residence do not apply to property held for investment, the investment property can't be sold tax free with the residence. But it may be possible to transfer the investment property separately in a transaction that qualifies as a tax-free like-kind exchange.

> **Example**
>
> Ms. Smith owns a country house located on a five-acre site. She purchased the property for $195,000 several years ago, and it is now worth $425,000. The property is adjacent to 45 acres of land that Ms. Smith bought for $50,000 when she purchased the house. The land is fenced off and rented to the farmer down the road for raising crops. The 45 acres have grown substantially in value since Ms. Smith acquired the acreage because the area is developing into a second home Mecca. The acreage is now worth $400,000. Ms. Smith made the country home her principal residence two years ago but is getting on in years and wants to move to a place in town for retirement. If she sold the house on the five-acre site, her gain would be covered by the $250,000 exclusion ($425,000 − $195,000 = $230,000). But a sale of the land would produce a $350,000 taxable profit (value of the land, $400,000, less tax basis of land [cost], $50,000).

This special situation affords Ms. Smith the opportunity to completely avoid tax by combining the use of the home sale exclusion and the exchange provisions. Assuming the numbers work out, she can find the in-town house she wants, then do a three-way exchange using her appreciated land to acquire the in-town house without any tax on the appreciation in value of her land.

The exchange arrangement would be much the same as the one described above. Specifically:

1. Ms. Smith would transfer her 45 acres of land held for rental use to a cash buyer (probably a local developer).
2. The cash buyer would transfer $400,000 to the owner of the in-town house.
3. The owner of the in-town house would transfer it to Ms. Smith.

Ms. Smith would then immediately rent her in-town house to a tenant, so that she will have exchanged one rental property, her land, for another, the rented in-town house, in a qualifying "like-kind" exchange. After the in-town rental property is held for a respectable period, she can sell her country home tax free under the personal residence exclusion provisions. Then she can move into the in-town house, with retirement cash she received tax free under the exclusion provisions from the sale of her country house.

Tax Danger. In exchange transactions, both the property you transfer and the property you receive must be "held" for use in a trade or business or for investment, such as rental. When the property received in the exchange is first rented, then converted to personal use, as in the case of the in-town house in the example, the IRS could argue that the property received in the exchange was really not "held" for rental, but for personal use. A two- or three-year waiting period should be sufficient to overcome this argument, especially if the property received is an economically viable rental property that could be held indefinitely for rental and conversion to personal use is merely a possibility, not a definite plan.

> **Caution**
>
> As noted above, exchange transactions should be undertaken only with the counsel of a lawyer who has expertise in both taxation and the real estate law aspects of exchanges.

7.5 Your Appreciated Residence Is a Tax Treasure: How to Trade Up and Get Tax-Free Cash

The great English jurist Lord Coke declared, "A man's home is his castle." He might have added that if the home has appreciated, it could also be his *treasury*.

If your residence has appreciated substantially in value above your mortgage, the untapped equity in your residence is a source of cash. As explained in Section 3.3, this source of cash can be tapped with a home equity loan, the interest on which is fully deductible. But there's another way to use this equity that may be more appealing. You may be able to "trade up" to a new, more expensive home and, in the process, pocket funds from the sale of your present residence, all tax free.

You usually can avoid tax on gain from the sale of your principal residence under the exclusion rules, as explained in Sections 4.3 through 4.9. If the proceeds from the sale exceed the amount you need to pay off any existing mortgage on your present home and make the down payment on your new home, you can keep the excess proceeds, *free of tax*.

> **Example**
>
> Suppose you purchased your residence some years ago for $145,000 and have paid your mortgage down to $30,000. You now sell the residence for $280,000. Disregarding selling expenses, this provides cash proceeds to you of $250,000 ($280,000 − $30,000 = $250,000). (The gain on the sale is well within the $250,000 [or $500,000] exclusion.) Now you trade up to a more expensive home costing $425,000, making a down payment of $80,000, with the balance being financed with a new mortgage. You pocket $170,000 in tax-free cash, consisting of the $250,000 cash proceeds you netted on the sale of your old home after paying off its mortgage, less the $80,000 down payment on your new home.

As the example illustrates, at the cost of taking on a larger mortgage, possibly with increased monthly payments, you can "cash in" on appreciation in the value of your old residence without incurring tax, assuming your gain does not exceed the $250,000 (or $500,000) exclusion limits. By cashing in on the appreciation, you generate tax-free funds with which you can both trade up to a more desirable home and create a cash nest egg for future use.

7.6 Home Improvements: Handyman's Special Tax Shelter

Congress didn't mean to, but when it passed the home sale exclusion rules it created a "handyman's special" tax shelter. If you're handy with tools and can make your own home improvements, the exclusion of up to $250,000 of gain on the sale of a principal residence for single individuals or up to $500,000 for marrieds (discussed in Sections 4.3 through 4.9) creates a tax break that can be used by you in an unintended but completely legitimate way.

Gain that may be excluded from tax when you sell your home is not limited to gain from market appreciation. It includes any gain that may result from home improvements you may make while you own the home. Thus, if you can personally install improvements to your home that increase its value beyond your cost for materials, you can pocket the increase in value from your labor tax free when you sell the home. In effect, you are selling your labor but don't have to pay tax on the payment you receive for it. It's like receiving tax-free compensation for work.

> **Example**
>
> Assume you're good with tools and decide to add a room to your house. You use $8,000 worth of materials and build the room with your own labor, and maybe with a little help from handy friends. The extra room brings you $15,000 more for your house when the house is sold three years later. You receive the $7,000 "income" from your labor ($15,000 − $8,000) tax free under the home sale exclusion rules.

This loophole can be taken a step further.

Handyman's Special House. The exclusion can be used to eliminate taxable gain even if you completely renovate a home. Suppose, for example, that you buy a "handyman's special" house, move in, renovate it over a two-year period, then sell it at a profit. If the renovated house is your principal residence, the gain on the sale can be wholly tax free, assuming it doesn't exceed the $250,000 (or $500,000) exclusion limits. This would be true even if you house-hopped every two years after a renovation.

House Hopping. This extraordinary tax break may lead some homeowners to house hopping—that is, buying, improving, and then selling house after house. The strategy would be workable in areas of the country where home prices are rising. Carried out over a period of years, it would permit earning large amounts of tax-free income. Of course, family and social considerations have to be taken into account, in addition to the career and economic aspects.

But suppose you're not handy or don't have the time or inclination to make home improvements. There may be another opportunity.

High-Priced Housing Areas. If you live in a high-priced housing area with appreciating values or plan to move to one, you might be able to shield substantial amounts of gain from tax without doing much in improvements. For example, suppose you live in a house you bought for $200,000, all cash, in an area with rapidly appreciating values, and the house is now worth $450,000. You might make out well if you sell the house, invest $300,000 of the proceeds in a new house in the area, pocket $150,000 in tax-free cash, and hope to repeat the process in two or more years when the new home has appreciated in value to, say, $400,000. On an after-tax basis, house hopping could be highly profitable in an area with fast-rising home prices.

> **Observation**
>
> If you use a mortgage to finance the purchase of the house, you "leverage" your investment by reducing the amount of cash you need to purchase the house. This means that when you sell the house, the return on your out-of-pocket cash investment is higher, perhaps dramatically so. But there is a downside to mortgage leverage, and the bigger the mortgage the greater the downside. If the housing market falls so that the house is hard to sell at an acceptable price, you have to keep making the mortgage payments until the market recovers, or the lender can foreclose on the house.

7.7 Home Improvement Business: Tax-Free Income for Renovators

As a practical matter, the home improvement and house-hopping strategy just described is best suited for small builders, home renovators, or carpenters who know how to renovate a house in a cost-effective way.

For them, it can be a tax-free business.

> **Example**
>
> A carpenter working for a home renovation company purchases a run-down house in a good neighborhood for $125,000, moves in with his family, and does extensive renovation and repair work. He keeps his day job, working on the house evenings and weekends. At the end of two years after investing $50,000 in materials and hundreds of hours of his own labor, the renovations are complete. Now the house looks great and shows well. He sells it for $235,000, pocketing a profit of $60,000 (sale price, $235,000, less cost, $125,000, and materials, $50,000 = $60,000). Since the profit is on the sale of a home he owned and occupied as his principal residence for more than two years out of the five years preceding the sale, *his profit is tax free!*

What's more, he can immediately buy another run-down house and repeat the renovation and sale procedure, sheltering the profit on the sale by the home sale exclusion rules. In effect, he has found the Holy Grail of income taxation: a business that's not subject to tax.

Can the Loophole Last? Probably not. It's fair to say that this escape from taxation is an abusive—though legitimate—use of the exclusion rules. If the practice becomes widespread, or even just to forestall its use, it's a good bet that Congress will close the loophole as an "unintended benefit."

In the meantime it's a perfectly legal tax-savings technique—and, it might be noted, a strong incentive for renovating run-down housing.

7.8 When a House Is Not a Home— How to Deduct Loss on Sale of Home

Except for real estate taxes and mortgage interest, you generally can't deduct home maintenance expenses. This is so even though you put your home on the market, move out, and live elsewhere. Likewise, a loss on the sale of your home generally is not deductible. Both the home maintenance expenses and the loss are normally considered nondeductible "personal" expenses.

That's the general rule. But the tax planner's hand may be quicker than the tax collector's eye. Maintenance expenses and a loss on a sale may become deductible if you convert the residence to income-producing use before the sale. The idea is to switch from a "personal" motivation for your ownership of the home to a "profit" motivation for your ownership.

It's not easy, and convincing the IRS that a conversion from personal to income-producing use has occurred can be uphill work. Usually, you have to show some affirmative profit-motivated act—such as renting the home or at least holding it out for rent. Actual rental at a market rental is the best proof.

But other approaches are possible. Two court cases illustrate how, under the right "surrounding circumstances," a mere change of a homeowner's intention may produce a conversion of a home to income-producing use, permitting the deduction of either a loss or maintenance expenses, or both.

The Case of the Deceased Spouse. A husband inherited the house in which he and his deceased wife had lived. The kids moved in to live with him rent free, and he continued to live in the house for four months. He didn't mourn long. He met a lady, decided to remarry, placed his house on the market, and purchased another house. He claimed long-term capital loss on the sale of the house. The IRS said no, claiming his ownership and decision to sell the house didn't have the necessary profit motive.

Persistence Pays. The homeowner insisted his ownership had a profit motive, rather than a residential motive, because he never intended to live in the house after his wife's death. He went to court and swore to it. The court believed his testimony that shortly after his wife's death he decided not to use the house as his personal residence. Consequently, his acquisition of ownership of the house as a result of his wife's death produced the requisite switch from a residential to a profit motive. While the mere offering of the house for sale wasn't a switch, here the intent to use the house as a personal residence vanished almost simultaneously with his acquisition of ownership from his deceased wife.

The Case of the Summer Home. The second case involved a decision to hold a former summer home as an investment. The homeowner ceased using his summer house at Martha's Vineyard and placed it on the market for sale. He was stubborn: He held out for his asking price for six years. Finally, appreciation in value brought him his price. During the interim, he made no attempt to rent the house because he believed renting would be economically disadvantageous. But he still claimed deductions for the maintenance expenses of the house.

Persistence Pays Again. The IRS said no. Undeterred, the homeowner went to court. The court was more sympathetic. It rejected renting as the "litmus test" for determining whether a home is converted to income-producing use. It found a sufficient conversion because the homeowner held the house for appreciation in value. Property may be held for the requisite "production of income" even though the income results from gain on the sale of the property from appreciation in value.

Unless you rent the home, it's not easy to get deductions for the expenses of maintaining the home after you put it on the market and move out, or to deduct a loss on the sale of the home. But as the two cases show, it's not impossible if you have the right facts.

How Much Can You Deduct? Determining how much you can deduct for expenses and depreciation if you convert your home to rental use requires some figuring. This subject is discussed in Section 8.7.

Determining whether you can claim a deductible loss on a sale also takes some figuring. You may not be able to deduct the difference between what you paid for the home and the sale price. This is because your tax basis in your home for purposes of figuring a loss after a conversion to income-producing use is the *lower* of the basis of the home, usually your cost plus improvements, or the fair market value of the home, on the date of the conversion. If fair market value on the date of conversion is lower than basis, then only the difference between such fair market value and the sales price can be deducted.

> **Example**
>
> You purchased your home for $150,000 and added a bathroom that cost $15,000, so your adjusted tax basis for your home now is $165,000. You convert your home to rental property at a time when its fair market value is $155,000. You sell the home a year later for $140,000. Your deductible loss is limited to $15,000, the difference between the fair market value of the home on the date of the conversion, $155,000, and the sale price, $140,000.

Watch Out for Valuation Trap. Deducting a loss on the sale of your home after you convert it to rental use may be stymied by a valuation problem. As indicated in the example, the basis of a converted personal residence for purposes of determining loss is the *lower* of its adjusted basis or fair market value on the date of conversion. If fair market value on the date of conversion is below the adjusted basis but it cannot be shown that the sale price was *below* such fair market value, no loss is allowed. An example based on a court case tells a cautionary tale.

> **Example**
>
> The adjusted basis of a converted personal residence was $382,000. The homeowner asserted its fair market value was $350,000 on the date of its conversion to rental use. The residence was subsequently sold for $295,000, producing an apparent loss of $55,000 ($350,000 – $295,000). The entire loss was disallowed. The reason: The homeowner failed to prove that the fair market value of the home on the date of conversion was more than $295,000.

Don't get caught in this trap. If you convert your home to rental use, obtain an appraisal of its fair market value on the date of the conversion. If the homeowner in the court case had obtained an appraisal substantiating the $350,000 fair market value of the home on the date of the conversion, the loss probably would have been allowed in full.

7.9 How to Get a Charitable Deduction for Your Home— And Still Live in It

It's like having your cake and eating it too.

This tax-planning idea is not for everyone. It's only for individuals who have genuine and substantial charitable objectives and have reached an age at which they want to do something significant about them. Also, to make the idea work, you have to own your own home and not be interested in leaving it to your children.

If this description fits you, you may be ready to consider an idea that can produce both a good deed and good tax results. The idea is for you to donate a "remainder interest" in your personal residence to a charity. You not only do good by the donation, but you also can get a charitable deduction with no out-of-pocket cost. The deduction can provide worthwhile tax savings.

> **Tax Tip**
>
> *What's a Remainder Interest?* Virtually all homeowners own their homes in "fee simple." This means that they have outright, 100 percent ownership of the real estate, even if there's a mortgage on the property. This so-called "fee" ownership can be split into other, smaller interests. For example, you can transfer your fee interest in your home to another party, retaining the right to live in the home for the rest of your life or a period of years. By doing so, you create a retained interest (in yourself), known as a "life estate" or "term of years," and create a remainder interest in the home in the person to whom you made the transfer. When you die or at the end of the term of years, the remainder interest belongs to the person to whom you transferred it and becomes a fee-simple interest, since your life estate or term of years is over.

Live Home for Life. You can get a charitable deduction for your home while you still live in it by transferring a remainder interest in the home to a qualifying charity, retaining the right to exclusive use of the home for your life or whatever period of years you want to remain in the home. This means you can live in your home for the rest of your life or the specified period of years, but when you die or at the end of the specified period, the home automatically goes to the charity. When you make this type of contribution upon creating the remainder interest (by changing the deed to your home), you get a charitable deduction for the value of the remainder interest. Of course, the charity involved has to be a tax-exempt charity, contributions to which are deductible for tax purposes.

This type of charitable gift isn't likely to spark controversy with the IRS. The IRS has approved it and even has illustrated how you figure the amount of the deduction.

150 TAX SHELTER FROM HOMEOWNER LOOPHOLES AND VACATION HOMES

> **Example**
>
> A homeowner donated a remainder interest in his personal residence to his church, retaining the exclusive right, for himself and his estate, to use the house and land for 20 years. At the time of the donation the house had a value of $60,000 and an expected useful life of 45 years, at the end of which period it was expected to be worth $10,000. The land was worth $8,000.

> **Caution**
>
> Since determining the amount of the deduction takes some relatively sophisticated math, you should get professional help with the numbers unless you are a math whiz. The process is shown here in case you want to know what is involved. You can skip it if you want to leave it to a tax professional.

Figuring the value of the contribution requires several steps:

1. Figure the present value and useful life of the house. Useful life is the period the house will last. Present value in the preceding example is assumed to be $68,000, and useful life is assumed to be 45 years. When these amounts must be determined in real life, a good appraisal should be obtained both for value and useful life.

2. Figure the value of the remainder after 20 years by deducting 20 years of straight-line depreciation. Straight-line depreciation requires deduction of the same amount of depreciation each year, as shown in the example below. This is the value of what actually will go to the charity at the end of the 20-year period.

3. Figure the present value of the remainder (its value today), using the appropriate discount factor. You use a discount factor to take into account the fact that the charity has to wait 20 years to get possession of its gift. In the preceding example, the IRS figures the value of the remainder interest to be $14,273 with the following computation. You have to take this step because what you are allowed to deduct is not the current value of the remainder, but its current value decreased to reflect the fact that the charity has to wait 20 years to get it—a much smaller value.

Present value, house and land		$68,000
Value of house	$60,000	
Less: Value in 45 years	$10,000	
Aggregate depreciation	$50,000	
Depreciation, 20-year term (20/45 × $50,000)		22,222
Value less allocable depreciation		$45,778
Discount factor		× 0.311805
Value of remainder interest		$14,273

The discount factor is based on tables set forth in IRS regulations.

How to Increase the Charitable Deduction. You can increase the amount of your charitable deduction by increasing the present value of the remainder that goes to charity. An increased present value for the remainder produces a larger deduction because the amount of your charitable deduction is the value of the property, the remainder, that is given to the charity. To increase the value of the remainder when you are retaining a term of years, you shorten the term of years, because the shorter the term of years, the sooner the remainder will take effect, and the sooner it will take effect, the higher its value. This assumes, of course, that a shorter term is consistent with your personal objectives.

Observation

Retained Interest for Life. If you use your life instead of a term of years as your retained interest, the older you are, the larger the deduction will be. This is because the older you are, the shorter your life expectancy and the sooner the charity will receive the remainder.

Practical Point. As previously indicated, use of this tax idea makes sense only in special situations. It is useful only when the transfer of a remainder interest is consistent with present tax and financial needs, as well as family living arrangements and estate plans. Usually, it is suitable only for older homeowners with important charitable goals who wish to live in their present homes until death.

7.10 Every Homeowner's Hidden Loophole: Nontaxable "Imputed" Income

Every homeowner enjoys a hidden loophole, buried like Captain Kidd's treasure. Known to tax professionals as "imputed income," this hidden loophole is the invisible income you receive from the untaxed value of living rent free in your own home.

Maybe you don't think living rent free in your own home is income, imputed or otherwise.

To check it out, let's first explore some tax theory illustrated by an exchange of services. It may seem silly at first, but it's not.

Mr. Jones and Mr. Smith each mows his own lawn. No income here, because each is just doing personal work for himself. But now suppose Jones mows Smith's lawn and Smith mows Jones's lawn. The situation changes here because each has received something of value in exchange for his services. For mowing Smith's lawn, Jones has received Smith's services, and for mowing Jones's lawn, Smith has received Jones's services. In the tax world, this receipt of "consideration" for the performance of services is taxable income, even though it's not paid in money. You don't have to be paid in money to have income. Payment in kind is just as taxable as payment in cash, assuming a value can be placed on the in-kind payment.

Now let's consider the in-kind value of owning your home. The untaxed imputed income you receive is best illustrated by an example.

> **Example**
>
> Let's assume that for the entire year you have a taxable investment of $200,000 earning 5 percent annually, or $10,000. Let's also assume that your other income is such that this $10,000 of taxable income is taxed at a combined federal and state rate of 30 percent, producing income tax of $3,000 for the year. Now let's assume you cash in the $200,000 investment and purchase a house with it. You live in the house for the entire year. How much is your taxable income for the year from your $200,000 investment in your house?

Zero, of course. You are no longer receiving the taxable investment income. But you *are* receiving the value of the $200,000 you invested in your home because you can live in the home rent free. In effect, you are receiving an in-kind payment from your $200,000 of capital in the form of living accommodations, except that this counterpart of the $10,000 investment income has become invisible—it has become imputed income that is not taxable. So you have converted your fully taxable $10,000 investment income on the $200,000 into fully sheltered nontaxable imputed income on the $200,000.

But suppose you don't have a $200,000 investment but must use a mortgage to purchase your home. Do you still get the benefit of imputed income from purchasing a home?

Yes, with a different twist.

Example

You purchase the same $200,000 home. Assume, for simplicity, that you finance the entire purchase price with a $200,000 mortgage. Disregarding the relatively small principal payments on the mortgage, your entire mortgage payment is deductible as home mortgage interest. If instead of purchasing the home you had rented it, the rent you would pay would be an entirely nondeductible personal expense. In effect, then, by purchasing the home instead of renting it, you have converted nondeductible rent into deductible interest. If the interest amounted to $10,000 and your income placed you in a combined federal and state income tax bracket of 30 percent, the purchase of the home would save you $3,000 in taxes for the year, the same amount saved by purchasing the home for cash.

The proof of the windfall for homeowners is demonstrated by viewing the situation through the tax collectors' eyes. Whether you purchase your home for all cash or finance the entire purchase price, you pay $3,000 less in taxes. The fact that most homes are financed with a down payment does not basically change the situation.

What does this seemingly theoretical discussion mean to you as a home purchaser?

Just this. Over the many years you will own your home you will receive tens of thousands of dollars in imputed income, all tax free. For many homeowners the tax savings from nontaxable imputed income can exceed $100,000 over the period they own their homes. This escape from tax on the imputed income of home ownership is one of the most important tax shelter features of home ownership.

Congressional tax writers are well aware of the imputed income received every year by some 65 million homeowners. If that income were taxed, the tax revenues would be huge and do much to reduce the national debt. But taxing the imputed income of homeowners is never even mentioned by politicians.

Why? The answer is simple: 67 million homeowners who can and will vote.

CHAPTER 8

Your Vacation Home Is a Tax Shelter

> No man's property is safe while Congress is in session.
>
> **Mark Twain**

8.1 Overview

Your vacation or "second" home is a tax chameleon. Under certain circumstances there are loopholes that permit it to provide you with a substantial tax shelter. Under other circumstances these loopholes can be pulled almost into a knot. It all depends on how you use your vacation home.

In this chapter we'll explain the rules by discussing four possible scenarios for the use of your vacation home. To help explain the applicable rules, we'll use the same basic example to illustrate each scenario:

- Scenario 1: You use the home exclusively as a vacation home for you and your family.
- Scenario 2: You use the home as a vacation home for you and your family but you rent it to others for 14 days or less.
- Scenario 3: You use the home as a vacation home for you and your family, but you rent it to others for more than 15 days but less than the entire year.
- Scenario 4: You rent your vacation home to others for the entire year.

> **Observation**
>
> *Type of Home.* The rules discussed apply regardless of whether your vacation home is a single-family house, condominium, or other type of residence.

TABLE 8.1 Quick Reference Table

	Deduction of Taxes and Interest Permitted	Deduction of Rental Costs Permitted	Deduction of Rental Loss Permitted
Scenario 1			
Use of Vacation Home Exclusively as Vacation Home	Yes	No—not applicable	No—not applicable
Scenario 2			
Use for Vacation and Rent for 14 Days or Less	Yes	No—but any rent received is nontaxable	No
Scenario 3			
Use for Vacation and Rent for More Than 14 Days	Yes	Yes—but not in excess of rental income.	No
Scenario 4			
Rent to Others for the Entire Year	Yes	Yes	Yes—subject to passive loss limits

Table 8.1 summarizes the rules applicable in the four scenarios.

> **Example**
>
> *Basic Example.* You bought a lakeside vacation home some years ago in a resort area for $250,000. You pay annual real estate taxes of $8,000 on the home. You financed the purchase of the home with a mortgage on which you pay interest amounting to $10,000 annually. Both the real estate taxes and interest qualify for deduction under the rules discussed in Sections 2.3 and 2.4, respectively.

8.2 Scenario 1: Use of Vacation Home Exclusively as Vacation Home

Assume you use your vacation home three months during the summer for yourself and your family and for occasional getaway weekends during the fall and spring. No other use is made of the home.

As pointed out in Section 2.1, the tax law says you can't take deductions for "personal, living or family expenses." As examples of these nondeductible expenses, the IRS lists the costs of maintaining a household and homeowner's insurance.

But these restrictions don't apply to two of the heaviest expenses of vacation home ownership: mortgage interest and real estate taxes. Even though these costs are personal in nature when associated with your vacation home, they generally are fully deductible. The same is generally true for the amount of any loss from damage to your vacation home from fire, storm, and other so-called "casualties." (See Section 2.4.)

So, based on the facts in the example, even though the vacation home is used for purely personal reasons, it shelters salary and other taxable income with offsetting deductions for the $8,000 real estate taxes you pay and the $10,000 interest, aggregating $18,000 yearly.

The rules governing these deductions are discussed in Sections 2.3 and 2.4.

8.3 Scenario 2: Use for Vacation and Rent for 14 Days or Less

Assume again that you use your lakeside vacation home three months during the summer for yourself and your family and for occasional getaway weekends during the fall and spring. But you also rent it to skiers on winter weekends for a total of 14 days for $250 a day. Your aggregate rental receipts are $3,500. No other use is made of the home.

The tax rules can become complicated if you combine too much personal use and rental use of your vacation home. When this occurs, the tax law places limitations on the amount you can deduct. As shown in Section 8.4 (Scenario 3), figuring the amount deductible is a pleasure only for the mathematically inclined.

But to save homeowners the trouble of going through these computations when they have only minor amounts of rental income, the tax law provides a sensible exemption for short-term rentals. It provides that if your home is used by you as a residence and the rental use of the home during the taxable year is less than 15 days, then rental income is not taxable. In other words, if you rent your vacation home for less than 15 days, your rental income is completely tax sheltered. The income becomes like interest on a municipal bond—*it is entirely tax free.*

In the example, you have tax-free rental income of $3,500. This is the equivalent of owning a $70,000 tax-free municipal bond yielding 5 percent (.05 ×

$70,000 = $3,500$). And you can still deduct all your interest and taxes, aggregating $18,000.

The rules for short-term rentals are discussed in Section 3.2.

8.4 Scenario 3: Use for Vacation and Rent for More Than 14 Days

As explained above, if you either don't rent your vacation home at all during the year or rent it for less than 15 days, the tax treatment of your vacation home is straightforward.

But this changes if you rent your vacation home for 15 days or more and your personal use of the home exceeds a specific limit. When you have this type of combined rental and personal use, figuring your deductions becomes more complicated. It brings to mind the words of a famous judge; Judge Learned Hand:

> The words of the income tax merely dance before my eyes in a meaningless procession, cross-reference to cross-reference, exception upon exception couched in abstract terms that offer no handle to seize hold of . . .

The following pages give you "a handle to seize hold of," explaining how you can use and benefit from the mixed use rules.

Tax Tip

Shortcut. As suggested previously, when you rent your vacation home for more than 15 days and also make substantial personal use of your vacation home, as illustrated in Section 8.4 (Scenario 3), figuring the amount deductible is a pleasure only for the mathematically inclined. The following discussion explains the complicated procedure for determining the amount deductible. For those who prefer to skip the details and just get to the "bottom line," reference should be made to Table 8.1 and to the "fill-in-the-blanks" IRS worksheet in Figure 8.1.

8.5 Tax Loss from Rental Not Allowed

While a tax loss from the year-round rental of a vacation home may be permitted, as explained in Section 8.7 (Scenario 4), Congress thought it was not a good idea to permit the deduction of tax losses from rental of vacation homes when the home also was used to a large extent for personal purposes. To pre-

YOUR VACATION HOME IS A TAX SHELTER

Table 2. Worksheet for Figuring the Limit on Rental Deductions for a Dwelling Unit Used as a Home

Use this worksheet only if you answer "yes" to all of the following questions.
- Did you use the dwelling unit as a home this year? (See *Dwelling Unit Used as Home*.)
- Did you rent the dwelling unit 15 days or more this year?
- Is the total of your rental expenses and depreciation more than your rental income?

1. Enter rents received . . . . _____
2a. Enter the rental portion of deductible home mortgage interest (see instructions) . . . . _____
  b. Enter the rental portion of real estate taxes . . . . _____
  c. Enter the rental portion of deductible casualty and theft losses (see instructions) . . . . _____
  d. Enter direct rental expenses (see instructions) . . . . _____
  e. **Fully deductible rental expenses.** Add lines 2a–2d . . . . _____
3. Subtract line 2e from line 1. If zero or less, enter zero . . . . _____
4a. Enter the rental portion of expenses directly related to operating or maintaining the dwelling unit (such as repairs, insurance, and utilities) . . . . _____
  b. Enter the rental portion of excess mortgage interest (see instructions) . . . . _____
  c. Add lines 4a and 4b . . . . _____
  d. **Allowable operating expenses.** Enter the smaller of line 3 or line 4c . . . . _____
5. Subtract line 4d from line 3. If zero or less, enter zero . . . . _____
6a. Enter the rental portion of excess casualty and theft losses (see instructions) . . . . _____
  b. Enter the rental portion of depreciation of the dwelling unit . . . . _____
  c. Add lines 6a and 6b . . . . _____
  d. **Allowable excess casualty and theft losses and depreciation.** Enter the smaller of line 5 or line 6c . . . . _____
7a. Operating expenses to be carried over to next year. Subtract line 4d from line 4c . . . . _____
  b. Excess casualty and theft losses and depreciation to be carried over to next year. Subtract line 6d from line 6c . . . . _____

Enter the amounts on **lines 2e, 4d, and 6d** on the appropriate lines of Schedule E (Form 1040), Part I.

Worksheet Instructions

Follow these instructions for the worksheet above. If you were unable to deduct all your expenses last year, because of the rental income limit, add these unused amounts to your expenses for this year.

Line 2a. Figure the mortgage interest on the dwelling unit that you could deduct on Schedule A (Form 1040) if you had not rented the unit. **Do not** include interest on a loan that did not benefit the dwelling unit. For example, **do not** include interest on a home equity loan used to pay off credit cards or other personal loans, buy a car, or pay college tuition. Include interest on a loan used to buy, build, or improve the dwelling unit, or to refinance such a loan. Enter the rental portion of this interest on line 2a of the worksheet.

Line 2c. Figure the casualty and theft losses related to the dwelling unit that you could deduct on Schedule A (Form 1040) if you had not rented the dwelling unit. To do this, complete Section A of Form 4684, *Casualties and Thefts*, treating the losses as personal losses. On line 17 of Form 4684, enter 10% of your adjusted gross income figured without your rental income and expenses from the dwelling unit. Enter the rental portion of the result from line 18 of Form 4684 on line 2c of this worksheet.

Note. Do **not** file this Form 4684 or use it to figure your personal losses on Schedule A. Instead, figure the personal portion on a separate Form 4684.

Line 2d. Enter the total of your rental expenses that are directly related only to the rental activity. These include interest on loans used for rental activities other than to buy, build, or improve the dwelling unit. Also include rental agency fees, advertising, office supplies, and depreciation on office equipment used in your rental activity.

Line 4b. On line 2a, you entered the rental portion of the mortgage interest you could deduct on Schedule A if you had not rented the dwelling unit. Enter on line 4b of this worksheet the rental portion of the mortgage interest you could not deduct on Schedule A because it is **more than** the limit on home mortgage interest. **Do not** include interest on a loan that did not benefit the dwelling unit (as explained in the line 2a instructions).

Line 6a. To find the rental portion of excess casualty and theft losses, use the Form 4684 you prepared for line 2c of this worksheet.

  A. Enter the amount from line 10 of Form 4684 . . . . _____
  B. Enter the rental portion of A . . . _____
  C. Enter the amount from line 2c of this worksheet . . . _____
  D. Subtract C from B. Enter the result here and on line 6a of this worksheet . . . . _____

Allocating the limited deduction. If you cannot deduct all of the amount on line 4c or 6c this year, you can allocate the allowable deduction in any way you wish among the expenses included on line 4c or 6c. Enter the amount you allocate to each expense on the appropriate line of Schedule E, Part I.

FIGURE 8.1 Determining the Limit on Rental Deductions

vent the deduction of tax losses arising from the deduction of home ownership expenses in these situations, such as interest, taxes, maintenance, and repairs, the tax law places limits on the amount of such deductions allowed. The limits become applicable when both of the following occur:

- Rental use of the residence is 15 or more days during the taxable year.
- Personal use of the residence exceeds the greater of 14 days per year or 10 percent of the number of days during the year that the residence is rented.

When these rental use and personal use limits are exceeded, the limitations on the deduction of home ownership expenses discussed below become applicable.

In applying the 10-percent test, only the number of days during the year that the residence is rented "at a fair rental" are taken into account. A "fair rental" does not necessarily have to be high enough to permit you to ultimately make a taxable profit. "Fair rental" is rental at current local market rates for comparable property.

The tax law is tough on what constitutes *personal use*, stretching the term to cover some unexpected users of your vacation home. It covers use by you and members of your family, extending to your grandparents, parents, children, spouse, and siblings. In addition, if any of these relatives have an interest in the vacation home, the same collection of relatives of *that* relative are included. Thus, for example, it is possible that if your spouse owns an interest in the vacation home, use by your mother-in-law would be considered personal use by you. (Who says Congress doesn't have a sense of humor?)

The way the tax law prevents you from having a tax loss from the deduction of home ownership expenses if you exceed the personal use/rental use limits is to restrict the amount of home ownership expenses you can deduct. The amount of home ownership expenses you can deduct generally is limited to the amount of your rental income. If deductible home ownership expenses cannot exceed rental income, a loss from the deduction of home ownership expenses simply cannot occur.

IRS regulations require that you figure the limit on deductions using a four-step procedure. Each step shows the amount deductible against rent for particular expenses, progressively reducing the amount of rent left over against which further expenses can be offset. The computation is illustrated below.

The four steps are as follows:

- Step 1: Deduction of expenses strictly for rental
- Step 2: Deduction of interest and taxes allocable to rental use

- Step 3: Deduction of home maintenance expenses allocable to rental use
- Step 4: Deduction of depreciation allocable to rental use

If this seems to you like a complicated process, you are not alone in your reaction. In coping with these provisions even the Tax Court has complained about having to thread its way "through the tortuous path of exasperatingly convoluted provisions."

> **Tax Tip**
>
> *Splitting Interest and Taxes.* As illustrated in the example below, the limits on deductions do not limit your deductions for real estate taxes and mortgage interest. However, your deductions for real estate taxes and mortgage interest are split between the portion of interest and taxes allocable to the rental of your vacation home and the portion allocable to your personal use. The portion allocable to rental is deducted in figuring your rental deductions, and the portion allocable to personal use is deducted as an itemized deduction on Schedule A of Form 1040.

8.6 Figuring the Amount Deductible

Now, the illustration.

Note in the example that rental use of the residence is more than 14 days and personal use of the residence exceeds the greater of 14 days per year or 10 percent of the number of days during the year that the residence is rented. Consequently, since the rental use and personal use limits are exceeded, the deduction limitations described above become applicable.

> **Example**
>
> You rent your lakeside home at a fair rental for 90 days during the taxable year at, say, $250 per day. To obtain your tenant, you pay $2,000 for advertising and a real estate agent's fee. These costs are strictly rental expenses, having nothing to do with the cost of owning your home. You use the home for personal purposes on 20 other days during the taxable year and also rent it to a friend at a discount for 10 days at, say, $150 per day. Thus, your vacation home is used for some purpose (other than repair or maintenance) on 120 days
>
> *(Continued)*

> **Example** *(Continued)*
>
> during the taxable year. Under the fair share rule (discussed later), you determine the rental ratio by dividing the number of days your home is rented at a fair rental by the number of days it is used, 90/120. Accordingly, the rental percentage is 75 percent. As will be shown, you use this percentage later when figuring the amount of home ownership expenses you can deduct.

Before you get to the limitations on the deduction of home ownership expenses, you are allowed to deduct expenses incurred strictly for rental. This is Step 1.

Step 1: Deduction of Expenses Strictly for Rental

Gross receipts from rental:	
90 days at $250 per day	$22,500
10 days at $150 per day	1,500
Total rent	$24,000
Less: advertising and agent's fee	2,000
Rental limit on home ownership expense deductions	$22,000

Based on the above facts, the rental limitation is $22,000 and deductible home ownership expenses cannot exceed this amount. This prevents a tax loss from being created from vacation home ownership expenses. The expenses that are strictly rental expenses, the advertising cost and agent's fee, are not part of home ownership expenses and are deductible without regard to the rental limitation.

Fair Share Rule. In figuring your rental deductions in steps 2, 3, and 4, you also are permitted to deduct only the portion of your home ownership expenses that relate to the rental use of the home. This is fair, because if you could deduct all your year-round expenses for the home when you rent it for only part of the year, you would be deducting as "rental expenses" costs that actually were your personal expenses. This fair share rule provides that your deductions attributable to rental use are limited by a rental ratio. This ratio is the number of actual rental days for the year over the total days of use for the year, and it is applied against total expenses for each category of expense to figure the amount of such expense allocable to rental use. As indicated in the example, your rental percentage is 75 percent. This percentage is used in figuring the allowable rental deductions in the following steps.

Step 2: Deduction of Interest and Taxes Allocable to Rental Use

As shown in Table 8.1, interest and taxes are fully deductible in all four scenarios. In Scenario 3, however, part of the aggregate interest and taxes is deducted in figuring your rental deductions, the balance being deducted in figuring your personal deductions. In step 2, you break out the portion of interest and taxes allocable to the rental use of your residence to get the amount of interest and taxes deductible as rental expenses. This amount is determined by using the fair share percentage of interest and taxes, 75 percent in the example. As indicated previously, the balance of your interest and taxes is deductible on Schedule A of Form 1040.

	Deductions Otherwise Allowable	*Allocable to Rental (75%)*	
Rental income limitation (above)			$22,000
Mortgage interest	$10,000	$7,500	
Real estate taxes	8,000	6,000	
Amount allowable			$13,500
Remaining limit on home ownership expense deductions			$8,500

As shown, the amount of interest and taxes deductible as rental expense is $13,500 ($7,500 + $6,000). The balance of interest and taxes, $4,500 ($2,500 + $2,000) is deductible as regular itemized deductions on Form 1040. The rental limit on deductions, $22,000, is reduced by the allowable interest and taxes, $13,500, to $8,500.

Step 3: Deduction of Home Maintenance Expenses Allocable to Rental Use

In this step, you have to figure the fair share amount of home ownership expenses other than interest and taxes allocable to the rental of your vacation home that are allowable as rental deductions.

	Home Expense Deductions	Allocable to Rental (75%)	
Remaining limit on further deductions (above)			$8,500
Insurance	$4,000	$3,000	
Utilities and repairs	6,000	4,500	
Amount allowable			$7,500
Remaining limit on further home ownership deductions			$1,000

As shown, the amount of home ownership expenses deductible as rental expenses is $7,500. The ceiling limitation, $8,500, is reduced by these allowable rental expenses, $7,500, to $1,000.

Step 4: Deduction of Depreciation Allocable to Rental Use

Finally, you have to figure the amount of depreciation allowed on the vacation home, and then the amount of such depreciation that is allowable as a rental deduction. (The manner in which the depreciation deduction is figured is explained below.)

	Depreciation Deduction	Allocable to Rental (75%)	
Limit on further deductions			$1,000
Depreciation	$6,970	$5,228	
Amount allowable			$1,000

The amount of depreciation allowed as a rental deduction is only $1,000, because the allowance of any larger amount would produce a tax loss from home ownership expenses. Thus, to prevent a tax loss from occurring, $4,228 of depreciation is disallowed as a deduction ($5,228 − $1,000), and is carried over to the following year.

Bottom Line. While the intricate limits on deductions prevent the creation of a tax loss, the permitted deductions nevertheless wipe out all the rental income. Thus, even in Scenario 3, your home is a tax shelter.

Financial and Tax Planning. As an examination of the illustration will show, the deduction limitation rules reward success. The larger the gross receipts from your rents, the less likely the deduction limitation rules for home ownership expenses will reduce allowable deductions. In other words, the higher your rent, the more of your home ownership expenses are deductible because of the increase in the rental ceiling on deductions. Thus, from both a financial-planning and tax-planning viewpoint, it is desirable to increase rents because your income is increased and because such income may be tax sheltered from the higher rental deductions, especially the deduction for depreciation that involves no out-of-pocket cost.

> **Tax Tip**
>
> *IRS Worksheet.* The IRS has provided a worksheet for figuring the limit on rental deductions for a vacation home when the rules described above are applicable. The worksheet appears in IRS Publication 527, "Residential Rental Property," and is reproduced above in Figure 8.1.

8.7   Scenario 4: Rent to Others for the Entire Year

Personal factors, such as financial pressure or a change in place of employment, sometimes cause individuals to rent their vacation homes for the entire year. While this may be a cause of personal regret, it can produce attractive financial advantages, namely, increased personal cash flow from the rental that is tax sheltered, *plus* a tax loss with which to shelter other income. These substantial tax benefits are a consequence of the fact that, for tax purposes, renting your vacation home for the entire year puts you in the real estate business. This combination of benefits is illustrated in the example below.

> **Caution**
>
> While being in the real estate business may assure you that your cash flow from the rental of your vacation home will be tax sheltered, it doesn't guarantee that you will be able to use any tax losses to offset your other income, such as salary. To do that you have to elude the "passive loss" rules, discussed in Section 8.12.

8.8   Need for Profit Motive

To get full rental expense and depreciation deductions from the rental of your vacation home, you need to have a profit motive for renting the vacation home. If the rental use is "an activity not engaged in for profit," rental-type deductions may either be restricted or entirely lost.

Whether or not you are engaged in the rental activity for profit depends on the facts. Facts supporting a profit motive include carrying out the rental activity in a businesslike manner, spending significant time on the rental activity, little personal or recreational use of the property, and making a profit from the rental. If these facts are present, you are likely to be deemed to be engaged in the rental activity for profit.

The courts have been reasonable on this "for-profit" question. For example, the deduction of all expenses and depreciation claimed by a condominium owner has been allowed, despite losses for several years, when the purchase of the unit was part of a pattern of investment in real estate, substantial and continuing efforts were made to rent the unit, and personal use was minimal. Likewise, a condominium acquired for investment has been deemed held for the production of income where the developer represented that rental opportunities were good, diligent attempts were made to find tenants, and no personal use was made of the unit. However, personal use and an unbusinesslike approach to rental have been held to indicate that participation in a condominium rental program was to minimize the expenses of a personal, recreational facility.

Years of losses may not be fatal if the losses are caused by unforeseen circumstances. For example, rental of a ski lodge in a businesslike fashion has been treated as having a profit motive, despite 12 consecutive years of losses, where the losses resulted from a fortuitous series of adverse business conditions and no use was made of the lodge for personal enjoyment. Likewise, despite continuing losses and occasional personal use, the businesslike rental of a beach house has qualified where there was a reasonable expectation that profit would be realized from appreciation in value of the property.

If you rent property to a relative at less than fair rental value, you will not be deemed to have the requisite profit motive.

8.9 Figuring Amount of Tax Shelter

Assuming you rent your vacation home for the entire year with the necessary profit motive, how much tax shelter can you get? The answer depends on your gross rentals, expenses, and depreciation for the year.

Example

Assume that you rent your lakefront vacation home for the entire year to a tenant for $30,000 and pay the rental expenses shown below. You make no personal use of the vacation home. Accordingly, the deduction limitation rules discussed in Section 8.4 (Scenario 3) are inapplicable, and you are entitled to deduct all your rental expenses and depreciation for the year.

Example *(Continued)*

Figuring Cash Profit

Rental income		$30,000
Expenses		
Advertising and realtor's fee	$2,500	
Mortgage interest	10,000	
Insurance	500	
Repairs and maintenance	6,500	
Real estate taxes	7,500	
Total expenses		27,000
Cash profit		$ 3,000

Figuring Tax Loss

Rental income		$30,000
Expenses	$27,000	
Depreciation	6,970	
Expenses plus depreciation		33,970
Tax loss		($3,970)

In this scenario, your vacation home becomes both an investment asset *and* a tax shelter. It produces a cash profit of $3,000 that is entirely tax sheltered by depreciation, plus an additional $3,970 of depreciation that creates a tax loss. In other words, you pay no tax on the $3,000 cash flow and have $3,970 in depreciation left over, creating a tax loss that can shelter your other income.

If you can get by the passive loss rules, discussed below, the tax loss is reported on Schedule E of Form 1040, and is used to offset your income from other sources, such as salary. If you can't get by the passive loss rules, you can only use the loss to

Tax Tip

Partial-Year Allocation. If you change the use of your vacation home from personal use to rental use at any time other than the beginning of the year, you must divide yearly expenses, such as depreciation, taxes, and insurance, between personal use and rental use. You can deduct as rental expenses only the portion of total expenses allocable to the portion of the year the property was used or held for rental.

offset your $3,000 cash profit from the rental. The additional $3,970 loss that is nondeductible because of the passive loss rules is suspended and carried forward to future tax years. In the future years it may be used either to offset passive income or be deducted when the property is sold.

8.10 Hidden Nugget: A Little Personal Use

There's a little-known tax aspect of year-round vacation home rental that can let you get some personal vacation use out of your rented vacation home. This can be done *without* limiting the tax shelter it can provide from rental expense deductions and depreciation. While you have to restrict your personal use of the rented vacation home to get this benefit, the personal use allowance is still a valuable home ownership perk. It only works, of course, if the dates of your tenant's occupancy leave you a little time to slip in some personal use.

Here's the requirement for this perk: Your personal use of the rented vacation home must not exceed the greater of 14 days or 10 percent of the number of days during the year that the residence is rented.

Suppose, in the above example, that you use the vacation home for 10 days just before the tenant moves in. This 10-day use does not exceed the personal use limitation of the greater of 14 days per year or 10 percent of the number of days during the year that the residence is rented. Thus, since you didn't use your rented vacation home more than the proscribed number of days during the taxable year, you can escape application of the deduction limiting rules described in Section 8.4 (Scenario 3) and deduct all your rental expenses and depreciation.

8.11 Depreciation: The Deduction without Cash Outlay

An individual usually has to make an out-of-pocket payment of an expense to get a tax deduction for the expense. If you could get a deduction without paying for it, it would be an especially valuable deduction.

Depreciation is such a deduction. It's an annual allowance to owners of depreciable business property that recognizes that such property gradually wears out. To properly reflect income, a percentage of the cost of such property is allowed as a depreciation deduction each year.

When you rent your vacation home year round, it becomes depreciable business property eligible for the depreciation deduction. The amount of your annual depreciation deduction is a prescribed percentage of your cost or other tax basis for your vacation home. If you rented your vacation home from the time you acquired it, your tax basis for depreciation would be your cost of the vacation home. If you converted your vacation home from personal vacation home use to business use, your tax basis for depreciation would be the lower of your cost for the home or its fair market value on the date of the conversion. The portion of cost or fair market value allocable to land is not depreciable.

> **Example**
>
> You paid $250,000 for your vacation home and 20 percent of such cost, or $50,000, is allocable to the value of the land. You convert your vacation home to year-round rental use four years later, when the value of the entire property is $300,000. Since your $250,000 cost is lower than the fair market value of $300,000, your basis for depreciation is your cost, $250,000, less the portion of cost allocable to land, $50,000, or $200,000.

How to Figure the Deduction. The IRS has provided a table (Table 8.2) that gives you a short-cut way to figure depreciation on your vacation home used as rental property. The table appears in IRS Publication 527, "Residential Rental Property," and is used for figuring the depreciation for residential rental property with a recovery period of 27.5 years, such as your vacation home. To use the table, find the row for the month you commenced renting the property. Then look under the column for the year involved opposite the month you commenced using the property.

TABLE 8.2 Determining the Depreciation on Your Vacation Home

	Year 1	Year 2	Year 3	Year 4	Year 5	Year 6
Jan.	3.485%	3.636%	3.636%	3.636%	3.636%	3.636%
Feb.	3.182	3.636	3.636	3.636	3.636	3.636
March	2.879	3.636	3.636	3.636	3.636	3.636
Apr.	2.576	3.636	3.636	3.636	3.636	3.636
May	2.273	3.636	3.636	3.636	3.636	3.636
June	1.970	3.636	3.636	3.636	3.636	3.636
July	1.667	3.636	3.636	3.636	3.636	3.636
Aug.	1.364	3.636	3.636	3.636	3.636	3.636
Sept.	1.061	3.636	3.636	3.636	3.636	3.636
Oct.	0.758	3.636	3.636	3.636	3.636	3.636
Nov.	0.455	3.636	3.636	3.636	3.636	3.636
Dec.	0.152	3.636	3.636	3.636	3.636	3.636

For the recovery periods for various types of property you may use in your business, see Table 8.3.

> **Example**
>
> You first placed your vacation home in service in January of this year by renting it to a year-round tenant. Your depreciation deduction is $6,970 ($200,000 × .03485).

As the example illustrates, the depreciation deduction does not require any current outlay. It is based on the original cost of the residence and it makes no difference that the original cost was paid for in part with a mortgage. Accordingly, since depreciation deductions reduce taxable income without any current cash outlay, they can be viewed as a "costless" deduction that can both shelter cash flow from property and create a tax loss that shelters other income.

> **Observation**
>
> *What's Depreciable Property?* Depreciation deductions are allowed only for property used in a trade or business or held for the production of income, such as a vacation home held for rental. Depreciation deductions are not allowed for property used exclusively for personal purposes, such as the vacation home use illustrated in Scenario 1 in Section 8.2 and Scenario 2 in Section 8.3.

> **Tax Tip**
>
> *Check Collateral Damage.* While depreciation deductions reduce your taxes, they also reduce the tax basis for the property. On a future sale of the property, gain is measured for tax purposes by the difference between your tax basis and the sales price for the property. Since depreciation deductions reduce your tax basis each year, it follows that gain on a later sale will be larger that it would have been in the absence of depreciation deductions.

Personal Property. So-called "personal" property, unlike "real" property, generally is anything that is movable, such as furniture and kitchen appliances. When you rent your vacation home together with personal property such as kitchen appliances and furniture, you can separately depreciate such property if you can establish its cost. The method for depreciating such personal property is described in IRS Publication 527, "Residential Rental Property." This publication can be obtained at the IRS web site, *www.irs.gov*.

Table 8.3 shows the period for depreciation for various items of personal property as adapted from a table appearing in Publication 527, which should be consulted for determining how the deduction is computed.

TABLE 8.3 Depreciation Recovery Periods for Property Used in Rental Activities

Type of Property	Recovery Period to Use General Depreciation System
Computers and their peripheral equipment	5 years

Office machinery, such as:
  Typewriters
  Calculators
  Copiers
	5 years

Appliances, such as:
  Stoves
  Refrigerators
	5 years

Carpets	5 years
Furniture used in rental property	5 years

Office furniture and equipment, such as:
  Desks
  Files
	7 years

Roads	15 years
Shrubbery	15 years
Fences	15 years
Residential rental property (buildings or structures) and structural components such as furnaces, water pipes, venting, etc.	27.5 years
Additions and improvements, such as a new roof	The recovery period of the property to which the addition or improvement is made, determined as if the property were placed in service at the same time as the addition or improvement

8.12 Tax Shelter Rules

In the 1980s there was a flood of tax shelter deals for high-income taxpayers, so many and so large that they threatened to overwhelm the income tax system. To stem this tide of tax avoidance, Congress passed antishelter legislation. While not aimed specifically at rented vacation homes, such homes occasionally may be caught in the cross-fire of these rules.

The principal antishelter rules that may apply to rented vacation homes are the "passive loss" rules. These rules may limit the deduction of losses from rental of your vacation home. A second set of antishelter rules, the "at-risk" rules, are normally unlikely to restrict losses from the rental of your vacation home.

Passive Loss Rules. In general, the passive loss rules prevent you from claiming deductions from passive activities to the extent such deductions exceed your income from passive activities. The rental of real estate generally is considered a passive activity, so that if your deductions from the rental of your vacation home exceed your income from such rental, producing a tax loss, the loss cannot be used to offset your other taxable income, such as salary.

There is a $25,000 exception to the passive loss rules that may protect owners of rental vacation homes from becoming subject to the passive loss rules, but this exception applies only if their adjusted gross income does not exceed $150,000.

How to Qualify for the $25,000 Exemption. Subject to a phase-out rule, if you or your spouse actively participate in the vacation home rental activity, you can deduct up to $25,000 of loss from the rental activity from your nonpassive income, such as salary. To qualify for this relief, you or your spouse must "actively" participate in the rental activity. This requires that you participate in making management decisions and providing services, or arranging for others to provide services, such as repairs, in a significant manner. The management decisions you must be involved in include the selection of tenants, setting rental terms, approving capital or repair expenditures, and similar decisions. A rental agent may be used to provide repair and other services, provided you supervise the rental agent's services.

The $25,000 exemption is subject to a phase-out keyed to your adjusted gross income. The $25,000 amount is reduced by 50 percent of the amount by which your adjusted gross income for the year exceeds $100,000. Accordingly, the exemption is wiped out when your adjusted gross income reaches $150,000. If you are married and don't file a joint return, the $25,000 exemption generally is reduced to $12,500 and the $100,000 adjusted gross income threshold is reduced to $50,000.

Tax Tip

Adjusted Gross Income. Your adjusted gross income generally is all your income, minus specified deductions such as alimony payments, capital loss deductions, the deduction for IRA contributions, and moving expense deductions. For purposes of the phase-out, adjusted gross income is figured without taking into account IRA contributions, taxable Social Security benefits, and any passive activity losses.

In Scenario 3 in Section 8.4, the vacation home was rented for more than 14 days and the owner made substantial personal use of the vacation home. This resulted in a "rental limitation" on the deduction of rental expenses. The passive loss rules are inapplicable when these rental limitation rules apply.

Tax Tip

Real Estate Professionals. There also is an exemption from the passive loss rules for real estate professionals. But you cannot qualify as a real estate professional unless, among other things, more than half of your time is devoted to real estate businesses.

At-Risk Rules. The at-risk rules generally suspend the deduction of any tax loss to the extent the tax loss exceeds the amount for which you are at risk at the end of the taxable year. This rule is unlikely to affect you as a vacation homeowner. This is so because you usually are at risk for the amount of the cash down payment you made on the purchase of your vacation home, as well as the amount of the mortgage on the home for which you are personally liable. These amounts normally will greatly exceed any losses you will claim.

Tax Tip

Three or More Homes. If you are one of the fortunate few who has three or more personal residences, only interest on a mortgage on your principal residence and one designated second home may constitute qualified residence interest. The interest on mortgages on additional homes is nondeductible personal interest. (See Section 2.4.) This rule would not affect the deduction of interest on a home used year round as rental property, as in Scenario 4 in Section 8.7.

PART IV

Retirement Benefits and Estate Planning

CHAPTER 9

How to Get Tax-Free Dollars in Retirement from Your Home

> I feel honored to pay taxes in America. The thing is, I could feel just as honored at half the price.
>
> Arthur Godfrey

9.1 Overview

A home is an asset for all seasons.

After it has sheltered you during your working life, your home can be a valuable nest egg when you retire. If you've paid down or paid off your mortgage, there will be substantial equity in your home that you can tap in retirement to help meet your cash flow needs.

From the tax viewpoint, it's better than an IRA or other retirement plan. You can tap the equity value in your home without paying *any* income tax. Your home is a tax shelter for life.

For many older homeowners, the investment in their home has proven to be the best investment of their lifetimes. It's commonplace that the value of a home bought 25 years ago has doubled and then redoubled, and sometimes even redoubled again. Thus, a home purchased for $50,000 or $60,000 years ago now may be worth hundreds of thousands of dollars. Owners who have purchased and sold a series of homes over the years may have similar accumulations of equity. If history repeats itself, younger homeowners also will enjoy substantial appreciation in value.

The family home often represents a retiree's most valuable asset, especially if the mortgage has been paid down over the years or paid off. For this reason, the home can be an important source of retirement funds. This source of retirement cash flow can be tapped either by trading down or using a reverse mortgage. The choice depends on the homeowner's individual circumstances, as explained below.

> **Observation**
>
> *Home Equity Loan.* As explained in Section 3.3, the equity in a home can be tapped by use of a home equity loan. But if you are retired, this usually is not the best choice for enhancing retirement cash flow. This is because a home equity loan must be paid back, and if you are retired, this may be difficult or impossible. However, you do not have to pay back funds raised from trading down or a reverse mortgage.

Younger Owners. If you're relatively new to home ownership and have not built up substantial equity, consider the following discussion a preview of possible future benefits. Moreover, if your parents or in-laws own a substantially appreciated home, the discussion may provide you with useful financial planning ideas that you can pass along to them.

9.2   Tax-Free Trading Down

If you are an older individual or retiree with a home larger than you need, tax-free trading down to a smaller home can be an attractive means for increasing your cash flow. Trading down tax free is feasible for most individuals because gain on the sale of their principal residence can be avoided under the exclusion rules. As explained in Sections 4.3 through 4.9, single individuals can exclude up to $250,000 of gain on the sale of their principal residences and married couples can exclude up to $500,000. Even if gain exceeds these ceilings, there are approaches to avoiding or reducing tax on the excess. (See Sections 5.4 through 5.7.)

9.3   How Trading Down Increases Cash Flow

The reason that trading down can increase your cash flow is that the difference between the net sales price of your present larger and more expensive home and the cost of your smaller and less expensive new home can be added to your retirement capital. This increase in your retirement capital often can provide a marked increase in your investment income. In addition, cost savings from living in a smaller home can be substantial and can further enhance your cash flow. Thus, trading down provides a double benefit for enhancing retirement cash flow because it both increases income and reduces expenses.

If you purchased your home years ago, the untapped equity in your home may be large.

> **Example**
>
> A home purchased for $40,000 in the early 1960s in a good suburban neighborhood in a growing area now could be worth $400,000 as a result of growing values and inflation. If the owner sold the home for $400,000 and purchased a replacement condominium for $250,000, $150,000 could be added to income-producing investment assets, such as a bond portfolio, increasing the owner's cash flow markedly. Moreover, the smaller home purchased would have lower real estate taxes and smaller bills for heating, cooling, insurance, and maintenance costs. If the move is from a single-family house to a condominium, as often will be the case, cost will be reduced even more: outside painting, roof repair, landscaping, and similar "common" costs disappear into monthly common charges that usually are much lower than the monthly cost of maintaining a single-family home.

9.4 How Much Cash from Trading Down?

The amount of cash you can get by trading down depends on the value of your present home, the cost of purchasing a new home, and the incidental costs involved in the trade. These incidental costs include brokerage commissions, legal fees, closing costs, and moving expenses, as well as any fixing up expenses you pay for either the present home or the new home. You should estimate these amounts to approximate the net amount you will receive from trading down.

To check the present value of your home, you should get an estimate of its selling price from two or three local realtors. You also should get an estimate of the cost of your replacement home by shopping for the desired type of home.

In addition to estimating the amount of cash you will net from trading down, you also should estimate the annual housing cost savings that trading down will provide for you. To make the estimate, compare the annual costs of maintaining your present home with the annual costs of maintaining the new home. Estimating the annual cost of maintaining a home should include a prorated portion of expenses that do not occur regularly, such as indoor and outdoor painting and roof repairs.

> **Caution**
>
> It usually is advisable not to purchase your replacement home until after you sell your present home, or at least enter into a contract to sell your present home. If you purchase your replacement home before you sell your present home and don't quickly find a buyer for your present home, you would incur costs for maintaining *two* homes.

If you choose to rent rather than purchase a new home, the amount of cash that can be added to your income-producing assets will be further enhanced—$400,000 in the preceding example. Figuring the benefits of trading down then must take into account the enhanced investment income, eliminated house expenses, and future estimated rent.

9.5 The Tax Benefit

Even after you retire, your home remains a tax shelter.

While payouts from individual retirement accounts (IRAs) and pension and profit-sharing plans generally are subject to substantial current income

> **Observation**
>
> *Balancing Burdens and Benefits.* There can be disadvantages in trading down, such as an unwelcome reduction in living space or a less attractive home. Perhaps the most common problem with trading down occurs if you are strongly attached to your present home. If you are familiar and comfortable with both your house and your neighborhood, you may not want to be "uprooted" from your present home and its surrounding social network. Nevertheless, regardless of how attached you may be to your home, you probably also are troubled by the worries that afflict most older homeowners. These include rising property taxes, the threat of escalating insurance, utility and repair costs, and the lurking, unexpected cost of major repairs such as a new roof or plumbing. You may decide that trading down from a larger house to a smaller house or condominium is warranted to lighten not only your financial burden, but also the worry of home ownership.

tax, the cash produced from selling your principal residence at a gain when you trade down normally will be completely free of income tax. This is because the gain on the sale will qualify for the exclusion of gain on the sale of a principal residence, up to $250,000 for single individuals or $500,000 for married couples. (See Sections 4.3 through 4.9.) The principal residence gain exclusion break will make most trade-down transactions entirely free of federal income taxes.

9.6 Tax-Free Reverse Mortgages

They say there's no free lunch, but the reverse mortgage seems to come close. It provides the homeowner with a stream of tax-free income that the homeowner need never repay, and it permits the homeowner to continue living in the home for life. For many retirees, this happy combination of increased cash flow and secure home ownership seems to create the ideal way to supplement retirement income.

For many retirees, it is. But to understand if it works for you, you should understand what a reverse mortgage is, take a close look at the critical question of how much cash flow you can get from a reverse mortgage, and know about the different types of reverse mortgages. The discussion that follows presents a concise overview of these factors. Then, if it seems that a reverse mortgage is right for you, you should get additional information about reverse mortgages. A good starting point for this is at the web site of AARP (formerly the American Association of Retired Persons) at *www.aarp.org/revmort*.

Observation

AARP Web Site. AARP's web site includes an online calculator permitting an estimate of the amount of funds that can be provided by a reverse mortgage. The estimate is obtained simply by inputting your birth date and the zip code for your home and its value. The site also has a collection of other useful information about reverse mortgages.

9.7 What Is a Reverse Mortgage, Anyway?

A reverse mortgage is a regular home mortgage turned on its head. With a regular mortgage you make monthly payments to the lender, reducing the amount of the mortgage with each payment. The reverse mortgage is, as the name implies, the reverse: You receive monthly payments from the lender, increasing the amount of the mortgage with each payment you receive.

If you are an older individual and have either a small regular mortgage on your home or no mortgage at all, the reverse mortgage can be an attractive way to increase your cash flow. This is because the reverse mortgage permits you to remain in your home for life while creating a supplemental stream of income for you from the built-up equity in your home, and you never have to repay the reverse mortgage. In effect, you can have your cake and eat it too.

At a price, of course. You must mortgage your home to the lender, and each payment you receive from the lender increases the amount of principal and interest owed to the lender on the reverse mortgage. This reduces the equity value of your home (its value in excess of the mortgage), as each payment is made to you. But if you need to increase your cash flow, this equity reduction usually will be far preferable to a marked reduction in your standard of living. In the typical case, the reverse mortgage cannot become "due" so long as you live in the home.

Especially for older individuals who intend to remain in their homes for life, the reverse mortgage may be the ideal way to deal with a cash flow shortfall. As will be explained, the size of annual payments that can be obtained from a reverse mortgage rises dramatically as the age of the retiree increases. Moreover, payments from a reverse mortgage are advances under a mortgage loan, and this makes the payments especially valuable for purposes of enhancing cash flow, for two reasons:

1. As explained below, the receipt of loan payments is not subject to income tax. Hence, the entire amount of cash flow received is retained, free of tax.
2. The character of the payments as loans also prevents them from counting as "earnings" that can reduce the amount of Social Security benefits for individuals under age 65.

9.8 The Tax Benefit

It seems like anytime you receive money, the IRS wants to tax it. But the receipt of money from reverse mortgages provides an often-overlooked tax break.

Like the proceeds from trading down, the payments under a reverse mortgage are *not* taxable, but for a different reason. The reason is quite simple: Payments by the lender to you under a reverse mortgage are a loan to you, and a loan is not subject to income tax.

So, again, your home is a tax shelter.

9.9 How Much Cash Flow Can You Get?

Especially for older individuals who intend to remain in their homes for the rest of their lives, the reverse mortgage may be the ideal way to deal with a cash shortfall. As shown in Table 9.1, the amount of monthly payments available from a reverse mortgage rises substantially as the age of the homeowner increases.

How much cash flow will a reverse mortgage provide? The answer to this question depends on four factors:

1. The homeowner's age
2. The amount of equity in the home available to support the loan (the market value of the home in excess of any regular mortgage on the home)
3. The interest rate
4. Closing costs

The older the homeowner, the higher the home equity, and the lower the costs and interest, the more the payments. If the homeowner is younger than 70, the payment rate usually is unattractive. But as age increases beyond age 70, the payment rate rises markedly, especially for larger loan amounts. This suggests that younger retirees may want to look more to other assets for cash flow during earlier years of retirement, saving the reverse mortgage as a source of funds for later years.

Table 9.1 illustrates the relationship between age, loan amounts, and monthly payments. (The table is from Fannie Mae's *Money from Home: A Guide to Understanding Reverse Mortgages*, which can be found at *www.fanniemae.com*.)

TABLE 9.1 Typical Monthly Payments for a Tenure Plan

Age	Maximum Claim Amount				
	$50,000	$85,000	$110,000	$125,000	$155,250
62	$ 76	$161	$221	$ 258	$ 331
65	90	185	253	294	376
70	119	234	316	365	464
75	154	295	396	456	577
80	203	378	503	578	729
85	272	498	659	755	950
90	396	711	937	1,072	1,344

The table assumes an 8.5 percent average interest rate, financing of $2,000 in closing costs and the initial insurance premium (2 percent of the maximum claim amount), and the deduction of an initial set-aside sufficient to pay a $30 monthly servicing fee for the duration of the loan. The "maximum claim amount" is the lesser of a home's appraised value or the maximum loan amount that can be insured by the Federal Housing Authority (FHA). The table shows the monthly amounts payable for a "tenure plan," under which you receive equal monthly payments for as long as you occupy your home as your principal residence. Under a tenure plan, you continue to receive payments until your death or until you sell your home, convey title, or permanently move away.

Refinancing a Reverse Mortgage. The rapid real estate inflation of recent years has increased the value of many homes subject to reverse mortgages. When this occurs, the reverse mortgage often can be refinanced to provide more funds for the homeowner. As when shopping for the original reverse mortgage, it's important to be a Black Belt shopper when shopping for the best deal on a reverse mortgage refinancing, including the interest rate and fees.

Observation

Keeping Your Present Home for Life. As indicated above, you may not want to increase your income by trading down for a variety of reasons, including attachment to your present home. With a reverse mortgage, you can increase your income while continuing to live in your present home for life. A reverse mortgage generally becomes due only when you move out of the home or die. Then the home is sold and the mortgage is paid off out of the sales proceeds.

9.10 What Type of Reverse Mortgage Is Best for You?

What type of reverse mortgage is the most suitable for you?

There are basically three types of cash advances under reverse mortgages: lump sums, credit lines, and monthly advances.

1. *Lump sum.* The total available amount of the reverse mortgage loan is paid to you in a single lump sum at the loan closing.
2. *Credit line.* The total available amount of the reverse mortgage loan is placed into a line of credit that you can draw upon on demand. This works much like a checking account.

3. *Monthly advances.* Fixed monthly advances are made to you, either by check or deposit to your checking account. The payments may last for a fixed term of years selected by you (*term advances*), for so long as you live in the home (*tenure advances*), or for your life regardless of where you live (*annuity advances*).

Reverse mortgage lenders often allow you to combine different types of loan advances. For many retirees with a cash flow shortage, the best combination will be monthly tenure advances linked with a credit line. While the credit line will reduce the amount available for monthly advances, the availability of the credit line assures a source of funds for emergencies. It also provides a source of funds to meet increased living costs from future inflation. This format will permit you to remain in your home for life with both an assured stream of income and a reserve nest egg.

Reverse mortgages have disadvantages. They usually involve substantial up-front costs and do not produce any reduction in home ownership expenses. Perhaps more important to many, they increase home mortgage debt, reducing the amount that will be left to children and other heirs. This effect brings to mind the ambivalent humor in the bumper sticker seen on some retirees' cars:

> We're out spending our children's inheritance.

As with many financial decisions, the pros and cons should be weighed. The disadvantages should be compared to the great benefit of the reverse mortgage: It permits you to remain in your home for life while giving you a supplemental stream of income that you never have to repay.

Observation

Older Americans have billions of dollars of equity in their homes, much of which could be used for reverse mortgages. Indeed, according to the National Council on the Aging, over 13 million households could qualify for an average of $72,128 each in reverse mortgage loans. In addition to being used for home upkeep or property taxes or to supplement meager retirement incomes, cash flow from this potentially vast pool of reverse mortgage funds also could be used to help defray the cost of a growing problem for the elderly: long-term care.

CHAPTER 10
Reducing Estate Tax on Home

> The difference between death and taxes is that death is frequently painless.
> **Anonymous**

10.1 Overview

It's been said that the difference between death and taxes is that death is frequently painless. Doubtless the pain of estate taxes is responsible for the preoccupation of many wealthier Americans with estate planning.

This chapter deals with estate planning for personal residences and vacation homes. The estate-planning objective for a personal residence or vacation home is basically the same as the estate-planning objective for other assets. The objective for both is to create and implement a program for the transfer of assets to children or other beneficiaries at the minimum tax cost.

If you're married, estate tax planning for your personal residence or vacation home is usually simple. The tax law generally lets your estate deduct the entire value of property that you leave outright or in a special trust for your spouse. So if your leave your personal residence or vacation home to your spouse, it entirely escapes estate tax. You can do this, if you wish, by joint ownership of the home (discussed in Section 10.2).

Even if you're unmarried, you may not need to worry about estate taxes. Everyone is entitled to an estate tax exemption, and this exemption is large enough to exempt most homeowners from estate tax. The estate tax exemption is $1.5 million for 2004, and increases in stages to $3.5 million in 2009. Even without the marital deduction, this exemption will completely exempt most homeowners' estates from tax. The question of whether you need estate tax planning is discussed in Section 10.3.

If your estate is large enough to be subject to estate taxes, which range up to 48 percent in 2004 on taxable estates over $2.5 million, you may have a problem. This is especially so if you are unmarried, since you have no marital deduction to shield your property from estate tax. This is when some estate-planning techniques can be useful. For example, in some situations, a variety of "time-share" arrangements can be created between a parent and children for use of a vacation home that serves to reduce estate taxes. (See Section 10.5.) In other situations, potential estate taxes on a residence can be reduced by a sale and leaseback transaction with children or by setting up a personal residence trust. (See Sections 10.6 and 10.7, respectively.)

> **Caution**
>
> The personal residence often is only a small portion of the estate-planning picture, and you should consult with a lawyer experienced in estate matters concerning an estate plan for your *entire* estate. While in some cases simple, do-it-yourself arrangements for transferring your assets at death will suffice, in other cases sophisticated planning with wills, trusts, and other documents will be warranted. Also, state tax considerations, not discussed here, should be taken into account. Of course, you should have a will that is up to date.

10.2   Should Spouses Own Home Jointly?

Sentimental considerations may lead you to want to own your home jointly with your spouse. Joint ownership is tangible evidence of trust and confidence and, on the death of a spouse, guarantees automatic ownership of the home to the other spouse.

But joint ownership of a home by spouses (known as a "tenancy by the entirety" in some states), may present a practical danger.

Possible Horror Story.   The classic joint tenants horror story involves inadvertent disinheritance of children.

> **Example**
>
> Suppose spouses with children jointly own their home and other assets. The wife dies, and the home and other assets go automatically to the husband. He promptly remarries, again placing the home and his other assets in joint ownership with his new wife. Then *he* dies, and the home and other jointly owned assets automatically pass to the new wife, leaving *nothing* for the children. The first wife may spin in her grave, but it doesn't help.

This potential danger can be readily avoided by a properly drafted will. To illustrate, suppose that in the example that title to the residence and other property is placed in the wife's name alone and that she makes a will leaving the property to her husband in trust for life, and after his death to their children. This makes the problem of disinherited children disappear. This is because the wife's will controls who ultimately gets the property. Even though the husband has the use of the residence and other property for life, both the residence and other property ultimately go to the children under the trust set up in the wife's will.

Estate Tax Planning Pointer. Property left to a surviving spouse can qualify for the marital deduction that exempts its entire value from estate tax. For most people who don't have the "horror story"–type problem discussed above, leaving the principal residence to a spouse through a joint tenancy arrangement works fine for estate tax purposes. But as explained in Section 10.4, leaving a principal residence to a spouse through a joint tenancy arrangement or by will may not be the most tax-efficient thing to do for some couples with larger estates.

Tax Tip

Joint Tenancy and Income Taxes. For income tax purposes, joint ownership of your residence with your spouse generally will not provide any tax advantage. If you file a joint income tax return, interest and taxes are deductible on the joint return regardless of whether the home is owned jointly or by one spouse alone. Similarly, eligibility for exclusion of gain up to $500,000 on the sale of the home (discussed in Sections 4.3 through 4.9) generally is equally available to you whether you own property jointly or separately.

10.3 Do You Need Estate Tax Planning?

The federal estate tax starts at 18 percent on the first dollar of taxable estate and rises to 48 percent in 2004 on taxable estates over $2 million. Unless you have a relatively large net worth, however, you don't need estate planning. This is because there is a federal estate tax exemption that exempts most estates from the federal estate tax.

Background. The present estate tax law has a now-you-see-it, now-you-don't feature. Congress repealed the estate tax in 2001, effective for estates of decedents dying after December 31, 2009. But in a tactic designed to permit compliance with budget requirements, the repeal was accompanied by a remarkable exercise of legislative legerdemain. The repeal of the estate tax was itself repealed for years beginning after December 31, 2010. In effect, then, the estate tax repeal applies only during 2010.

In the meantime, the law provides a phased-in reduction in gift and estate tax rates and increases in the estate tax exemption amounts. The phase-in commenced in 2002 when the top rate became 50 percent and the exemption increased to $1 million. It culminates in 2009 with a top rate of 45 percent and an exemption of $3.5 million, as shown in Table 10.1.

Based on the table, if an individual dies in 2006 and doesn't have net assets exceeding $2 million, no estate tax is payable. For most Americans, these estate tax thresholds completely eliminate federal estate tax, and often state tax as well.

While the gift tax rates were also reduced as shown in the table, the gift tax was not repealed and the gift tax exemption amount was increased to $1 million permanently.

Since existing law provides only a one-year window for escaping estate tax,

TABLE 10.1 Exemption and Rate Table

Calendar Year	Estate Tax Exemption	Highest Estate and Gift Tax Rates
2002	$1 million	50%
2003	$1 million	49%
2004	$1.5 million	48%
2005	$1.5 million	47%
2006	$2 million	46%
2007	$2 million	45%
2008	$2 million	45%
2009	$3.5 million	45%
2010	N/A (taxes repealed)	Top individual rate (gift tax only)

the tax minimization techniques discussed in this chapter generally continue to be useful estate-planning tools.

Marital Deduction and Lifetime Exemption. If you are married, both you and your spouse are entitled to separate lifetime exemptions, as shown in Table 10.1. Moreover, the value of all property left to a surviving spouse outright usually is eligible for a marital deduction for estate tax purposes, so that in most cases, even with large estates, where most assets are left to the surviving spouse there is no estate tax on the death of the first spouse to die.

For estate tax purposes, joint ownership of your residence is usually a neutral factor. Whether you own the home jointly so that it passes automatically to your surviving spouse as a joint tenant, or you or your spouse alone owns the house and leave it to the other by will, the entire value of the home will be shielded from estate tax by the marital deduction.

But if you have a large estate, there's a catch. Leaving a personal residence to a spouse, through joint ownership or by will, can cost the couple one of their lifetime exemptions.

We discuss this next. If you don't have to worry about getting both exemptions, you can skip the next section.

10.4 Larger Estates: How Not to Lose the Second Exemption

While the marital deduction usually will shield the estate of the first spouse to die from estate tax, using the marital deduction for all your assets may not produce the maximum tax economy if the value of your estate exceeds your lifetime exemption. This results from the fact that if you leave all your assets to your surviving spouse in a manner that qualifies for the marital deduction, *your* lifetime exemption may be wasted.

What's the problem?

If the couple's entire estate, including jointly owned property, passes to the surviving spouse on the death of the first to die, there is no estate tax because of the marital deduction. But the entire estate (assuming no reduction in value) is included in the surviving spouse's estate on the surviving spouse's death and only one lifetime exemption is used—the surviving spouse's. However, if an amount equal to the exemption in the estate of the first spouse to die is transferred in a manner that avoids its inclusion in the surviving spouse's estate, two exemptions are available: one in the estate of the first spouse to die and one in the estate of the surviving spouse. These permutations can best be illustrated by an example.

> **Example**
>
> A husband has $3 million in assets, including jointly owned property, and his wife has no assets. The husband dies first, leaving all of his individually owned assets to his wife. The property they owned jointly passes to her automatically, by operation of law. The husband's entire estate escapes estate tax, shielded by his unlimited marital deduction. The wife's estate, assuming no reduction in value and an exemption of $1.5 million, is $1.5 million ($3 million left to her by her husband, minus her $1.5 million lifetime exemption). Thus, the wife's taxable estate is $1.5 million.
>
> Suppose, instead, that the husband leaves $1.5 million in trust for the benefit of his children, with the balance of his assets left to his wife outright or in a trust that qualifies for the marital deduction. The husband's $1.5 million exemption and his marital deduction would entirely shield the husband's $3 million estate from estate tax. But, since the amount included in the wife's estate would be only $1.5 million ($3 million minus the $1.5 million trust for the children), her taxable estate would be zero ($1.5 million, the amount included in her estate, minus her $1.5 million exemption). The aggregate taxable estate of the spouses is reduced from $1.5 million to zero.

As the example illustrates, estate taxes are reduced when a well-to-do married couple makes an estate-planning arrangement that causes the exemption amount to bypass the surviving spouse's estate. What's known in legalese as a *credit shelter trust* or *bypass trust* often is used for this purpose, the assets in which bypass the surviving spouse's estate for estate tax purposes. A home may be placed in a bypass trust.

While a marital deduction is allowed for property you leave to your spouse outright, an outright bequest to a spouse may not always be appropriate. For example, if your spouse is inexperienced in handling substantial assets or has children from a prior marriage, you may prefer a transfer in trust to an outright transfer. A so-called QTIP (qualified terminable interest property) trust is often used in these situations. With a QTIP trust, all income from property can be left to your spouse for life, with provisions for the use of principal in the trustees' discretion if you wish, and the remainder of the property on your spouse's death goes to your children. Even though your spouse cannot reach the assets in the QTIP trust, a full marital deduction is allowed for this type of gift. A home also may be placed in a QTIP trust.

Whenever a home is placed in a trust, special rules apply, and the draftsman of the trust should be an experienced estate-planning attorney.

> **Observation**
>
> *The Bird's-Eye-View Problem.* The discussion here of estate tax planning has provided only a bird's-eye view of the subject. The trouble with bird's-eye views is that while they may provide a useful broad outline of a subject, they can miss critical detail. If you are married and the combined value of your assets and the assets of your spouse, including your home, exceeds the amount of a single estate tax exemption, you should consult with counsel experienced in estate-planning matters to determine how to approach taking full advantage of each spouse's federal estate tax exemption.

10.5 How Parent Can Cut Taxes on Vacation Home

A parent with a vacation home who wants to reduce estate taxes may be able to do some innovative tax planning with the vacation home. By splitting the ownership of the vacation home with children, part of the value of the vacation home may be removed from the parent's estate.

A parent's ownership of a vacation home can be split by deeding a part interest in the vacation home to children or a trust for children. As illustrated in the example below, the part interest transferred can consist of a right to use the vacation property during particular months of the year.

> **Caution**
>
> The real estate conveyancing required for this type of transfer requires the counsel of a lawyer with expertise in real estate.

Before the plan is discussed, a few technical features of the estate and gift tax must be mentioned.

How Is It Done? One of the basic approaches to saving estate taxes is to make gifts of cash or property to children. A parent can give up to $11,000 to each child each year without paying any gift tax. This "annual exclusion" amount is increased to $22,000 for each child for spouses who want to make gifts together, so-called gift splitting. In addition, each parent has a lifetime exemption from estate tax and gift tax as shown in the table and discussion above. No part of this lifetime exemption is used up by gifts within the $11,000 (or $22,000) annual exclusion limits.

Property given away is not included in a parent's estate for estate tax purposes. In addition, if the property given away appreciates in value, all the better, since the appreciation also escapes tax in the parents' estates. The federal estate tax can run up to 45 percent or more. So the idea is for parents to give property away during life to keep it out of their estates and free from federal estate tax. Of course, giving property away has to be consistent with parents' personal planning objectives.

To avoid current federal *gift* tax on property given away, its value has to be covered by the annual $11,000 exclusions or the lifetime exemptions.

Vacation Home Tax Planning. A vacation home owned by parents can play a role in their estate planning. Properly planned, a gift of a part interest in the vacation home to children has a unique double advantage:

1. It removes the interest in the vacation home given to the children and any appreciation in value of that interest from the grasp of the estate tax.
2. Since the parents retain a part interest in the vacation home, it permits the parents to continue to enjoy ownership and use of the vacation home.

In addition, there's another unusual advantage to the plan. The IRS has not only approved it, but has also given an example of how to figure the amount of the gift for gift tax purposes. It has issued a ruling showing how a portion of a vacation home can be given to children, subject to the parents' retained rights to use it during part of the vacation season.

> **Example**
>
> A father owned a residence worth $70,000 that he used for vacation purposes in December, January, and February each year. The property was rented to others the rest of the year. He deeded the property to his children, but *retained* the right to use or rent out the property during January. The IRS said that on the father's death only the value of the *retained* interest is includable in his estate.

That sounds good, but what does it mean in dollars? What you want to know is, how much of the $70,000 value is eliminated from the father's estate for estate tax purposes?

Figuring the Benefit. To figure the benefit, you figure backwards. To get the amount eliminated from the father's estate for estate tax purposes, you figure the amount includable in the father's estate after the gift, then subtract that amount from the value of the property, as illustrated below. To do this, you have to know both the fair market value of the property and its rental value at the time of the father's death.

The Numbers. In the example, the value of the property was assumed to be $70,000. It also was assumed that the rental value for the months of December, January, and February was $600 per month, and $300 per month for the rest of the year. Thus, the annual rental value was $4,500 (3 × $600 = $1,800, plus 9 × $300 = $2,700, and $1,800 plus $2,700 = $4,500) The rental value for January, $600, divided by the total rental value, $4,500, gives the percentage of total value represented by the retained interest, or 13.3 percent. Thus, the value of the interest retained by the father is $9,310 (13.3 percent of $70,000). Only this portion of the total $70,000 value is included in the father's gross estate. The amount eliminated from the father's estate is the balance, the amount of the gift, $60,690 ($70,000 − $9,310).

Gift Tax Pointer. If the gift in the example was given by parents who "split" the gift of interests in the vacation home equally among three children, the entire amount of the $60,690 gift would fit within the annual exclusions available to the parents (3 × $22,000 = $66,000), so that no part of either parent's lifetime exemption would have to be used up to eliminate gift tax on the gift. This saves the parents' full exemption amounts for later use. Married individuals can make "split" gifts regardless of which of them owns the property to be given away. If the amount of the gift was larger and the parents wanted to cover the gift *entirely* with their annual exclusions, they could divide it into two parts, giving one part immediately and the second part in the following year. The gift tax exclusions are *annual* exclusions. The effect of this would be to *double* the exclusions available for the gift from $66,000 to $132,000 (2 × $66,000).

That's the way the rich do it.

Observation

Additional Attraction of Plan. There is another feature of the vacation home gift idea that can be attractive to parents: It doesn't require the transfer of cash or an interest in a business. Accordingly, it may especially appeal to parents who are reluctant to make gifts of cash or business property.

10.6 Estate Planning for a Parent's Home: Using Sale–Leaseback to Shift Appreciation in Value

Like other assets, personal residences of parents with sufficiently large estates may be subject to heavy estate taxes. The tax burden may be particularly severe for homes owned by widows and widowers.

When a parent dies, leaving the marital abode to his or her surviving spouse, the estate tax marital deduction shields the entire value of the home from estate tax. But it is a different story when the surviving spouse dies. Since the marital deduction is available only for property passing to a surviving spouse, no marital deduction for the value of the home is available to the estate of a widow or widower.

The federal estate tax on estates with a value above the lifetime exemption amount ranges from 18 percent to 48 percent in 2004. (The lifetime exemption amount is discussed in Section 10.3.) If a parent will have an estate substantially in excess of the lifetime exemption amount, it may be appropriate to consider some estate planning for the parent's residence.

There are two approaches to mitigating the impact of estate taxes on a personal residence, both of which usually involve a transfer of the residence, sooner or later, to children. The first, the sale and leaseback with children, discussed in this section, may serve to remove future appreciation in the value of the residence from the grasp of the estate tax. For example, if a home now worth $500,000 appreciates in value to $1 million at the date of a parent's death, it may be possible to avoid tax on the $500,000 in appreciation with a sale-and-leaseback transaction.

The second approach is use of a qualified personal residence trust. With this approach, the residence is placed in a trust, under the provisions of which the parent continues to occupy the house for a period of years, after which the residence passes automatically to children. This approach, which may serve to entirely remove the residence from the grasp of the estate tax, is discussed in Section 10.7.

The approach chosen will depend on the personal preferences of the parents.

Why a Sale and Leaseback? If a parent's home appreciates in value between the present and the date when the parent dies, the parent's estate tax liability may increase beyond its present level. This is because, in addition to the present value of the home, the appreciation in value of the home also will be included in the parent's estate for estate tax purposes, increasing the estate tax bill. In other words, both its current value and any appreciation over its current value will be subject to estate tax.

A sale-and-leaseback transaction may serve to avoid this problem. To illustrate, suppose a parent enters into a sale-and-leaseback transaction with a child, under which the parent sells the parent's home to the child, then rents it back from the child and continues to live in the home as a tenant. The parent lends the child the money required to purchase the home.

With this sale-and-leaseback arrangement, the parent can transfer the home to the child even though the parent continues to live in the home for life. Assuming the transaction is properly structured, when the parent dies, the home is not included in the parent's estate for estate tax purposes. Instead, the parent's estate includes only the amount of the balance of any unpaid purchase price that the child owes the parent at the time of the parent's death. Thus, appreciation in the value of the home escapes estate taxation in the parent's estate.

The Family Situation. Estate planning for a parent's residence should take the family aspects of any proposed transaction into account. In many cases, a parent will have no interest whatsoever in parting with ownership of the home, regardless of tax savings. Or it may be that there are children who will not share the view that estate tax savings is such an important goal. There could be a variety of other personal factors that make this estate-planning idea inappropriate. Accordingly, the plan, and the personal residence trust discussed in the next section, should be considered only if it will not cause significant family problems. If family considerations are no problem, then the tax-saving features of the plan warrant consideration.

Let's assume a well-to-do widowed mother lives in a valuable home, that her other assets will more than use up her lifetime exemption from estate tax, and that each of the concerned family members agrees that estate tax planning for the home is a good idea. The next step is to consider how to go about getting the home out of her taxable estate while she still lives in it.

It may not be easy.

The "Retained Interest" Problem. If the mother is to continue to live in the home after the sale-and-leaseback transfer, the home nevertheless may be included in her estate for estate tax purposes despite the transfer. There's a rule that provides, in effect, that if a person makes a transfer of property, except for a regular sale, and the person retains the possession or enjoyment of the property for life, then the value of the entire property is swept back into the person's estate for estate tax purposes. If this happens in the mother's case, nothing will be gained by the sale and leaseback. An example based on a court case is instructive.

> **Example**
>
> A mother sells her residence to her son for its $270,000 fair market value. She lends her son the whole purchase price, taking a mortgage on the house from the son to secure the loan, and simultaneously rents the residence back from her son in a leaseback transaction at fair market rental. Her gain on the sale of the house is not subject to tax because it is entirely covered by the rule permitting the exclusion of gain on the sale of a principal residence (discussed in Sections 4.3 through 4.9). Each year during her life, the mother cancels a part of the mortgage debt equal to her available gift tax exclusion (now $11,000 per year, per donee). The unpaid balance of the mortgage at her death is $210,000, and is entirely forgiven in her will. On her death, she is still living in the residence, which then is worth $550,000.

Question: Is the amount includable in her taxable estate only the $210,000 remaining unpaid balance on the mortgage, or the $550,000 appreciated value of the residence?

According to the court, the entire $550,000 value of the residence is included in her estate. The residence is dragged back into the mother's estate because the transfer was not a real sale for full value, since both mother and son did not intend that the mortgage would ever be paid. It didn't help that the interest on the mortgage and the rent paid under the leaseback were approximately equal, and that the mother's estate neglected to pay rent after her death. According to the court:

> The "sale" and "leaseback" were merely components of a single, integrated transaction having very little substance that in reality amounted basically to a transfer of decedent's home to her son ... retaining the right by agreement, express or implied, to remain in possession for the remainder of her life.

The result was that the home was taxed in the mother's estate.

> **Tax Tip**
>
> *Gift and Leaseback.* A *gift* and leaseback between a parent and a child would be as vulnerable to an IRS challenge as a *sale* and leaseback.

Proper Structure Is Critical. While both sale-and-leaseback and gift-and-leaseback transactions invite close scrutiny by the IRS, they may be structured to withstand attack. The foundation of such a structure is a legally binding and economically genuine conveyance of property, linked with a legally binding and economically genuine leaseback.

An example of a plan that worked based on another court case will illustrate how it can be done.

> **Example**
>
> Parents made a gift of a 372-acre farm to their children and immediately leased it back. The transfer was made by the parents by a legally executed and recorded deed that was reported as a gift on a gift tax return. The leaseback to the parents was at fair market rental under a recorded lease containing terms normally found in leases of similar property. There was no indication that there was any express or implied understanding between the parents and the children regarding the property that would vary the written terms of the lease. The lease was to continue until the death of the parents.

Plan Stands Up. The IRS claimed the farm was includable in the parents' taxable estate because they retained the right to possess the farm. Clearly, the parents had possession of the farm after the leaseback, but was it the kind of "retained" possession that would drag the property back into their estate for estate tax purposes?

In the court's view, the parents did not "retain" possession. Instead, they acquired possession as tenants under a lease compelling them "to pay a fair, customary rental for the rights which they enjoyed, and the children were entitled, as landlords, to require the rent to be paid." There was no unwritten understanding secretly changing the terms of the deed or lease. Under these circumstances, the parents didn't retain the prohibited possession or enjoyment and the farm was not included in their taxable estate.

> **Caution**
>
> In the successful court case, the parents did *not* reside on the farm. It may be that where the leaseback involves a parent's principal residence, there is more likelihood that an implied agreement exists that the parent can remain in the house for life. This could be a negative factor. However, mere continued occupancy by the parent, standing alone, doesn't show an agreement for retained enjoyment that would prevent the home from escaping estate tax.

Planning Note. The sale and leaseback usually won't make tax sense unless any gain on the sale will qualify for the $250,000 (or $500,000) home sale exclusion (explained in Sections 4.3 through 4.9). Also, an economically genuine transfer is essential if the transaction is to have reasonable assurance of standing up for tax purposes.

The transfer and leaseback of a parent's personal residence is a tempting estate-planning mechanism because it is relatively easy to implement and holds the promise of removing appreciation in the value of the home from the parent's taxable estate. While it may be more vulnerable to attack than other planning techniques, it can be a useful tool if handled correctly. It is essential to get professional help in implementing it.

10.7 How Parents Can Escape Estate Tax on Their Homes: The Qualified Personal Residence Trust

There is a legitimate tax-avoidance technique that may permit parents to entirely escape estate tax on their homes. The technique, known as the *qualified personal residence trust*, permits parents to continue to live in their homes for whatever period of years they choose, after which the home passes to their children, completely free of estate tax.

The personal residence trust can be used for either a principal residence or a vacation home. And while the trust arrangement isn't a simple procedure, it has the virtue of IRS approval when it's done right.

Background. You normally don't think of a home as property that can be split into separate legal pieces, and usually it isn't. But real estate law lets the owner of property create separate legal interests in the property. For example, the ownership of a single-family house can be split in a manner that lets the owner continue to live in it for a period of years, after which ownership of the house passes to someone else, such as the owner's child.

This arrangement, referred to in legalese as a " term for years and remainder," can be the basis for a valuable estate tax reduction technique.

How It Works. The term for years and remainder interest plan works like this. Say a widow transfers her home to a personal residence trust. Under the terms of the trust, she retains the right to continue to live in the home for a specified period, say 15 years. At the end of the 15-year term, the trust agreement provides that ownership of the home automatically passes to her beneficiary, such as a child, the "remainderman."

The tax attraction of this split-ownership arrangement is that it permits a parent to ultimately transfer the full value of the parent's home to children (or other beneficiaries) at a transfer tax cost based only on the relatively small value of the remainder. The personal attraction of the plan compared to an outright gift is that the parent can remain in the home rent free for whatever period of years the parent chooses and, with cooperative children, lease it back from them at the end of the term if the parent chooses to do so.

What's the Tax Advantage? Just this: Assuming the parent outlives the term of years for which the home is retained, the home passes to the children at the end of the term of years without any estate tax. This means that both the present value of the home, plus all appreciation in the value of the home since it was put into the trust, escape the estate tax, as illustrated in the following example. The only tax cost involved is a reduction in the parent's lifetime gift and estate tax exemption (discussed in Section 10.3) or the gift tax the parent would have to pay on the remainder interest when the trust is set up. In most cases, gift tax is avoided by use of the parent's lifetime exemption.

The tax attraction of this technique can best be illustrated by an example.

Example

Say a parent is 65 years old and owns a vacation home worth $500,000. The parent gives the vacation home to a trust, the terms of which provide that the parent has the right to continue to live in the home for a period of 15 years, at the end of which period the home is transferred to an only child, either outright or in trust. If the parent doesn't outlive the 15-year term, the home returns to the parent's estate.

Under this scenario, the parent has made a gift in trust of a remainder interest in the vacation home to the child, and it is necessary to determine if the gift of the remainder interest is subject to gift tax. To determine if the gift of the remainder interest is subject to gift tax, it is necessary to compare the value of the gift of the remainder interest to the parent's gift tax lifetime exemption amount. If the parent has not yet used any part of the parent's $1 million lifetime exemption amount and, as will almost always be the case, the value of the remainder interest is less than $1 million, there will be no gift tax. Even if the parent has used part of the parent's exemption amount to shelter prior gifts, say $500,000, the remaining amount, $500,000, usually is more than enough to cover the amount of the remainder gift.

Here's How It's Figured. The value of the child's remainder interest in the vacation home is the present value of the entire home, minus the value of the parent's retained term of 15 years. Thus, to figure the value of the gift of the remainder interest to the child, it is first necessary to value the home, then subtract the value of the parent's retained 15-year term of years.

To get the value of the retained term of years, it is necessary to use an actuarial table provided by the IRS, based on a specified rate of return. Specialized math is required to figure the value of the retained term of years, a task that should be given to a tax professional.

Assume in our case that, using the IRS tables, the parent's tax professional figures the value of the retained term of years is $375,000. Thus, the value of the gift of the remainder interest to the child is $125,000 (value of home, $500,000, minus value of retained interest, $375,000 = $125,000 remainder interest gift).

What Has Been Accomplished? Assuming the parent lives beyond the 15-year term, the parent will have accomplished dramatic estate tax savings. The parent will have transferred the $500,000 home to the child at a transfer tax valuation of only $125,000, all of which was covered by the lifetime exemption, so that it was entirely gift tax free. Moreover, if the home appreciates at the rate of, say, 4 to 5 percent per year, it will be worth approximately $1 million at the end of the 15-year term. Thus, the parent will have transferred roughly another $500,000 worth of value to the child, also completely free of estate tax. Accordingly, at the tax cost of using up $125,000 of the parent's lifetime exemption for the remainder interest gift, the parent will have escaped estate tax on property worth approximately $1 million.

Is It Too Good to Be True? They say there's no free lunch, and that wisdom applies to estate planning. The qualified personal residence trust has several drawbacks that can discourage its use.

- *The parent has to outlive the term.* The benefits of the plan are obtained only if the parent outlives the term of years for which the home is placed in trust. If the parent dies during the term of years, the value of the home is dragged back into the parent's estate, destroying the tax saving. Accordingly, when the trust is set up, the parent should make sure the term of years is not so long that it is likely the parent will die before the end of the term.

    There's a catch to making the term short: The shorter the term of the trust, the higher the value of the remainder, and the higher the value of the remainder, the larger the amount of the gift. This hurts because the larger the amount of the gift, the larger the amount of the lifetime exemption that must be used up to shield the remainder interest from gift tax. Thus, a dilemma is presented: Should the term be short to be sure the parent will outlive it, or should it be long to decrease the value of the remainder as much as possible? Like many choices in life, it's usually a compromise ending up somewhere in between.

- *Cost and complexity.* Planning and preparing the papers for a qualified personal residence trust is not a do-it-yourself project. It requires the skills of a trained tax lawyer, and their hourly rates are high. And for those who like to keep their life simple, the trust arrangement for their home doesn't help.

- *The tax price.* The part of the transfer to the personal residence trust that is taken into account for gift tax purposes is the remainder interest. Since this is an interest that will vest in the beneficiaries in the future, it is known as a "future interest." Future interests don't qualify for the $11,000 annual gift tax exclusions, discussed earlier. Thus, it is necessary to rely on the lifetime exemption to shield the gift from current gift tax. While the exemption, currently $1 million, is large enough to shield most remainder gifts from tax, the portion of the lifetime exemption used to shield the gift is "used up" and not available to either shield future gifts or to reduce estate tax.

- *Dealing with children.* If the parent wants to continue to live in the home following the end of the retained term of years, the parent has to count on cooperative beneficiaries, usually children. The parent may have to work out a lease or some other type of arrangement with them that permits the parent to continue to live in the home. Many parents do not relish the prospect of negotiating with their children about where they will live.

One or more of these drawbacks may cool a parent's interest in a personal residence trust, despite its tax attractions. But for those who view the tax benefits as outweighing the drawbacks, the personal residence trust can be a uniquely attractive tax-planning technique. For them, their home is a tax shelter even in estate planning.

Epilogue

In the preface to this book, I said it would be a book of revelations—tax revelations. I have done my best to fulfill this promise. I hope you have been rewarded with many revelations showing how your home can be tax treasure.

Many of the tax-saving ideas described in these pages will arise only by chance—an unexpected rental opportunity, a casualty loss, a bargain refinancing offer, or a need for a medical home improvement. But, as Louis Pasteur observed, chance favors the prepared mind. I hope that when you have completed this book you will have the prepared mind that enables you to discover the tax-saving opportunities provided by such chance events.

Appendix A

2003
Instructions for Form 8829
Expenses for Business Use of Your Home

Section references are to the Internal Revenue Code.

General Instructions

Note: *If you are claiming expenses for business use of your home as an **employee** or a **partner**, or you are claiming these expenses on **Schedule F** (Form 1040), **do not** use Form 8829. Instead, complete the worksheet in **Pub. 587**, Business Use of Your Home (Including Use by Daycare Providers).*

Purpose of Form

Use Form 8829 to figure the allowable expenses for business use of your home on **Schedule C** (Form 1040) and any carryover to 2004 of amounts not deductible in 2003.

If all of the expenses for business use of your home are properly allocable to inventory costs, do not complete Form 8829. These expenses are figured in Part III of Schedule C and not on Form 8829.

You must meet specific requirements to deduct expenses for the business use of your home. Even if you meet these requirements, your deductible expenses may be limited. For details, see Pub. 587.

Who May Deduct Expenses for Business Use of a Home

Generally, you may deduct business expenses that apply to a part of your home **only** if that part is exclusively used on a regular basis:

1. As your **principal place of business** for any of your trades or businesses; or
2. As a place of business used by your patients, clients, or customers to meet or deal with you in the normal course of your trade or business; or
3. In connection with your trade or business if it is a separate structure that is not attached to your home.

As explained on this page, exceptions to this rule apply to space used on a regular basis for:
- Storage of inventory or product samples and
- Certain daycare facilities.

Principal Place of Business

Your home office will qualify as your principal place of business for deducting expenses for its use if you meet the following requirements.
- You use it exclusively and regularly for administrative or management activities of your trade or business.
- You have no other fixed location where you conduct substantial administrative or management activities of your trade or business.

Administrative or management activities. There are many activities that are administrative or managerial in nature. The following are a few examples.
- Billing customers, clients, or patients.
- Keeping books and records.
- Ordering supplies.
- Setting up appointments.
- Forwarding orders or writing reports.

Administrative or management activities performed at other locations. The following activities performed by you or others will *not* disqualify your home office from being your principal place of business.
- You have others conduct your administrative or management activities at locations other than your home. (For example, another company does your billing from its place of business.)
- You conduct administrative or management activities at places that are not fixed locations of your business, such as in a car or a hotel room.
- You occasionally conduct minimal administrative or management activities at a fixed location outside your home.
- You conduct substantial nonadministrative or nonmanagement business activities at a fixed location outside your home. (For example, you meet with or provide services to customers, clients, or patients at a fixed location of the business outside your home.)
- You have suitable space to conduct administrative or management activities outside your home, but choose to use your home office for those activities instead.

More information. For information on other ways to qualify to deduct business use of the home expenses, see Pub. 587.

Storage of Inventory or Product Samples

You may also deduct expenses that apply to space within your home used on a regular basis to store inventory or product samples from your trade or business of selling products at retail or wholesale. Your home must be the **only** fixed location of your trade or business.

Daycare Facilities

If you use space in your home on a regular basis in the trade or business of providing daycare, you may be able to deduct the business expenses even though you use the same space for nonbusiness purposes. To qualify for this exception, you must have applied for (and not have been rejected), been granted (and still have in effect), or be exempt from having a license, certification, registration, or approval as a daycare center or as a family or group daycare home under state law.

Cat. No. 15683B

At press time, the 2004 instructions were not available.

Expenses Related to Tax-Exempt Income

Generally, you cannot deduct expenses that are allocable to tax-exempt income. However, if you receive a tax-exempt parsonage allowance or a tax-exempt military housing allowance, your expenses for mortgage interest and real property taxes are deductible under the normal rules. No deduction is allowed for other expenses allocable to the tax-exempt allowance.

Specific Instructions

Part I

Lines 1 and 2

To determine the area on lines 1 and 2, you may use square feet or any other reasonable method if it accurately figures your business percentage on line 7.

Do not include on line 1 the area of your home you used to figure any expenses allocable to inventory costs. The business percentage of these expenses should have been taken into account in Part III of Schedule C.

Special Computation for Certain Daycare Facilities

If the part of your home used as a daycare facility included areas used exclusively for business as well as other areas used only partly for business, you **cannot** figure your business percentage using Part I. Instead, follow these three steps:

1. Figure the business percentage of the part of your home used exclusively for business by dividing the area used exclusively for business by the total area of the home.
2. Figure the business percentage of the part of your home used only partly for business by following the same method used in Part I of the form, but enter on line 1 of your computation only the area of the home used partly for business.
3. Add the business percentages you figured in the first two steps and enter the result on line 7. Attach your computation and write "See attached computation" directly above the percentage you entered on line 7.

Line 4

Enter the total number of hours the facility was used for daycare during the year.

Example. Your home is used Monday through Friday for 12 hours per day for 250 days during the year. It is also used on 50 Saturdays for 8 hours per day. Enter 3,400 hours on line 4 (3,000 hours for weekdays plus 400 hours for Saturdays).

Line 5

If you started or stopped using your home for daycare in 2003, you must prorate the number of hours based on the number of days the home was available for daycare. Cross out the preprinted entry on line 5. Multiply 24 hours by the number of days available and enter the result.

Part II

Line 8

If all the gross income from your trade or business is from the business use of your home, enter on line 8 the amount from Schedule C, line 29, **plus** any net gain or (loss) derived from the business use of your home and shown on Schedule D or Form 4797. If you file more than one Form 8829, include only the income earned and the deductions attributable to that income during the period you owned the home for which Part I was completed.

If some of the income is from a place of business other than your home, you must first determine the part of your gross income (Schedule C, line 7, and gains from Schedule D and Form 4797) from the business use of your home. In making this determination, consider the amount of time you spend at each location as well as other facts. After determining the part of your gross income from the business use of your home, subtract from that amount the **total expenses** shown on Schedule C, line 28, plus any losses from your business shown on Schedule D or Form 4797. Enter the result on line 8 of Form 8829.

Columns (a) and (b)

Enter as direct or indirect expenses only expenses for the business use of your home (i.e., expenses allowable only because your home is used for business). If you did not operate a business for the entire year, you can only deduct the expenses paid or incurred for the portion of the year you used your home for business. Other expenses not allocable to the business use of your home, such as salaries, supplies, and business telephone expenses, are deductible elsewhere on Schedule C and should not be entered on Form 8829.

Direct expense benefit only the business part of your home. They include painting or repairs made to the specific area or rooms used for business. Enter 100% of your direct expenses on the appropriate line in column (a).

Indirect expenses are for keeping up and running your entire home. They benefit both the business and personal parts of your home. Generally, enter 100% of your indirect expenses on the appropriate line in column (b).

Exception. If the business percentage of an indirect expense is different from the percentage on line 7, enter only the business part of the expense on the appropriate line in column (a), and leave that line in column (b) blank. For example, your electric bill is $800 for lighting, cooking, laundry, and television. If you reasonably estimate $300 of your electric bill is for lighting and you use 10% of your home for business, enter $30 on line 19 in column (a). **Do not** make an entry on line 19 in column (b) for any part of your electric bill.

Lines 9, 10, and 11

Enter only the amounts that would be deductible whether or not you used your home for business (i.e., amounts allowable as itemized deductions on **Schedule A** (Form 1040)).

Treat **casualty losses** as personal expenses for this step. Figure the amount to enter on line 9 by completing Form 4684, Section A. When figuring line 17 of Form 4684, enter 10% of your adjusted gross income excluding the gross income from business use of your home and the deductions attributable to that income. Include on line 9 of Form 8829 the amount from Form 4684, line 18. See line 27 below to deduct part of the casualty losses not allowed because of the limits on Form 4684.

Do not file or use that Form 4684 to figure the amount of casualty losses to deduct on Schedule A. Instead, complete a separate Form 4684 to deduct the personal portion of your casualty losses.

On line 10, include only **mortgage interest** that would be deductible on Schedule A and that qualifies as a direct or indirect expense. **Do not** include interest on a mortgage loan that did not benefit your home (e.g., a home equity loan used to pay off credit card bills, to buy a car, or to pay tuition costs).

If you itemize your deductions, be sure to claim **only** the personal portion of your deductible mortgage interest and real estate taxes on Schedule A. For example, if your business percentage on line 7 is 30%, you can claim 70% of your deductible mortgage interest and real estate taxes on Schedule A.

Line 16

If the amount of home mortgage interest you deduct on Schedule A is limited, enter the part of the excess mortgage interest that qualifies as a direct or indirect expense. **Do not** include mortgage interest on a loan that did not benefit your home (explained earlier).

Line 20

Include on this line any 2003 operating expenses not included on lines 9 through 19.

If you rent rather than own your home, include the rent you paid on line 20, column (b). If your housing is provided free of charge and the value of the housing is tax exempt, you cannot deduct the rental value of any portion of the housing.

Line 27

Multiply your casualty losses in excess of the amount on line 9 by the business percentage of those losses and enter the result.

Line 34

If your home was used in more than one business, allocate the amount shown on line 34 to each business using any method that is reasonable under the circumstances. For each business, enter on Schedule C, line 30, only the amount allocated to that business.

Part III

Lines 35 Through 37

Enter on line 35 the cost or other basis of your home, or, if less, the fair market value of your home on the date you first used the home for business. **Do not** adjust this amount for depreciation claimed or changes in fair market value after the year you first used your home for business. Allocate this amount between land and building values on lines 36 and 37.

Attach your own schedule showing the cost or other basis of additions and improvements placed in service after you began to use your home for business. **Do not** include any amounts on lines 35 through 38 for these expenditures. Instead, see the instructions for line 40.

Line 39

IF you first used your home for business in the following month in 2003...	THEN enter the following percentage on line 39*...
January	2.461%
February	2.247%
March	2.033%
April	1.819%
May	1.605%
June	1.391%
July	1.177%
August	0.963%
September	0.749%
October	0.535%
November	0.321%
December	0.107%

IF you first used your home for business...	THEN the percentage to enter on line 39 is...
After May 12, 1993, and before 2003 (except as noted below)	2.564%*
After May 12, 1993, and before 1994, and you either started construction or had a binding contract to buy or build that home before May 13, 1993	The percentage given in Pub. 946
After May 12, 1993, and you stopped using your home for business before the end of the year	The percentage given in Pub. 946 as adjusted by the instructions under Sale or Other Disposition Before the Recovery Period Ends in that publication
After 1986 and before May 13, 1993	The percentage given in Pub. 946
Before 1987	The percentage given in **Pub. 534**, Depreciating Property Placed in Service Before 1987

*Exception. If the business part of your home is qualified Indian reservation property (as defined in section 168(j)(4)), see **Pub. 946**, How To Depreciate Property, to figure the depreciation.

Line 40

If no additions and improvements were placed in service after you began using your home for business, multiply line 38 by the percentage on line 39. Enter the result on lines 40 and 28.

IF additions and improvements were placed in service...	THEN figure the depreciation allowed on these expenditures by multiplying the business part of their cost or other basis by...
During 2003 (but after you began using your home for business)	The percentage in the line 39 instructions for the month placed in service*
After May 12, 1993, and before 2003 (except as noted below)	2.564%*
After May 12, 1993, and before 1994, and you either started construction or had a binding contract to buy or build that home before May 13, 1993	The percentage given in Pub. 946
After May 12, 1993, and you stopped using your home for business before the end of the year	The percentage given in Pub. 946 as adjusted by the instructions under Sale or Other Disposition Before the Recovery Period Ends in that publication
After 1986 and before May 13, 1993	The percentage given in Pub. 946
Before 1987	The percentage given in Pub. 534

*See the **Exception** on page 3.

Attach a schedule showing your computation and include the amount you figured in the total for line 40. Write "See attached" below the entry space.

Complete and attach **Form 4562**, Depreciation and Amortization, **only** if:

1. You first used your home for business in 2003 or
2. You are depreciating additions and improvements placed in service in 2003.

If you first used your home for business in 2003, enter the amounts from lines 38 and 40 of Form 8829 on the appropriate line of Form 4562. But **do not** include this amount on Schedule C, line 13.

Paperwork Reduction Act Notice. We ask for the information on this form to carry out the Internal Revenue laws of the United States. You are required to give us the information. We need it to ensure that you are complying with these laws and to allow us to figure and collect the right amount of tax.

You are not required to provide the information requested on a form that is subject to the Paperwork Reduction Act unless the form displays a valid OMB control number. Books or records relating to a form or its instructions must be retained as long as their contents may become material in the administration of any Internal Revenue law. Generally, tax returns and return information are confidential, as required by section 6103.

The time needed to complete and file this form will vary depending on individual circumstances. The estimated average time is: **Recordkeeping**, 52 min.; **Learning about the law or the form**, 7 min.; **Preparing the form**, 1 hr., 15 min.; and **Copying, assembling, and sending the form to the IRS**, 20 min.

If you have comments concerning the accuracy of these time estimates or suggestions for making this form simpler, we would be happy to hear from you. See the Instructions for Form 1040.

Appendix B

Appendix K

Department of the Treasury
Internal Revenue Service

Publication 521
Cat. No. 15040E

Moving Expenses

For use in preparing
2003 Returns

Get forms and other information faster and easier by:
Internet • www.irs.gov   or   **FTP** • ftp.irs.gov
FAX • 703–368–9694 (from your fax machine)

Contents

Important Change	1
Important Reminders	1
Introduction	2
Who Can Deduct Moving Expenses	2
Related to Start of Work	2
Distance Test	3
Time Test	4
Retirees or Survivors Who Move to the United States	6
Deductible Moving Expenses	7
Moves to Locations in the United States	7
Moves to Locations Outside the United States	7
Nondeductible Expenses	8
Reimbursements	8
Types of Reimbursement Plans	8
Tax Withholding and Estimated Tax	10
How and When To Report	10
Form 3903	10
When To Deduct Expenses	11
Illustrated Example	11
Members of the Armed Forces	14
How To Get Tax Help	15
Index	17

Important Change

Standard mileage rate. The standard mileage rate for moving expenses has been decreased from 13 cents to 12 cents a mile. See *Travel by car* under *Deductible Moving Expenses*.

Important Reminders

Change of address. If you change your mailing address, be sure to notify the IRS using Form 8822, *Change of Address*. Mail it to the Internal Revenue Service Center for your old address. Addresses for the service centers are on the back of the form.

Photographs of missing children. The Internal Revenue Service is a proud partner with the National Center for Missing and Exploited Children. Photographs of missing children selected by the Center may appear in this publication on pages that would otherwise be blank. You can help bring these children home by looking at the photographs and calling **1–800–THE–LOST (1–800–843–5678)** if you recognize a child.

At press time, the 2004 publication was not available.

Introduction

This publication explains the deduction of certain expenses of moving to a new home because you changed job locations or started a new job. It includes the following topics.

- Who can deduct moving expenses.
- What moving expenses are deductible.
- What moving expenses are not deductible.
- How a reimbursement affects your moving expense deduction.
- How and when to report moving expenses.
- Special rules for members of the Armed Forces.

An example, including a filled-in Form 3903, *Moving Expenses*, is shown near the end of the publication.

You may be able to deduct moving expenses whether you are self-employed or an employee. Your expenses generally must be related to starting work at your new job location. However, certain retirees and survivors may qualify to claim the deduction even if they are not starting work at a new job location. See *Who Can Deduct Moving Expenses*.

Comments and suggestions. We welcome your comments about this publication and your suggestions for future editions.

You can e-mail us at *taxforms@irs.gov. Please put "Publications Comment" on the subject line.

You can write to us at the following address:

Internal Revenue Service
Individual Forms and Publications Branch
SE:W:CAR:MP:T:I
1111 Constitution Ave. NW
Washington, DC 20224

We respond to many letters by telephone. Therefore, it would be helpful if you would include your daytime phone number, including the area code, in your correspondence.

Useful Items
You may want to see:

Publication

❏ **3** Armed Forces' Tax Guide

Form (and Instructions)

❏ **1040** U.S. Individual Income Tax Return

❏ **1040X** Amended U.S. Individual Income Tax Return

❏ **3903** Moving Expenses

❏ **8822** Change of Address

Page 2

See *How To Get Tax Help*, near the end of this publication, for information about getting the publication and the forms listed.

Who Can Deduct Moving Expenses

You can deduct your moving expenses if you meet all three of the following requirements.

1) Your move is closely related to the start of work.
2) You meet the distance test.
3) You meet the time test.

After you have read these rules, you may want to use *Figure B* to help you decide if you can deduct your moving expenses.

Retirees, survivors, and Armed Forces members. Different rules may apply if you are a member of the Armed Forces or a retiree or survivor moving to the United States. These rules are discussed later in this publication.

Related to Start of Work

Your move must be closely related, both in time and in place, to the start of work at your new job location.

Closely related in time. You can generally consider moving expenses incurred within 1 year from the date you first reported to work at the new location as closely related in time to the start of work. It is not necessary that you arrange to work before moving to a new location, as long as you actually do go to work.

If you do not move within 1 year of the date you begin work, you ordinarily cannot deduct the expenses unless you can show that circumstances existed that prevented the move within that time.

Example. Your family moved more than a year after you started work at a new location. You delayed the move for 18 months to allow your child to complete high school. You can deduct your moving expenses.

Closely related in place. You can generally consider your move closely related in place to the start of work if the distance from your new home to the new job location is not more than the distance from your former home to the new job location. If your move does not meet this requirement, you may still be able to deduct moving expenses if you can show that:

1) You are required to live at your new home as a condition of your employment, or
2) You will spend less time or money commuting from your new home to your new job location.

Home defined. Your **home** means your main home (residence). It can be a house, apartment, condominium, houseboat, house trailer, or similar dwelling. It does not include other homes owned or kept up by you or members of your family. It also does not include a seasonal home, such as a summer beach cottage. Your **former home** means your home before you left for your new job location. Your **new home** means your home within the area of your new job location.

Retirees or survivors. You may be able to deduct the expenses of moving to the United States or its possessions even if the move is not related to the start of work at a new job location. You must have worked outside the United States or be a survivor of someone who did. See *Retirees or Survivors Who Move to the United States*, later.

Distance Test

Your move will meet the distance test if your new main job location is *at least 50 miles* farther from your former home than your old main job location was from your former home. For example, if your old main job location was 3 miles from your former home, your new main job location must be at least 53 miles from that former home.

The distance between a job location and your home is the shortest of the more commonly traveled routes between them. The distance test considers only the location of your former home. It does not take into account the location of your new home. See *Figure A*, below.

Example. You moved to a new home less than 50 miles from your former home because you changed main job locations. Your old main job location was 3 miles from your former home. Your new main job location is 60 miles from that home. Because your new main job location is 57 miles farther from your former home than the distance from your former home to your old main job location, you meet the distance test.

First job or return to full-time work. If you go to work full time for the first time, your place of work must be at least 50 miles from your former home to meet the distance test.

If you go back to full-time work after a substantial period of part-time work or unemployment, your place of work also must be at least 50 miles from your former home.

Armed Forces. If you are in the Armed Forces and you moved because of a permanent change of station, you do not have to meet the distance test. See *Members of the Armed Forces*, later.

Main job location. Your main job location is usually the place where you spend most of your working time. If there is no one place where you spend most of your working time, your main job location is the place where your work is centered, such as where you report for work or are otherwise required to "base" your work.

Union members. If you work for several employers on a short-term basis and you get work under a union hall system (such as a construction or building trades worker), your main job location is the union hall.

More than one job. If you have more than one job at any time, your main job location depends on the facts in each case. The more important factors to be considered are:

• The total time you spend at each place,

Figure A. **Illustration of Distance Test**

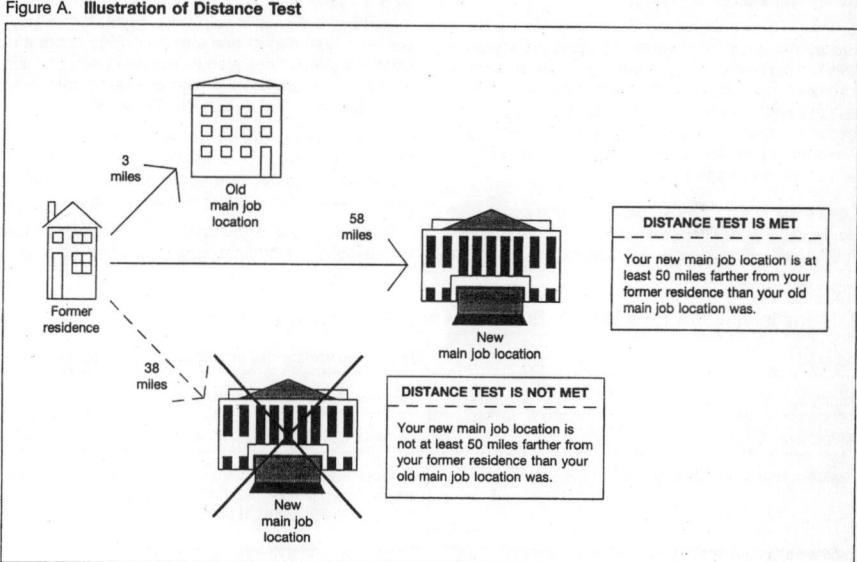

Page 3

215

- The amount of work you do at each place, and
- How much money you earn at each place.

Time Test

To deduct your moving expenses, you also must meet one of the following two time tests.

1) The time test for employees.
2) The time test for self-employed persons.

Both of these tests are explained below. See *Table 1*, below, for a summary of these tests.

Time Test for Employees

If you are an employee, you must work full time for at least **39 weeks during the first 12 months** after you arrive in the general area of your new job location (39-week test). Full-time employment depends on what is usual for your type of work in your area.

For purposes of this test, the following four rules apply.

1) You count only your full-time work as an employee, not any work you do as a self-employed person.
2) You do not have to work for the same employer for all 39 weeks.
3) You do not have to work 39 weeks in a row.
4) You must work full time within the same general commuting area for all 39 weeks.

Temporary absence from work. You are considered to have worked full time during any week you are temporarily absent from work because of illness, strikes, lockouts, layoffs, natural disasters, or similar causes. You are also considered to have worked full time during any week you are absent from work for leave or vacation provided for in your work contract or agreement.

Seasonal work. If your work is seasonal, you are considered to be working full time during the off-season only if your work contract or agreement covers an off-season period of less than 6 months. For example, a school teacher on a 12-month contract who teaches on a full-time basis for more than 6 months is considered to have worked full time for the entire 12 months.

Time Test for Self-Employed Persons

If you are self-employed, you must work full time for at least **39 weeks during the first 12 months AND** for a total of at least **78 weeks during the first 24 months** after you arrive in the general area of your new job location (78-week test).

For purposes of the time test for self-employed persons, the following three rules apply.

1) You count any full-time work you do either as an employee or as a self-employed person.
2) You do not have to work for the same employer or be self-employed in the same trade or business for the 78 weeks.
3) You must work within the same general commuting area for all 78 weeks.

Self-employment. You are self-employed if you work as the sole owner of an unincorporated business or as a partner in a partnership carrying on a business. You are not considered self-employed if you are semi-retired, are a part-time student, or work only a few hours each week.

Full-time work. You can count only those weeks during which you work full time as a week of work. Whether you work full time during any week depends on what is usual for your type of work in your area. For example, you are a self-employed dentist and maintain office hours 4 days a week. You are considered to perform services full time if maintaining office hours 4 days a week is not unusual for other self-employed dentists in your area.

Temporary absence from work. You are considered to be self-employed on a full-time basis during any week you are temporarily absent from work because of illness, strikes, natural disasters, or similar causes.

Seasonal trade or business. If your trade or business is seasonal, the off-season weeks when no work is re-

Table 1. **Satisfying the Time Test for Employees and Self-Employed Persons**

IF you are...	THEN you satisfy the time test by meeting the...
an employee	39-week test for employees.
self-employed	78-week test for self-employed persons.
both self-employed and an employee at the same time	78-week test for a self-employed person or the 39-week test for an employee. Your principal place of work determines which test applies.
both self-employed and an employee, but unable to satisfy the 39-week test for employees	78-week test for self-employed persons.

Figure B. Can You Deduct Expenses for a Non-Military Move Within the United States?[1]

```
Start Here:
┌─────────────────────────────┐
│ Was your move closely       │──No──────────────────────┐
│ related to a new or changed │                          │
│ job location?[2]            │                          │
└─────────────────────────────┘                          │
            │Yes                                         ▼
┌─────────────────────────────┐                  ┌──────────────┐
│ Is your new main job        │──No──────────────▶│ You cannot   │
│ location at least 50 miles  │                  │ deduct your  │
│ farther from your FORMER    │                  │ moving       │
│ HOME than your old main     │                  │ expenses     │
│ job location was?           │                  └──────────────┘
└─────────────────────────────┘                          ▲
            │Yes                                         │
┌─────────────────────────────┐    ┌──────────────────┐  │
│ Are you an employee?        │──No▶│ Are you self-    │──No
└─────────────────────────────┘    │ employed?        │
            │Yes                   └──────────────────┘
                                          │Yes
┌─────────────────────────────┐    ┌──────────────────────────┐
│ Did you or will you work    │    │ Did you or will you work │
│ full time as an employee    │    │ full time as an employee │──No
│ for at least 39 weeks in    │    │ or a self-employed person│
│ the first 12 months after   │No  │ for at least 78 weeks in │
│ you arrived in the new      │    │ the first 24 months      │
│ area?[3,4]                  │    │ (which includes 39 weeks │
└─────────────────────────────┘    │ in the first 12 months)  │
            │Yes                   │ after you arrived in the │
                                   │ new area?                │
                                   └──────────────────────────┘
                                          │Yes
┌─────────────────────────────┐
│ You may be able to deduct   │
│ your moving expenses        │
└─────────────────────────────┘
```

[1] Military persons should see *Members of the Armed Forces* for special rules that apply to them.
[2] Your move must be closely related to the start of work at your new job location. See *Related to Start of Work*.
[3] If you deduct expenses and do not meet this test later, you must either file an amended tax return or report your moving expense deduction as other income. See *Time test not yet met*.
[4] If you became self-employed during the first 12 months, answer YES if your combined time as a full-time employee and self-employed person equals or will equal at least 78 weeks in the first 24 months (including 39 weeks in the first 12 months) after you arrived in the new area.

quired or available may be counted as weeks during which you worked full time. The off-season must be less than 6 months and you must work full time before and after the off-season.

Example. You own and operate a motel at a beach resort. The motel is closed for 5 months during the off-season. You work full-time as the operator of the motel before and after the off-season. You are considered self-employed on a full-time basis during the weeks of the off-season.

If you were both an employee and self-employed, see *Table 1* (previous page) for the requirements.

Example. Justin quit his job and moved from the east coast to the west coast to begin a full-time job as a cabinet-maker for C and L Cabinet Shop. He generally worked at the shop about 40 hours each week. Shortly after the move, Justin also began operating a cabinet-installation business from his home for several hours each afternoon and all day on weekends. Because Justin's principal place of business is the cabinet shop, he can satisfy the time test by meeting the 39-week test.

If Justin is unable to satisfy the requirements of the 39-week test during the 12-month period immediately following his arrival in the general location of his new principal place of work, he can satisfy the 78-week test.

Joint Return

If you are married and file a joint return and both you and your spouse work full time, either of you can satisfy the full-time work test. However, you cannot combine the weeks your spouse worked with the weeks you worked to satisfy that test.

Time Test Not Yet Met

You can deduct your moving expenses on your 2003 tax return even if you have not yet met the time test by the date your 2003 return is due. You can do this if you expect to

Page 5

meet the 39-week test in 2004 or the 78-week test in 2004 or 2005. If you deduct moving expenses but do not meet the time test in 2004 or 2005, you must either:

1) Report your moving expense deduction as other income on your Form 1040 for the year you cannot meet the test, or

2) Amend your 2003 return using Form 1040X.

If you do not deduct your moving expenses on your 2003 return, and you later meet the time test, you can file an amended return for 2003 to take the deduction.

Example. You arrive in the general area of your new job location on September 15, 2003. You deduct your moving expenses on your 2003 return, the year of the move, even though you have not yet met the time test by the date your return is due. If you do not meet the 39-week test during the 12-month period following your arrival in the general area of your new job location, you must either:

1) Report as income on your 2004 return the amount you deducted as moving expenses on your 2003 return, or

2) Amend your 2003 return.

Exceptions to the Time Test

You do not have to meet the time test if one of the following applies.

1) You are in the Armed Forces and you moved because of a permanent change of station. See *Members of the Armed Forces*, later.

2) Your main job location was outside the United States and you moved to the United States because you retired. See *Retirees or Survivors Who Move to the United States*, in the next column.

3) You are the survivor of a person whose main job location at the time of death was outside the United States. See *Retirees or Survivors Who Move to the United States*, below.

4) Your job at the new location ends because of death or disability.

5) You are transferred for your employer's benefit or laid off for a reason other than willful misconduct. For this exception, you must have obtained full-time employment and you must have expected to meet the test at the time you started the job.

Retirees or Survivors Who Move to the United States

If you are a retiree who was working abroad or a survivor of a decedent who was working abroad and you move to the United States or one of its possessions, you do not have to meet the *time test*, discussed earlier. However, you must meet the requirements discussed below under *Retirees who were working abroad* or *Survivors of decedents who were working abroad*.

United States defined. For this section of this publication, the term "United States" includes the possessions of the United States.

Retirees who were working abroad. You can deduct moving expenses for a move to a new home in the United States when you permanently retire. However, both your former main job location and your former home must have been outside the United States.

Permanently retired. You are considered permanently retired when you cease gainful full-time employment or self-employment. If, at the time you retire, you intend your retirement to be permanent, you will be considered retired even though you later return to work. Your intention to retire permanently may be determined by:

1) Your age and health,

2) The customary retirement age for people who do similar work,

3) Whether you receive retirement payments from a pension or retirement fund, and

4) The length of time before you return to full-time work.

Survivors of decedents who were working abroad. If you are the spouse or the dependent of a person whose main job location at the time of death was outside the United States, you can deduct moving expenses if the following five requirements are met.

1) The move is to a home in the United States.

2) The move begins within 6 months after the decedent's death. (When a move begins is described below.)

3) The move is from the decedent's former home.

4) The decedent's former home was outside the United States.

5) The decedent's former home was also your home.

When a move begins. A move begins when one of the following events occurs.

1) You contract for your household goods and personal effects to be moved to your home in the United States, but only if the move is completed within a reasonable time.

2) Your household goods and personal effects are packed and on the way to your home in the United States.

3) You leave your former home to travel to your new home in the United States.

Deductible Moving Expenses

If you meet the requirements discussed earlier under *Who Can Deduct Moving Expenses*, you can deduct the reasonable expenses of:

1) Moving your household goods and personal effects (including in-transit or foreign-move storage expenses), and

2) Traveling (including lodging but not meals) to your new home.

 You cannot deduct any expenses for meals.

Reasonable expenses. You can deduct only those expenses that are reasonable for the circumstances of your move. For example, the cost of traveling from your former home to your new one should be by the shortest, most direct route available by conventional transportation. If during your trip to your new home, you stop over, or make side trips for sightseeing, the additional expenses for your stopover or side trips are not deductible as moving expenses.

Travel by car. If you use your car to take yourself, members of your household, or your personal effects to your new home, you can figure your expenses by deducting either:

1) Your *actual expenses*, such as gas and oil for your car, if you keep an accurate record of each expense, or

2) The *standard mileage rate* of 12 cents a mile.

Whether you use actual expenses or the standard mileage rate to figure your expenses, you can deduct parking fees and tolls you pay in moving. You *cannot deduct* any part of general repairs, general maintenance, insurance, or depreciation for your car.

Member of your household. You can deduct moving expenses you pay for yourself and members of your household. A member of your household is anyone who has both your former and new home as his or her home. It does not include a tenant or employee, unless that person is your dependent.

Moves to Locations in the United States

If you meet the requirements under *Who Can Deduct Moving Expenses*, earlier, you can deduct expenses for a move to the area of a new main job location within the United States or its possessions. Your move may be from one United States location to another or from a foreign country to the United States.

Household goods and personal effects. You can deduct the cost of packing, crating, and transporting your household goods and personal effects and those of the members of your household from your former home to your new home.

If you use your own car to move your things, see *Travel by car*, earlier.

You can deduct any costs of connecting or disconnecting utilities required because you are moving your household goods, appliances, or personal effects.

You can deduct the cost of shipping your car and your household pets to your new home.

You can deduct the cost of moving your household goods and personal effects from a place other than your former home. Your deduction is limited to the amount it would have cost to move them from your former home.

Example. Paul Brown is a resident of North Carolina and has been working there for the last 4 years. Because of the small size of his apartment, he stored some of his furniture in Georgia with his parents. Paul got a job in Washington, DC. It cost him $900 to move his furniture from North Carolina to Washington and $3,000 to move his furniture from Georgia to Washington. If Paul shipped his furniture in Georgia from North Carolina (his former home), it would have cost $1,800. He can deduct only $1,800 of the $3,000 he paid. The amount he can deduct for moving his furniture is $2,700 ($900 + $1,800).

 You cannot deduct the cost of moving furniture you buy on the way to your new home.

Storage expenses. You can include the cost of storing and insuring household goods and personal effects within *any period of 30 consecutive days* after the day your things are moved from your former home and before they are delivered to your new home.

Travel expenses. You can deduct the cost of transportation and lodging for yourself and members of your household while traveling from your former home to your new home. This includes expenses for the day you arrive.

You can include any lodging expenses you had in the area of your former home within one day after you could no longer live in your former home because your furniture had been moved.

You can deduct expenses for only one trip to your new home for yourself and members of your household. However, all of you do not have to travel together or at the same time. If you use your own car, see *Travel by car*, earlier.

Moves to Locations Outside the United States

To deduct expenses for a move outside the United States, you must move to the area of a new place of work outside the United States and its possessions. You must meet the requirements under *Who Can Deduct Moving Expenses*, earlier.

Page 7

Deductible expenses. If your move is to a location outside the United States and its possessions, you can deduct the following expenses.

- The cost of moving household goods and personal effects from your former home to your new home.
- The cost of traveling (including lodging) from your former home to your new home.
- The cost of moving household goods and personal effects to and from storage.
- The cost of storing household goods and personal effects while you are at the new job location.

The first two items were explained earlier under *Moves to Locations in the United States*. The last two items are discussed below.

Moving goods and effects to and from storage. You can deduct the reasonable expenses of moving your personal effects to and from storage.

Storage expenses. You can deduct the reasonable expenses of storing your household goods and personal effects for all or part of the time the new job location remains your main job location.

Moving expenses allocable to excluded foreign income. If you live and work outside the United States, you may be able to exclude from income part or all of the income you earn in the foreign country. You may also be able to claim a foreign housing exclusion or deduction. If you claim the foreign earned income or foreign housing exclusion, you cannot deduct the part of your moving expenses that relates to the excluded income.

Publication 54, *Tax Guide for U.S. Citizens and Resident Aliens Abroad*, explains how to figure the part of your moving expenses that relates to excluded income. You can get the publication from most United States Embassies and consulates, or see *How To Get Tax Help* at the end of this publication.

Nondeductible Expenses

You cannot deduct the following items as moving expenses.

- Any part of the purchase price of your new home.
- Car tags.
- Driver's license.
- Expenses of buying or selling a home.
- Expenses of getting or breaking a lease.
- Home improvements to help sell your home.
- Loss on the sale of your home.
- Losses from disposing of memberships in clubs.
- Meal expenses.
- Mortgage penalties.
- Pre-move househunting expenses.
- Real estate taxes.
- Refitting of carpets and draperies.
- Security deposits (including any given up due to the move).
- Storage charges except those incurred in transit and for foreign moves.
- Temporary living expenses.

No double deduction. You cannot take a moving expense deduction and a business expense deduction for the same expenses. You must decide if your expenses are deductible as moving expenses or as business expenses. For example, expenses you have for travel, meals, and lodging while *temporarily* working at a place away from your regular place of work may be deductible as business expenses if you are considered away from home on business. Generally, your work at a single location is considered temporary if it is realistically expected to last (and does in fact last) for one year or less.

See Publication 463, *Travel, Entertainment, Gift, and Car Expenses*, for information on deducting your business expenses.

Reimbursements

This section explains what to do when you receive a reimbursement (including advances and allowances) for any of your moving expenses discussed in this publication. It also explains the types of reimbursements on which your employer must withhold income tax, social security tax, and Medicare tax.

Types of Reimbursement Plans

If you receive a reimbursement for your moving expenses, how you report this amount and your expenses depends on whether the reimbursement is paid to you under an *accountable plan* or a *nonaccountable plan*. For a quick overview of how to report your reimbursement and moving expenses, see *Table 2* in the section on *How and When To Report*.

Your employer should tell you what method of reimbursement is used and what records are required.

Accountable Plans

To be an accountable plan, your employer's reimbursement arrangement must require you to meet *all* three of the following rules.

1) Your expenses must be of the type for which a deduction would be allowed had you paid them yourself. The reasonable expenses of moving your possessions from your former home to your new home, and traveling from your former home to your new home are two examples.

2) You must adequately account to your employer for these expenses within a reasonable period of time.

3) You must return any excess reimbursement or allowance within a reasonable period of time.

Adequate accounting. You adequately account for your moving expenses by giving your employer documentary evidence of those expenses, along with a statement of expense, an account book, a diary, or a similar record in which you entered each expense at or near the time you had it. Documentary evidence includes receipts, canceled checks, and bills.

Reasonable period of time. What constitutes a "reasonable period of time" depends on the facts and circumstances of your situation. However, regardless of those facts and circumstances, actions that take place within the time specified in the following list will be treated as taking place within a reasonable period of time.

1) You receive an advance within 30 days of the time you have an expense.

2) You adequately account for your expenses within 60 days after they were paid or incurred.

3) You return any excess reimbursement within 120 days after the expense was paid or incurred.

4) You are given a periodic statement (at least quarterly) that asks you to either return or adequately account for outstanding advances *and* you comply within 120 days of the statement.

Excess reimbursement. This includes any amount you are paid (including advances and allowances) that is more than the moving expenses that you adequately accounted for to your employer within a reasonable period of time. See *Returning excess reimbursements*, next, for information on how to handle these excess amounts.

Returning excess reimbursements. You must be required to return any excess reimbursement for your moving expenses to the person paying the reimbursement. Excess reimbursement includes any amount for which you did not adequately account within a reasonable period of time. For example, if you received an advance and you did not spend all the money on deductible moving expenses, or you do not have proof of all your expenses, you have an excess reimbursement.

You meet accountable plan rules. If for all reimbursements you meet the three rules for an accountable plan, your employer should not include any reimbursements of expenses in your income in box 1 of your **Form W–2**. Instead, your employer should include the reimbursements in box 12 of your **Form W–2**.

Example. You lived in Boston and accepted a job in Atlanta. Under an accountable plan, your employer reimbursed you for your actual traveling expenses from Boston to Atlanta and the cost of moving your furniture to Atlanta.

Your employer will include the reimbursement in box 12 of your Form W–2. If your moving expenses are more than your reimbursement, you may be able to deduct your additional expenses (see *How and When To Report*, later).

You do not meet accountable plan rules. You may be reimbursed by your employer, but you may not meet all three rules for part of your expenses.

If your deductible expenses are reimbursed under an otherwise accountable plan but you do not return, within a reasonable period, any reimbursement of expenses for which you did not adequately account, then only the amount for which you did adequately account is considered as paid under an accountable plan. The remaining expenses are treated as having been reimbursed under a nonaccountable plan (discussed below).

Reimbursement of nondeductible expenses. You may be reimbursed by your employer for moving expenses, some of which are deductible expenses and some of which are not deductible. The reimbursements received for the nondeductible expenses are treated as paid under a nonaccountable plan.

Nonaccountable Plans

A nonaccountable plan is a reimbursement arrangement that does not meet the three rules listed earlier under *Accountable Plans*.

In addition, the following payments will be treated as paid under a nonaccountable plan.

1) Excess reimbursements you fail to return to your employer.

2) Reimbursements of nondeductible expenses. See *Reimbursement of nondeductible expenses*, above.

If an arrangement pays for your moving expenses by reducing your wages, salary, or other pay, the amount of the reduction will be treated as a payment made under a nonaccountable plan. This is because you are entitled to receive the full amount of your pay regardless of whether you had any moving expenses.

If you are not sure if the moving expense reimbursement arrangement is an accountable or nonaccountable plan, ask your employer.

Your employer will combine the amount of any reimbursement paid to you under a nonaccountable plan with your wages, salary, or other pay. Your employer will report the total in box 1 of your **Form W–2**.

Example. To get you to work in another city, your new employer reimburses you under an accountable plan for the $7,500 loss on the sale of your home. Since this is a reimbursement of a nondeductible expense, it is treated as paid under a nonaccountable plan and must be included as pay in box 1 of your Form W–2.

Uniform Relocation Assistance and Real Property Acquisition Policies Act of 1970

Do not include in income any moving expense payment you received under the Uniform Relocation Assistance and

Page 9

Real Property Acquisition Policies Act of 1970. These payments are made to persons displaced from their homes, businesses, or farms by federal projects.

Tax Withholding and Estimated Tax

Your employer must withhold income tax, social security tax, and Medicare tax from reimbursements and allowances paid to you that are included in your income. See *Reimbursements included in income,* later.

Reimbursements excluded from income. Your employer should not include in your wages reimbursements paid under an accountable plan (explained earlier) for moving expenses that you:

1) Could deduct if you had paid or incurred them, and

2) Did not deduct in an earlier year.

These reimbursements are fringe benefits excludable from your income as qualified moving expense reimbursements. Your employer should report these reimbursements in box 12 of **Form W–2**.

 You **cannot** claim a moving expense deduction for expenses covered by reimbursements excluded from income (see Accountable Plans under Types of Reimbursement Plans, earlier).

Expenses deducted in earlier year. If you receive reimbursement this year for moving expenses deducted in an earlier year, and the reimbursement is not included as wages in box 1 of your **Form W–2**, you must include the reimbursement on line 21 of your Form 1040. Your employer should show the amount of your reimbursement in box 12 of **Form W–2**.

Reimbursements included in income. Your employer must include in your income any reimbursements made (or treated as made) under a nonaccountable plan, even if they are for deductible moving expenses. See *Nonaccountable Plans* under *Types of Reimbursement Plans,* earlier. Your employer must also include in your gross income as wages any reimbursements of, or payments for, nondeductible moving expenses. This includes amounts your employer reimbursed you under an accountable plan (explained earlier) for meals, househunting trips, and real estate expenses. It also includes reimbursements that exceed your deductible expenses and that you do not return to your employer.

Reimbursement for deductible and nondeductible expenses. If your employer reimburses you for both deductible and nondeductible moving expenses, your employer must determine the amount of the reimbursement that is not taxable and not subject to withholding. Your employer must treat any remaining amount as taxable wages and withhold income tax, social security tax, and Medicare tax.

Amount of income tax withheld. If the reimbursements or allowances you receive are taxable, the amount of income tax your employer will withhold depends on several factors. It depends in part on whether or not income tax is withheld from your regular wages, on whether or not the reimbursements and allowances are combined with your regular wages, and on any information you have given to your employer on **Form W–4**, *Employee's Withholding Allowance Certificate*.

Estimated tax. If you must make estimated tax payments, you need to take into account any taxable reimbursements and deductible moving expenses in figuring your estimated tax. For details about estimated tax, see Publication 505, *Tax Withholding and Estimated Tax*.

How and When To Report

This section explains how and when to report your moving expenses and any reimbursements or allowances you received for your move. For a quick overview, see *Table 2* on the next page.

Form 3903

Use **Form 3903** to figure your moving expense deduction. Use a separate Form 3903 for each move for which you are deducting expenses.

You do not have to complete Form 3903 if **all** of the following apply.

1) You moved to a location outside the United States in an earlier year.

2) You are claiming only storage fees while you are away from the United States.

3) Any amount your employer paid for the storage fees is included as wages in box 1 of your **Form W–2**.

Instead, enter the storage fees (after the reduction for the part that is allocable to excluded income) on line 27, **Form 1040**, and write "Storage" next to the amount.

If you meet the special rules for members of the Armed Forces, see *How to complete Form 3903 for members of the Armed Forces* under *Members of the Armed Forces,* later.

Completing the form. Complete the *Distance Test Worksheet* in the instructions for Form 3903 to see whether you meet the distance test. If so, complete lines 1–3 of the form using your actual expenses (except, if you use your own car, you can figure expenses based on a mileage rate of 12 cents a mile, instead of on actual amounts for gas and oil). Enter on line 4 the total amount of your moving expense reimbursement that was excluded from your wages. This excluded amount should be identified with code **P** in box 12 of **Form W–2**.

Expenses greater than reimbursement. If line 3 is more than line 4, subtract line 4 from line 3 and enter the result on line 5 and on **Form 1040**, line 27. This is your moving expense deduction.

Expenses equal to or less than reimbursement. If line 3 is equal to or less than line 4, you have no moving expense deduction. Subtract line 3 from line 4 and, if the

Page 10

Table 2. **Reporting Your Moving Expenses and Reimbursements**

IF your Form W-2 shows...	AND you have...	THEN...
your reimbursement reported **only** in box 12 with code **P**	moving expenses greater than the amount in box 12	file Form 3903 showing all allowable expenses* and reimbursements.
your reimbursement reported **only** in box 12 with code **P**	moving expenses equal to the amount in box 12	do not file Form 3903.
your reimbursement divided between box 12 and box 1	moving expenses greater than the amount in box 12	file Form 3903 showing all allowable expenses,* but only the reimbursements reported in box 12.
your entire reimbursement reported as wages in box 1	moving expenses	file Form 3903 showing all allowable expenses,* but no reimbursements.
no reimbursement	moving expenses	file Form 3903 showing all allowable expenses.*

* See *Deductible Moving Expenses* for allowable expenses.

result is more than zero, include it as income on **Form 1040**, line 7.

Where to deduct. Deduct your moving expenses on line 27 of Form 1040. The amount of moving expenses you can deduct is shown on line 5 of Form 3903.

 You cannot deduct moving expenses on Form 1040EZ or Form 1040A.

When To Deduct Expenses

You may have a choice of when to deduct your moving expenses and report any reimbursement.

Expenses not reimbursed. If you were not reimbursed, deduct your moving expenses either in the year you incurred them or in the year you paid them.

Example. In December 2002, your employer transferred you to another city in the United States, where you still work. You are single and were not reimbursed for your moving expenses. In 2002, you paid for moving your furniture and deducted these expenses on your 2002 tax return. In January 2003, you paid for travel to the new city. You can deduct these additional expenses on your 2003 tax return.

Expenses reimbursed. If you are reimbursed for your expenses, you may be able to deduct your expenses either in the year you incurred them or in the year you paid them. If you use the cash method of accounting, you can choose to deduct the expenses in the year you are reimbursed even though you paid the expenses in a different year. See *Choosing when to deduct*, next.

If you are reimbursed for your expenses in a year after you paid the expenses, you may want to delay taking the deduction until the year you receive the reimbursement. If you do not choose to delay your deduction until the year you are reimbursed and you deduct moving expenses that will be reimbursed, you must include the reimbursement in your income.

Choosing when to deduct. If you use the cash method of accounting, which is used by most individuals, you can choose to deduct moving expenses in the year your employer reimburses you if:

1) You paid the expenses in a year before the year of reimbursement, or

2) You paid the expenses in the year immediately after the year of reimbursement but by the due date, including extensions, for filing your return for the reimbursement year.

How to make the choice. You choose to deduct moving expenses in the year you received reimbursement by taking the deduction on your return, or amended return, for that year.

 You cannot deduct any moving expenses for which you received a reimbursement that was not included in your income.

Illustrated Example

Tom Smith is married and has two children. He owned his home in Detroit where he worked. On February 8, his employer told him that he would be transferred to San Diego as of April 10 that year. His wife, Peggy, flew to San Diego on March 1 to look for a new home. She put a down payment of $25,000 on a house being built and came back to Detroit on March 4. The Smiths sold their Detroit home for $1,500 less than they paid for it. They contracted to have their personal effects moved to San Diego on April 3. The family drove to San Diego where they found that their new home was not finished. They stayed in a nearby motel until the house was ready on May 1. On April 10, Tom went to work in the San Diego plant where he still works.

Page 11

His records for the move show:

1) Peggy's pre-move househunting trip:
   Travel and lodging .... $ 449
   Meals .... 75 $ 524
2) Down payment on San Diego home 25,000
3) Real estate commission paid on sale of Detroit home 3,500
4) Loss on sale of Detroit home (not including real estate commission) 1,500
5) Amount paid for moving personal effects (furniture, other household goods, etc.) 8,000
6) Expenses of driving to San Diego:
   Mileage (Start 14,278; End 16,478)
   2,200 miles at 12 cents a mile $ 264
   Lodging   180
   Meals   320   764
7) Cost of temporary living expenses in San Diego:
   Motel rooms $1,450
   Meals   2,280   3,730

Total $43,018

Tom was reimbursed $10,643 under an accountable plan. His employer gave him the following breakdown of the reimbursement.

Moving personal effects .... $ 6,800
Travel (and lodging) to San Diego   444
Travel (and lodging) for househunting trip   449
Lodging for temporary quarters 1,450
Loss on sale of home   1,500

Total reimbursement $10,643

The employer included this reimbursement on Tom's Form W–2 for the year. The reimbursement of deductible expenses, $7,244 ($6,800 + $444) for moving household goods and travel to San Diego, was included in box 12 of Form W–2. His employer identified this amount with code P.

The employer included the balance, $3,399 reimbursement of nondeductible expenses, in box 1 of Form W–2 with Tom's other wages. Tom must include this amount on line 7 of Form 1040. The employer withholds taxes from the $3,399, as discussed under *Reimbursement for deductible and nondeductible expenses* under *Tax Withholding and Estimated Tax*, earlier. Also, Tom's employer could have given him a separate Form W–2 for his moving reimbursement.

To figure his deduction for moving expenses, Tom enters the following amounts on **Form 3903**.

Item 5 — moving personal effects (line 1) $8,000

Item 6 — driving to San Diego ($264 + $180) (line 2) 444

Total deductible moving expenses (line 3) $8,444

Minus: Reimbursement included in box 12 of Form W–2 (line 4) 7,244

Deduction for moving expenses (line 5) $1,200

Tom's Form 3903 and *Distance Test Worksheet* are shown on the next page. He also enters his deduction, $1,200, on line 27, **Form 1040**.

Nondeductible expenses. Of the $43,018 expenses that Tom incurred, the following items cannot be deducted.

- Item 1 — pre-move househunting expenses.
- Item 2 — the down payment on the San Diego home. If any part of it were for payment of deductible taxes or interest on the mortgage on the house, that part would be deductible as an itemized deduction.
- Item 3 — the real estate commission paid on the sale of the Detroit home. The commission is used to figure the gain or loss on the sale.
- Item 4 — the loss on the sale of the Detroit home. The Smiths cannot deduct it even though Tom's employer reimbursed him for it.
- Item 6 — the expenses for meals while driving to San Diego. (However, the lodging and car expenses are deductible.)
- Item 7 — temporary living expenses.

Form 3903
Department of the Treasury
Internal Revenue Service

Moving Expenses

▶ Attach to Form 1040.

OMB No. 1545-0062

2003
Attachment Sequence No. **62**

Name(s) shown on Form 1040: Tom and Peggy Smith

Your social security number: 325 : 00 : 6437

Before you begin: ✓ See the **Distance Test** and **Time Test** in the instructions to find out if you can deduct your moving expenses.
✓ If you are a member of the armed forces, see the instructions to find out how to complete this form.

1	Enter the amount you paid for transportation and storage of household goods and personal effects (see instructions)	1	8,000 —
2	Enter the amount you paid for travel and lodging in moving from your old home to your new home (see instructions). **Do not** include the cost of meals	2	444 —
3	Add lines 1 and 2	3	8,444 —
4	Enter the total amount your employer paid you for the expenses listed on lines 1 and 2 that is **not** included in the wages box (box 1) of your Form W-2. This amount should be identified with code **P** in box 12 of your Form W-2	4	7,244 —
5	Is line 3 **more than** line 4?		
	☐ **No.** You **cannot** deduct your moving expenses. If line 3 is less than line 4, subtract line 3 from line 4 and include the result on Form 1040, line 7.		
	☑ **Yes. Moving expense deduction.** Subtract line 4 from line 3. Enter the result here and on Form 1040, line 27	5	1,200 —

General Instructions

A Change To Note
For 2003, the standard mileage rate for using your vehicle to move to a new home is 12 cents a mile.

Purpose of Form
Use Form 3903 to figure your moving expense deduction for a move related to the start of work at a new principal place of work (workplace). If the new workplace is outside the United States or its possessions, you must be a U.S. citizen or resident alien to deduct your expenses.

If you qualify to deduct expenses for more than one move, use a separate Form 3903 for each move.

For more details, see **Pub. 521**, Moving Expenses.

Who May Deduct Moving Expenses
If you move to a new home because of a new principal workplace, you may be able to deduct your moving expenses whether you are self-employed or an employee. But you must meet both the distance test and time test that follow.

Distance Test
Your new principal workplace must be at least 50 miles farther from your old home than your old workplace was. For example, if your old workplace was 3 miles from your old home, your new workplace must be at least 53 miles from that home. If you did not have an old workplace, your new workplace must be at least 50 miles from your old home. The distance between the two points is the shortest of the more commonly traveled routes between them.

 To see if you meet the distance test, you can use the worksheet below.

Distance Test Worksheet

Keep a Copy for Your Records

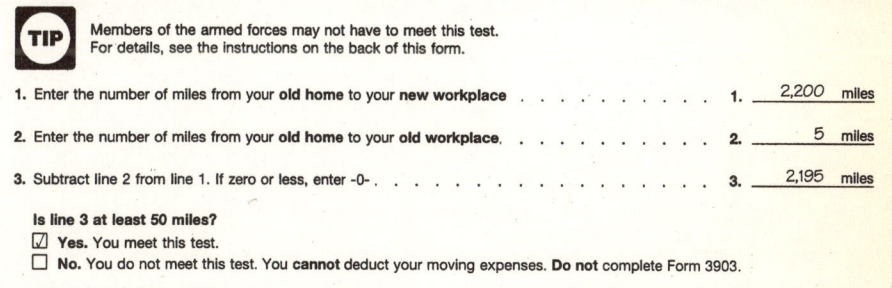

For Paperwork Reduction Act Notice, see back of form.   Cat. No. 12490K   Form **3903** (2003)

Members of the Armed Forces

If you are a member of the Armed Forces on active duty and you move because of a permanent change of station, you do not have to meet the *distance and time tests*, discussed earlier. You can deduct your unreimbursed moving expenses.

A permanent change of station includes:

- A move from your home to your first post of active duty,
- A move from one permanent post of duty to another, and
- A move from your last post of duty to your home or to a nearer point in the United States. The move must occur within one year of ending your active duty or within the period allowed under the Joint Travel Regulations.

Spouse and dependents. If a member of the Armed Forces dies, is imprisoned, or deserts, a permanent change of station for the spouse or dependent includes a move to:

- The place of enlistment,
- The member's, spouse's, or dependent's home of record, or
- A nearer point in the United States.

If the military moves you and your spouse and dependents to or from separate locations, the moves are treated as a single move to your new main job location.

Services or reimbursements provided by government. Do not include in income the value of moving and storage services provided by the government because of a permanent change of station. In general, if the total reimbursements or allowances you receive from the government because of the move are more than your actual moving expenses, the government should include the excess in your wages on **Form W–2**. However, the excess portion of a dislocation allowance, a temporary lodging allowance, a temporary lodging expense, or a move-in housing allowance is not included in income and should not be included in box 1 of **Form W–2**.

If your reimbursements or allowances are less than your actual moving expenses, do not include the reimbursements or allowances in income. You can deduct the expenses that are more than your reimbursements. See *Deductible Moving Expenses*, earlier.

How to complete Form 3903 for members of the Armed Forces. Take the following steps.

1) Complete lines 1–3 of the form, using your actual expenses. **Do not** include any expenses for moving services provided by the government. Also, do not include any expenses that were reimbursed by an allowance you do not have to include in your income.

2) Enter on line 4 the total reimbursements and allowances you received from the government for the expenses claimed on lines 1 and 2. **Do not** include the value of moving services provided by the government. Also, do not include any part of a dislocation allowance, a temporary lodging allowance, a temporary lodging expense, or a move-in housing allowance.

3) Complete line 5. If line 3 is more than line 4, subtract line 4 from line 3 and enter the result on line 5 and on **Form 1040**, line 27. This is your moving expense deduction. If line 3 is equal to or less than line 4, you do not have a moving expense deduction. Subtract line 3 from line 4 and, if the result is more than zero, enter it on **Form 1040**, line 7.

If the military moves you and your spouse and dependents to or from different locations, treat these moves as a single move.

Do not deduct any expenses for moving services provided by the government.

How To Get Tax Help

You can get help with unresolved tax issues, order free publications and forms, ask tax questions, and get more information from the IRS in several ways. By selecting the method that is best for you, you will have quick and easy access to tax help.

Contacting your Taxpayer Advocate. If you have attempted to deal with an IRS problem unsuccessfully, you should contact your Taxpayer Advocate.

The Taxpayer Advocate independently represents your interests and concerns within the IRS by protecting your rights and resolving problems that have not been fixed through normal channels. While Taxpayer Advocates cannot change the tax law or make a technical tax decision, they can clear up problems that resulted from previous contacts and ensure that your case is given a complete and impartial review.

To contact your Taxpayer Advocate:

- Call the Taxpayer Advocate at **1–877–777–4778**.
- Call, write, or fax the Taxpayer Advocate office in your area.
- Call **1–800–829–4059** if you are a TTY/TDD user.
- Visit the web site at **www.irs.gov/advocate**.

For more information, see Publication 1546, *The Taxpayer Advocate Service of the IRS*.

Free tax services. To find out what services are available, get Publication 910, *Guide to Free Tax Services*. It contains a list of free tax publications and an index of tax topics. It also describes other free tax information services, including tax education and assistance programs and a list of TeleTax topics.

Internet. You can access the IRS website 24 hours a day, 7 days a week at **www.irs.gov** to:

- *E-file.* Access commercial tax preparation and *e-file* services available for free to eligible taxpayers.
- Check the amount of advance child tax credit payments you received in 2003.
- Check the status of your 2003 refund. Click on "Where's My Refund" and then on "Go Get My Refund Status." Be sure to wait at least 6 weeks from the date you filed your return (3 weeks if you filed electronically) and have your 2003 tax return available because you will need to know your filing status and the exact whole dollar amount of your refund.
- Download forms, instructions, and publications.
- Order IRS products on-line.
- See answers to frequently asked tax questions.
- Search publications on-line by topic or keyword.

- Figure your withholding allowances using our Form W-4 calculator.
- Send us comments or request help by email.
- Sign up to receive local and national tax news by email.
- Get information on starting and operating a small business.

You can also reach us with your computer using File Transfer Protocol at **ftp.irs.gov**.

Fax. You can get over 100 of the most requested forms and instructions 24 hours a day, 7 days a week, by fax. Just call **703–368–9694** from your fax machine. Follow the directions from the prompts. When you order forms, enter the catalog number for the form you need. The items you request will be faxed to you.

For help with transmission problems, call the FedWorld Help Desk at **703–487–4608**.

Long-distance charges may apply.

Phone. Many services are available by phone.

- *Ordering forms, instructions, and publications.* Call **1–800–829–3676** to order current and prior year forms, instructions, and publications and prior-year forms and instructions. You should receive your order within 10 days.
- *Asking tax questions.* Call the IRS with your tax questions at **1–800–829–1040**.
- *Solving problems.* You can get face-to-face help solving tax problems every business day in IRS Taxpayer Assistance Centers. An employee can explain IRS letters, request adjustments to your account, or help you set up a payment plan. Call your local Taxpayer Assistance Center for an appointment. To find the number, go to **www.irs.gov** or look in the phone book under "United States Government, Internal Revenue Service."
- *TTY/TDD equipment.* If you have access to TTY/TDD equipment, call **1–800–829–4059** to ask tax or account questions or to order forms and publications.
- *TeleTax topics.* Call **1–800–829–4477** to listen to pre-recorded messages covering various tax topics.
- *Refund information.* If you would like to check the status of your 2003 refund, call **1–800–829–4477** for automated refund information and follow the recorded instructions or call **1–800–829–1954**. Be sure to wait at least 6 weeks from the date you filed your return (3 weeks if you filed electronically) and have your 2003 tax return available because you will need to know your filing status and the exact whole dollar amount of your refund.

Evaluating the quality of our telephone services. To

Page 15

ensure that IRS representatives give accurate, courteous, and professional answers, we use several methods to evaluate the quality of our telephone services. One method is for a second IRS representative to sometimes listen in on or record telephone calls. Another is to ask some callers to complete a short survey at the end of the call.

Walk-in. Many products and services are available on a walk-in basis.

- *Products.* You can walk in to many post offices, libraries, and IRS offices to pick up certain forms, instructions, and publications. Some IRS offices, libraries, grocery stores, copy centers, city and county governments, credit unions, and office supply stores have a collection of products available to print from a CD-ROM or photocopy from reproducible proofs. Also, some IRS offices and libraries have the Internal Revenue Code, regulations, Internal Revenue Bulletins, and Cumulative Bulletins available for research purposes.

- *Services.* You can walk in to your local Taxpayer Assistance Center every business day to ask tax questions or get help with a tax problem. An employee can explain IRS letters, request adjustments to your account, or help you set up a payment plan. You can set up an appointment by calling your local Center and, at the prompt, leaving a message requesting Everyday Tax Solutions help. A representative will call you back within 2 business days to schedule an in-person appointment at your convenience. To find the number, go to **www.irs.gov** or look in the phone book under "United States Government, Internal Revenue Service."

Mail. You can send your order for forms, instructions, and publications to the Distribution Center nearest to you and receive a response within 10 workdays after your request is received. Use the address that applies to your part of the country.

- **Western part of U.S.:**
  Western Area Distribution Center
  Rancho Cordova, CA 95743–0001

- **Central part of U.S.:**
  Central Area Distribution Center
  P.O. Box 8903
  Bloomington, IL 61702–8903

- **Eastern part of U.S. and foreign addresses:**
  Eastern Area Distribution Center
  P.O. Box 85074
  Richmond, VA 23261–5074

CD-ROM for tax products. You can order IRS Publication 1796, *Federal Tax Products on CD-ROM,* and obtain:

- Current tax forms, instructions, and publications.
- Prior-year tax forms and instructions.
- Frequently requested tax forms that may be filled in electronically, printed out for submission, and saved for recordkeeping.
- Internal Revenue Bulletins.

Buy the CD-ROM from National Technical Information Service (NTIS) on the Internet at **www.irs.gov/cdorders** for $22 (no handling fee) or call **1–877–233–6767** toll free to buy the CD-ROM for $22 (plus a $5 handling fee). The first release is available in early January and the final release is available in late February.

CD-ROM for small businesses. IRS Publication 3207, *Small Business Resource Guide,* is a must for every small business owner or any taxpayer about to start a business. This handy, interactive CD contains all the business tax forms, instructions and publications needed to successfully manage a business. In addition, the CD provides an abundance of other helpful information, such as how to prepare a business plan, finding financing for your business, and much more. The design of the CD makes finding information easy and quick and incorporates file formats and browsers that can be run on virtually any desktop or laptop computer.

It is available in early April. You can get a free copy by calling **1–800–829–3676** or by visiting the website at **www.irs.gov/smallbiz**.

Page 16

Index

To help us develop a more useful index, please let us know if you have ideas for index entries. See "Comments and Suggestions" in the "Introduction" for the ways you can reach us.

A
Accountable plans 8-9
Adequate accounting 9
Advances (See Reimbursements)
Allowances (See Reimbursements)
Armed Forces, members of 3, 14
Assistance (See Tax help)

C
Car expenses 7
Change of address 1
Choosing when to deduct 11
Comments on publication 2

D
Deductible moving expenses 7-8
  Household goods 7
  Member of your household 7
  Moves to locations in the United States 7
  Moves to locations outside the United States 7-8
  Personal effects 7
  Reasonable expenses 7
  Travel by car 7
  Travel expenses 7
  When to deduct 11
Distance test 3, 14

E
Estimated tax 10
Example, illustrated 11-13
Exceptions to the time test 6
Excess reimbursement 9
Excluded foreign income, moving expenses allocable to 8

F
Figures:
  Can You Deduct Expenses for a Non-Military Move Within the United States? 5
  Form 3903, illustrated 13
  Illustration of Distance Test 3
First job 3
Form:
  1040 .... 10, 12, 14
  3903 .... 10, 12-13, 14
  W–2 .... 9, 10
  W–4 10

Free tax services 15
Full-time work, defined 4

H
Help (See Tax help)
Home:
  Defined 2
  Former 3
  New 3
Household goods 7
How to report:
  Form 1040 .... 10, 12, 14
  Form 3903 .... 10, 12-13, 14

I
Illustrated example 11-13
Important change 1
Important reminders 1

J
Joint return 5

M
Main job location:
  Defined 3
  More than one job 3
  Union members 3
Member of your household 7
Members of the Armed Forces 3, 14
More information (See Tax help)
Moves to locations in the United States 7
Moves to locations outside the United States 7-8
Moving expenses:
  Allocable to excluded foreign income 8
  Deductible 7-8
  No double deduction 8
  Nondeductible 8
  Who can deduct 2-6, 14

N
Nonaccountable plans 9
Nondeductible expenses 8
Nondeductible expenses, reimbursement of 9

P
Personal effects 7
Publications (See Tax help)

R
Reasonable expenses 7
Reasonable period of time 9
Reimbursements:
  Accountable plans 8-9
  Armed Forces, members of ... 14
  Excess 9
  Excluded from income 10
  Included in income 10
  Nonaccountable plans 9
  Nondeductible expenses 9, 10
  Uniform Relocation Assistance and Real Property Acquisition Policies Act of 1970 9
  Withholding on 10
Residence (See Home)
Retirees who move to U.S. 3, 6
Return to full-time work 3

S
Seasonal trade or business ... 4-5
Self-employment, defined 4
Standard mileage rate 1, 7
Storage expenses 7, 8
Suggestions for publication 2
Survivors who move to U.S. 3, 6

T
Tables:
  Reporting Your Moving Expenses and Reimbursements 11
  Satisfying the Time Test for Employees and Self-Employed Persons 4
Tax help 15-16
Tax withholding 10
Taxpayer Advocate 15
Temporary absence from work 4
Time test:
  Armed Forces, member of 14
  Employees 4
  Exceptions 6
  Full-time work 4
  Joint return 5
  Not yet met 5-6
  Seasonal work 4
  Self-employed persons 4-5
  Temporary absence from work 4

Travel by car 7
Travel expenses 7
TTY/TDD information 15

U
Uniform Relocation Assistance and Real Property Acquisition Policies Act of 1970 9
Union members, main job location 3

W
When to deduct expenses:
Choosing when to deduct 11
Expenses not reimbursed 11
Expenses reimbursed 11
Where to deduct 11
Who can deduct:
Distance test 3
Members of the Armed Forces 14
Related to start of work 2-3

Retirees who move to U.S. ... 3, 6
Survivors who move to U.S. 3, 6
Time test 4-6
Withholding 10

∎

Tax Publications for Individual Taxpayers

See *How To Get Tax Help* for a variety of ways to get publications, including by computer, phone, and mail.

General Guides
- 1 Your Rights as a Taxpayer
- 17 Your Federal Income Tax (For Individuals)
- 334 Tax Guide for Small Business (For Individuals Who Use Schedule C or C-EZ)
- 509 Tax Calendars for 2004
- 553 Highlights of 2003 Tax Changes
- 910 Guide to Free Tax Services

Specialized Publications
- 3 Armed Forces' Tax Guide
- 54 Tax Guide for U.S. Citizens and Residents Aliens Abroad
- 225 Farmer's Tax Guide
- 378 Fuel Tax Credits and Refunds
- 463 Travel, Entertainment, Gift, and Car Expenses
- 501 Exemptions, Standard Deduction, and Filing Information
- 502 Medical and Dental Expenses (Including the Health Coverage Tax Credit)
- 503 Child and Dependent Care Expenses
- 504 Divorced or Separated Individuals
- 505 Tax Withholding and Estimated Tax
- 514 Foreign Tax Credit for Individuals
- 516 U.S. Government Civilian Employees Stationed Abroad
- 517 Social Security and Other Information for Members of the Clergy and Religious Workers
- 519 U.S. Tax Guide for Aliens
- 521 Moving Expenses
- 523 Selling Your Home
- 524 Credit for the Elderly or the Disabled
- 525 Taxable and Nontaxable Income
- 526 Charitable Contributions
- 527 Residential Rental Property
- 529 Miscellaneous Deductions
- 530 Tax Information for First-Time Homeowners
- 531 Reporting Tip Income
- 533 Self-Employment Tax
- 536 Net Operating Losses (NOLs) for Individuals, Estates, and Trusts
- 537 Installment Sales
- 541 Partnerships
- 544 Sales and Other Dispositions of Assets
- 547 Casualties, Disasters, and Thefts
- 550 Investment Income and Expenses
- 551 Basis of Assets
- 552 Recordkeeping for Individuals
- 554 Older Americans' Tax Guide
- 555 Community Property
- 556 Examination of Returns, Appeal Rights, and Claims for Refund
- 559 Survivors, Executors, and Administrators
- 561 Determining the Value of Donated Property
- 564 Mutual Fund Distributions
- 570 Tax Guide for Individuals With Income From U.S. Possessions
- 571 Tax-Sheltered Annuity Plans (403(b) Plans)
- 575 Pension and Annuity Income
- 584 Casualty, Disaster, and Theft Loss Workbook (Personal-Use Property)
- 587 Business Use of Your Home (Including Use by Daycare Providers)
- 590 Individual Retirement Arrangements (IRAs)
- 593 Tax Highlights for U.S. Citizens and Residents Going Abroad
- 594 What You Should Know About the IRS Collection Process
- 595 Tax Highlights for Commercial Fishermen
- 596 Earned Income Credit (EIC)
- 721 Tax Guide to U.S. Civil Service Retirement Benefits
- 901 U.S. Tax Treaties
- 907 Tax Highlights for Persons with Disabilities
- 908 Bankruptcy Tax Guide
- 911 Direct Sellers
- 915 Social Security and Equivalent Railroad Retirement Benefits
- 919 How Do I Adjust My Tax Withholding?
- 925 Passive Activity and At-Risk Rules
- 926 Household Employer's Tax Guide
- 929 Tax Rules for Children and Dependents
- 936 Home Mortgage Interest Deduction
- 946 How To Depreciate Property
- 947 Practice Before the IRS and Power of Attorney
- 950 Introduction to Estate and Gift Taxes
- 967 The IRS Will Figure Your Tax
- 968 Tax Benefits for Adoption
- 969 Medical Savings Accounts (MSAs)
- 970 Tax Benefits for Education
- 971 Innocent Spouse Relief
- 972 Child Tax Credit
- 1542 Per Diem Rates
- 1544 Reporting Cash Payments of Over $10,000 (Received in a Trade or Business)
- 1546 The Taxpayer Advocate Service of the IRS

Spanish Language Publications
- 1SP Derechos del Contribuyente
- 579SP Cómo Preparar la Declaración de Impuesto Federal
- 594SP Comprendiendo el Proceso de Cobro
- 596SP Crédito por Ingreso del Trabajo
- 850 English-Spanish Glossary of Words and Phrases Used in Publications Issued by the Internal Revenue Service
- 1544SP Informe de Pagos en Efectivo en Exceso de $10,000 (Recibidos en una Ocupación o Negocio)

Commonly Used Tax Forms

See *How To Get Tax Help* for a variety of ways to get forms, including by computer, fax, phone, and mail. For fax orders only, use the catalog number when ordering.

Form Number and Title		Catalog Number	Form Number and Title		Catalog Number
1040	U.S. Individual Income Tax Return	11320	2106	Employee Business Expenses	11700
Sch A&B	Itemized Deductions & Interest and Ordinary Dividends	11330	2106-EZ	Unreimbursed Employee Business Expenses	20604
Sch C	Profit or Loss From Business	11334	2210	Underpayment of Estimated Tax by Individuals, Estates, and Trusts	11744
Sch C-EZ	Net Profit From Business	14374	2441	Child and Dependent Care Expenses	11862
Sch D	Capital Gains and Losses	11338	2848	Power of Attorney and Declaration of Representative	11980
Sch D-1	Continuation Sheet for Schedule D	10424	3903	Moving Expenses	12490
Sch E	Supplemental Income and Loss	11344	4562	Depreciation and Amortization	12906
Sch EIC	Earned Income Credit	13339	4868	Application for Automatic Extension of Time To File U.S. Individual Income Tax Return	13141
Sch F	Profit or Loss From Farming	11346	4952	Investment Interest Expense Deduction	13177
Sch H	Household Employment Taxes	12187	5329	Additional Taxes on Qualified Plans (Including IRAs) and Other Tax-Favored Accounts	13329
Sch J	Farm Income Averaging	25513	6251	Alternative Minimum Tax—Individuals	13600
Sch R	Credit for the Elderly or the Disabled	11359	8283	Noncash Charitable Contributions	62299
Sch SE	Self-Employment Tax	11358	8582	Passive Activity Loss Limitations	63704
1040A	U.S. Individual Income Tax Return	11327	8606	Nondeductible IRAs	63966
Sch 1	Interest and Ordinary Dividends for Form 1040A Filers	12075	8812	Additional Child Tax Credit	10644
Sch 2	Child and Dependent Care Expenses for Form 1040A Filers	10749	8822	Change of Address	12081
Sch 3	Credit for the Elderly or the Disabled for Form 1040A Filers	12064	8829	Expenses for Business Use of Your Home	13232
1040EZ	Income Tax Return for Single and Joint Filers With No Dependents	11329	8863	Education Credits	25379
1040-ES	Estimated Tax for Individuals	11340	9465	Installment Agreement Request	14842
1040X	Amended U.S. Individual Income Tax Return	11360			

Page 19

Appendix C

Department of the Treasury
Internal Revenue Service

Publication 530
Cat. No. 15058K

Tax Information for First-Time Homeowners

For use in preparing
2003 Returns

Get forms and other information faster and easier by:

Internet • www.irs.gov   or   FTP • ftp.irs.gov
FAX • 703-368-9694 (from your fax machine)

As of publication, 2004 forms were not available.

Contents

Important Reminders	1
Introduction	1
What You Can and Cannot Deduct	2
Real Estate Taxes	2
Home Mortgage Interest	3
Mortgage Interest Credit	6
Figuring the Credit	6
Basis	8
Figuring Your Basis	8
Adjusted Basis	9
Keeping Records	9
How To Get Tax Help	11
Index	12

Important Reminders

District of Columbia first-time homebuyer credit. The credit for first-time homebuyers in the District of Columbia is not allowable for property purchased after 2003. For more information about this credit, see page 2.

Limit on itemized deductions. Certain itemized deductions (including real estate taxes and home mortgage interest) are limited if your adjusted gross income is more than $139,500 ($69,750 if you are married filing separately). For more information, see the instructions for Schedule A (Form 1040).

Limit on mortgage interest credit. Your mortgage interest credit for 2003 can offset both your regular tax (after reduction by any foreign tax credit) and your alternative minimum tax for the year, if any. See *Figuring the Credit* under *Mortgage Interest Credit.*

Photographs of missing children. The Internal Revenue Service is a proud partner with the National Center for Missing and Exploited Children. Photographs of missing children selected by the Center may appear in this publication on pages that would otherwise be blank. You can help bring these children home by looking at the photographs and calling 1-800-THE-LOST (1-800-843-5678) if you recognize a child.

Introduction

This publication provides tax information for first-time homeowners. Your first home may be a house, condominium, cooperative apartment, mobile home, houseboat, or house trailer.

The following topics are explained.

- How you treat items such as settlement and closing costs, real estate taxes, home mortgage interest, and repairs.
- What you can and cannot deduct on your tax return.

235

- The tax credit you can claim if you received a mortgage credit certificate when you bought your home.
- Why you should keep track of adjustments to the basis of your home. (Your home's basis generally is what it costs; adjustments include the cost of any improvements you might make.)
- What records you should keep as proof of the basis and adjusted basis.

District of Columbia first-time homebuyer credit. You may be able to claim a one-time tax credit of up to $5,000 ($2,500 if married filing separately) if you buy a main home in the District of Columbia. You must reduce the basis of your home by the amount of the credit you claim. Only purchases after August 4, 1997, and before January 1, 2004, qualify for this credit.

The credit is not allowed if you acquired your home from certain related persons or by gift or inheritance.

You qualify for the credit if you (and your spouse if you are married) did not have an ownership interest in a main home in the District of Columbia for at least 1 year before buying the new home. Individuals with modified adjusted gross income of $90,000 or more ($130,000 or more in the case of a joint return) cannot claim the credit. Individuals with modified adjusted gross income between $70,000 and $90,000 (between $110,000 and $130,000 in the case of a joint return) can claim only a reduced credit.

Use Form 8859, *District of Columbia First-Time Homebuyer Credit*, to figure your credit. See the form and its instructions for more information.

Comments and suggestions. We welcome your comments about this publication and your suggestions for future editions.

You can e-mail us at *taxforms@irs.gov*. Please put "Publications Comment" on the subject line.

You can write to us at the following address:

Internal Revenue Service
Individual Forms and Publications Branch
SE:W:CAR:MP:T:I
1111 Constitution Ave. NW
Washington, DC 20224

We respond to many letters by telephone. Therefore, it would be helpful if you would include your daytime phone number, including the area code, in your correspondence.

Useful Items

You may want to see:

Publication

- ❑ 523 Selling Your Home
- ❑ 527 Residential Rental Property
- ❑ 547 Casualties, Disasters, and Thefts
- ❑ 551 Basis of Assets
- ❑ 555 Community Property
- ❑ 587 Business Use of Your Home
- ❑ 936 Home Mortgage Interest Deduction

Form (and Instructions)

- ❑ 8396 Mortgage Interest Credit

See *How To Get Tax Help*, near the end of this publication, for information about getting publications and forms.

What You Can and Cannot Deduct

To deduct expenses of owning a home, you must file Form 1040 and itemize your deductions on Schedule A (Form 1040). If you itemize, you cannot take the standard deduction. See the Form 1040 instructions if you have questions about whether to itemize your deductions or claim the standard deduction.

This section explains what expenses you can deduct as a homeowner. It also points out expenses that you cannot deduct. There are two primary discussions: real estate taxes and home mortgage interest. Generally, your real estate taxes and home mortgage interest are included in your house payment.

Your house payment. If you took out a mortgage (loan) to finance the purchase of your home, you probably have to make monthly house payments. Your house payment may include several costs of owning a home. The only costs you can deduct are real estate taxes actually paid to the taxing authority and interest that qualifies as home mortgage interest. These are discussed in more detail later.

Here are some expenses, which may be included in your house payment, that cannot be deducted.

- Fire or homeowner's insurance premiums.
- FHA mortgage insurance premiums.
- The amount applied to reduce the principal of the mortgage.

Minister's or military housing allowance. If you are a minister or a member of the uniformed services and receive a housing allowance that is not taxable, you still can deduct your real estate taxes and your home mortgage interest. You do not have to reduce your deductions by your nontaxable allowance.

Nondeductible payments. You cannot deduct any of the following items.

- Insurance, including fire and comprehensive coverage, and title and mortgage insurance.
- Wages you pay for domestic help.
- Depreciation.
- The cost of utilities, such as gas, electricity, or water.
- Most settlement costs. See *Settlement or closing costs* under *Cost as Basis*, later, for more information.

Real Estate Taxes

Most state and local governments charge an annual tax on the value of real property. This is called a *real estate tax*. You can deduct the tax if it is based on the assessed value of the real property and the taxing authority charges a uniform rate on all property in its jurisdiction. The tax must be for the welfare of the general public and not be a payment for a special privilege granted or service rendered to you.

Deductible Taxes

You can deduct real estate taxes imposed on you. You must have paid them either at settlement or closing, or to a taxing authority (either directly or through an escrow account) during the year. If you own a cooperative apartment, see *Special Rules for Cooperatives*, later.

Where to deduct real estate taxes. Enter the amount of your deductible real estate taxes on line 6 of Schedule A (Form 1040).

Real estate taxes paid at settlement or closing. Real estate taxes are generally divided so that you and the seller each pay taxes for the part of the property tax year you owned the home. Your share of these taxes is fully deductible, if you itemize your deductions.

Division of real estate taxes. For federal income tax purposes, the seller is treated as paying the property taxes up to, but not including, the date of sale. You (the buyer) are treated as paying the taxes beginning with the date of sale. This applies regardless of the lien dates under local law. Generally, this information is included on the settlement statement you get at closing.

You and the seller each are considered to have paid your own share of the taxes, even if one or the other paid the entire amount. You each can deduct your own share, if you itemize deductions, for the year the property is sold.

Example. You bought your home on September 1. The property tax year (the period to which the tax relates) in your area is the calendar year. The tax for the year was $730 and was due and paid by the seller on August 15.

You owned your new home during the property tax year for 122 days (September 1 to December 31, including your date of purchase). You figure your deduction for real estate taxes on your home as follows.

1. Enter the total real estate taxes for the real property tax year $730
2. Enter the number of days in the property tax year that you owned the property 122
3. Divide line 2 by 365 .... .3342
4. Multiply line 1 by line 3. This is your deduction. Enter it on line 6 of Schedule A (Form 1040) $244

You can deduct $244 on your return for the year if you itemize your deductions. You are considered to have paid this amount and can deduct it on your return even if, under the contract, you did not have to reimburse the seller.

Delinquent taxes. Delinquent taxes are unpaid taxes that were imposed on the seller for an earlier tax year. If you agree to pay delinquent taxes when you buy your home, you cannot deduct them. You treat them as part of the cost of your home. See *Real estate taxes*, later, under *Cost as Basis*.

Escrow accounts. Many monthly house payments include an amount placed in escrow (put in the care of a third party) for real estate taxes. You may not be able to deduct the total you pay into the escrow account. You can deduct only the real estate taxes that the lender actually paid from escrow to the taxing authority. Your real estate tax bill will show this amount.

Refund or rebate of real estate taxes. If you receive a refund or rebate of real estate taxes this year for amounts you paid this year, you must reduce your real estate tax deduction by the amount refunded to you. If the refund or rebate was for real estate taxes paid for a prior year, you may have to include some or all of the refund in your income. For more information, see *Recoveries* in Publication 525, *Taxable and Nontaxable Income*.

Items You Cannot Deduct as Real Estate Taxes

The following items are not deductible as real estate taxes.

Charges for services. An itemized charge for services to specific property or people is not a tax, even if the charge is paid to the taxing authority. You cannot deduct the charge as a real estate tax if it is:

- A unit fee for the delivery of a service (such as a $5 fee charged for every 1,000 gallons of water you use),
- A periodic charge for a residential service (such as a $20 per month or $240 annual fee charged for trash collection), or
- A flat fee charged for a single service provided by your local government (such as a $30 charge for mowing your lawn because it had grown higher than permitted under a local ordinance).

 You must look at your real estate tax bill to decide if any nondeductible itemized charges, such as those listed above, are included in the bill. If your taxing authority (or lender) does not furnish you a copy of your real estate tax bill, ask for it.

Assessments for local benefits. You cannot deduct amounts you pay for local benefits that tend to increase the value of your property. Local benefits include the construction of streets, sidewalks, or water and sewer systems. You must add these amounts to the basis of your property.

You can, however, deduct assessments (or taxes) for local benefits if they are for maintenance, repair, or interest charges related to those benefits. An example is a charge to repair an existing sidewalk and any interest included in that charge.

If only a part of the assessment is for maintenance, repair, or interest charges, you must be able to show the amount of that part to claim the deduction. If you cannot show what part of the assessment is for maintenance, repair, or interest charges, you cannot deduct any of it.

An assessment for a local benefit may be listed as an item in your real estate tax bill. If so, use the rules in this section to find how much of it, if any, you can deduct.

Transfer taxes (or stamp taxes). You cannot deduct transfer taxes and similar taxes and charges on the sale of a personal home. If you are the buyer and you pay them, include them in the cost basis of the property. If you are the seller and you pay them, they are expenses of the sale and reduce the amount realized on the sale.

Homeowners association assessments. You cannot deduct these assessments because the homeowners association, rather than a state or local government, imposes them.

Special Rules for Cooperatives

If you own a *cooperative apartment*, some special rules apply to you, though you generally receive the same tax treatment as other homeowners. As an owner of a cooperative apartment, you own shares of stock in a corporation that owns or leases housing facilities. You can deduct your share of the corporation's deductible real estate taxes if the *cooperative housing corporation* meets all of the following conditions.

- The corporation has only one class of stock outstanding.
- Each stockholder, solely because of ownership of the stock, can live in a house, apartment, or house trailer owned or leased by the corporation.
- No stockholder can receive any distribution out of capital, except on a partial or complete liquidation of the corporation.
- The tenant-stockholders pay at least 80% of the corporation's gross income for the tax year. For this purpose, gross income means all income received during the entire tax year, including any received before the corporation changed to cooperative ownership.

Tenant-stockholders. A tenant-stockholder can be any entity (such as a corporation, trust, estate, partnership, or association) as well as an individual. The tenant-stockholder does not have to live in any of the cooperative's dwelling units. The units that the tenant-stockholder has the right to occupy can be rented to others.

Deductible taxes. You figure your share of real estate taxes in the following way.

1) Divide the number of your shares of stock by the total number of shares outstanding, including any shares held by the corporation.

2) Multiply the corporation's deductible real estate taxes by the number you figured in (1). This is your share of the real estate taxes.

Generally, the corporation will tell you your share of its real estate tax. This is the amount you can deduct if it reasonably reflects the cost of real estate taxes for your dwelling unit.

Refund of real estate taxes. If the corporation receives a refund of real estate taxes it paid in an earlier year, it must reduce the amount of real estate taxes paid this year when it allocates the tax expense to you. Your deduction for real estate taxes the corporation paid this year is reduced by your share of the refund the corporation received.

Home Mortgage Interest

This section of the publication gives you basic information about home mortgage interest, including information on interest paid at settlement, points, and Form 1098, *Mortgage Interest Statement*.

Most home buyers take out a mortgage (loan) to buy their home. They then make monthly payments to either the mortgage holder or someone collecting the payments for the mortgage holder. (See *Your house payment*, earlier, under *What You Can and Cannot Deduct*.)

Usually, you can deduct the entire part of your payment that is for mortgage interest, if you itemize your deductions on Schedule A (Form 1040). However, your deduction may be limited if:

- Your total mortgage balance is more than $1 million ($500,000 if married filing separately), or
- You took out a mortgage for reasons other than to buy, build, or improve your home.

If either of these situations applies to you, you will need to get Publication 936. You also may need Publication 936 if you later refinance your mortgage or buy a second home.

Refund of home mortgage interest. If you receive a refund of home mortgage interest that you deducted in an earlier year and that reduced your tax, you generally must include the refund in income in the year you receive it. For more information, see *Recoveries* in Publication 525. The amount of the refund will usually be shown on the mortgage interest statement you receive from your mortgage lender. See *Mortgage Interest Statement*, later.

Deductible Mortgage Interest

To be deductible, the interest you pay must be on a loan secured by your main home or a second home. The loan can be a first or second mortgage, a home improvement loan, or a home equity loan.

Prepaid interest. If you pay interest in advance for a period that goes beyond the end of the tax year, you must spread this interest over the tax years to which it applies. You can deduct in each year only the interest that qualifies as home mortgage interest for that year. However, there is an exception that applies to points, discussed later.

Late payment charge on mortgage payment. You can deduct as home mortgage interest a late payment charge if it was not for a specific service in connection with your mortgage loan.

Mortgage prepayment penalty. If you pay off your home mortgage early, you may have to pay a penalty. You can deduct that penalty as home mortgage interest provided the penalty is not for a specific service performed or cost incurred in connection with your mortgage loan.

Ground rent. In some states (such as Maryland), you may buy your home subject to a ground rent. A ground rent is an obligation you

Page 3

assume to pay a fixed amount per year on the property. Under this arrangement, you are leasing (rather than buying) the land on which your home is located.

Redeemable ground rents. If you make annual or periodic rental payments on a redeemable ground rent, you can deduct the payments as mortgage interest. The ground rent is a redeemable ground rent only if all of the following are true.

- Your lease, including renewal periods, is for more than 15 years.
- You can freely assign the lease.
- You have a present or future right (under state or local law) to end the lease and buy the lessor's entire interest in the land by paying a specified amount.
- The lessor's interest in the land is primarily a security interest to protect the rental payments to which he or she is entitled.

Payments made to end the lease and buy the lessor's entire interest in the land are not redeemable ground rents. You cannot deduct them.

Nonredeemable ground rents. Payments on a nonredeemable ground rent are not mortgage interest. You can deduct them as rent only if they are a business expense or if they are for rental property.

Cooperative apartment. You can usually treat the interest on a loan you took out to buy stock in a cooperative housing corporation as home mortgage interest if you own a cooperative apartment and the cooperative housing corporation meets the conditions described earlier under *Special Rules for Cooperatives*. In addition, you can treat as home mortgage interest your share of the corporation's deductible mortgage interest. Figure your share of mortgage interest the same way that is shown for figuring your share of real estate taxes in the *Example* under *Division of real estate taxes*. For more information on cooperatives, see *Special Rule for Tenant-Stockholders in Cooperative Housing Corporations* in Publication 936.

Refund of cooperative's mortgage interest. You must reduce your mortgage interest deduction by your share of any cash portion of a patronage dividend that the cooperative receives. The patronage dividend is a partial refund to the cooperative housing corporation of mortgage interest it paid in a prior year.

If you receive a Form 1098 from the cooperative housing corporation, the form should show only the amount you can deduct.

Mortgage Interest Paid at Settlement

One item that normally appears on a settlement or closing statement is home mortgage interest.

You can deduct the interest that you pay at settlement if you itemize your deductions on Schedule A (Form 1040). This amount should be included in the mortgage interest statement provided by your lender. See the discussion under *Mortgage Interest Statement*, later. Also,

Page 4

if you pay interest in advance, see *Prepaid interest,* earlier, and *Points,* next.

Points

The term *points* is used to describe certain charges paid, or treated as paid, by a borrower to obtain a home mortgage. Points also may be called loan origination fees, maximum loan charges, loan discount, or discount points.

A borrower is treated as paying any points that a home seller pays for the borrower's mortgage. See *Points paid by the seller,* later.

General rule. You cannot deduct the full amount of points in the year paid. They are prepaid interest, so you generally must deduct them over the life (term) of the mortgage.

Exception. You can deduct the full amount of points in the year paid if you meet all the following tests.

1) Your loan is secured by your main home. (Generally, your main home is the one you live in most of the time.)

2) Paying points is an established business practice in the area where the loan was made.

3) The points paid were not more than the points generally charged in that area.

4) You use the cash method of accounting. This means you report income in the year you receive it and deduct expenses in the year you pay them. Most individuals use this method.

5) The points were not paid in place of amounts that ordinarily are stated separately on the settlement statement, such as appraisal fees, inspection fees, title fees, attorney fees, and property taxes.

6) The funds you provided at or before closing, plus any points the seller paid, were at least as much as the points charged. The funds you provided do not have to have been applied to the points. They can include a down payment, an escrow deposit, earnest money, and other funds you paid at or before closing for any purpose. You cannot have borrowed these funds from your lender or mortgage broker.

7) You use your loan to buy or build your main home.

8) The points were computed as a percentage of the principal amount of the mortgage.

9) The amount is clearly shown on the settlement statement (such as the Uniform Settlement Statement, Form HUD-1) as points charged for the mortgage. The points may be shown as paid from either your funds or the seller's.

Note. If you meet all of the tests listed above and you itemize your deductions in the year you get the loan, you can either deduct the full amount of points in the year paid or deduct them over the life of the loan, beginning in the year you get the loan. If you do not itemize your deductions in the year you get the loan, you can spread the points over the life of the loan and

deduct the appropriate amount in each future year, if any, when you do itemize your deductions.

Home improvement loan. You can also fully deduct in the year paid points paid on a loan to improve your main home, if tests (1) through (6) are met.

Points not fully deductible in year paid. If you do not qualify under the exception to deduct the full amount of points in the year paid (or choose not to do so), see *Points* in chapter 5 of Publication 535, *Business Expenses,* for the rules on when and how much you can deduct.

Figure A. You can use *Figure A* as a quick guide to see whether your points are fully deductible in the year paid.

Amounts charged for services. Amounts charged by the lender for specific services connected to the loan are not interest. Examples of these charges are:

- Appraisal fees,
- Notary fees,
- Preparation costs for the mortgage note or deed of trust,
- Mortgage insurance premiums, and
- VA funding fees.

You cannot deduct these amounts as points either in the year paid or over the life of the mortgage. For information about the tax treatment of these amounts and other settlement fees and closing costs, see *Basis,* later.

Points paid by the seller. The term points includes loan placement fees that the seller pays to the lender to arrange financing for the buyer.

Treatment by seller. The seller *cannot* deduct these fees as interest; but, they are a selling expense that reduces the seller's amount realized. See Publication 523 for more information.

Treatment by buyer. The buyer treats seller-paid points as if he or she had paid them. If all the tests under *Exception* (discussed earlier) are met, the buyer can deduct the points in the year paid. If any of those tests is not met, the buyer must deduct the points over the life of the loan.

The buyer must also reduce the basis of the home by the amount of the seller-paid points. For more information about the basis of your home, see *Basis,* later.

Funds provided are less than points. If you meet all the tests under *Exception* (discussed earlier) except that the funds you provided were less than the points charged to you (test 6), you can deduct the points in the year paid up to the amount of funds you provided. In addition, you can deduct any points paid by the seller.

Example 1. When you took out a $100,000 mortgage loan to buy your home in December, you were charged one point ($1,000). You meet all the tests for deducting points in the year paid (see *Exception*), except the only funds you provided were a $750 down payment. Of the $1,000 you were charged for points, you can deduct

Figure A. **Are My Points Fully Deductible This Year?**

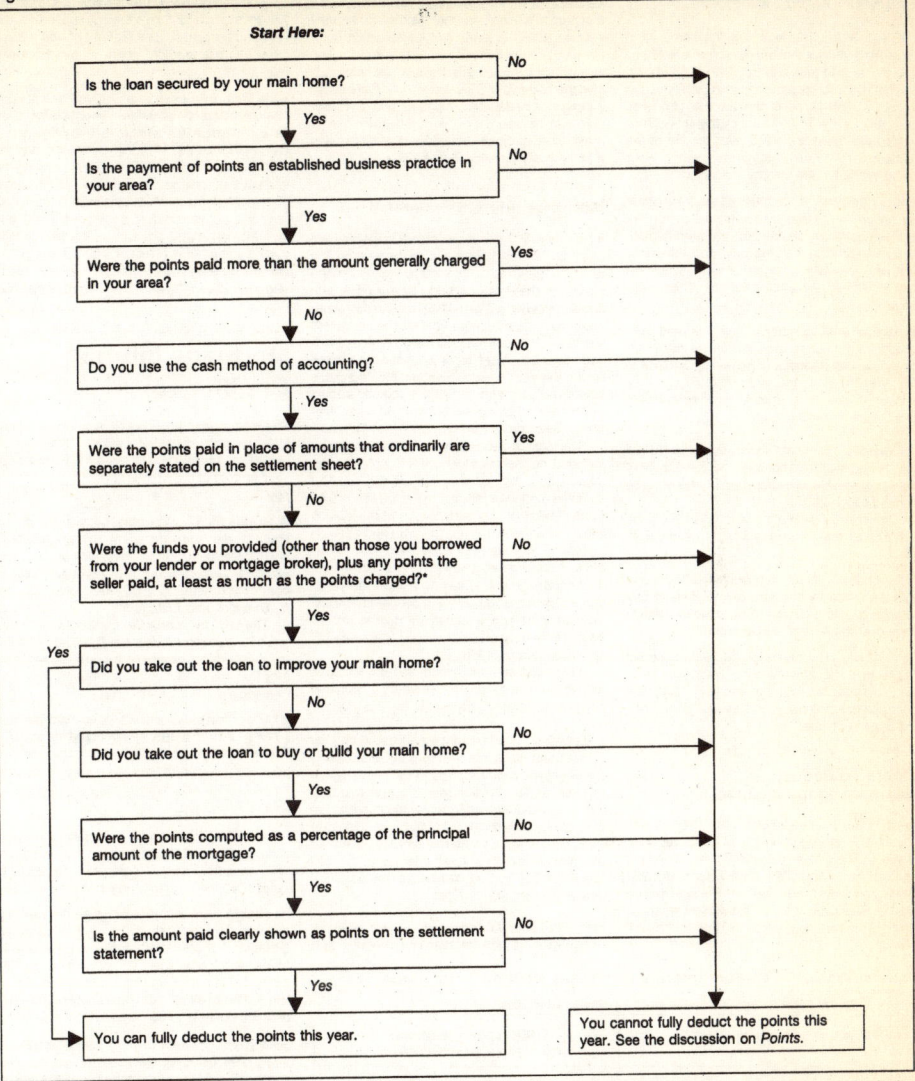

* The funds you provided do not have to have been applied to the points. They can include a down payment, an escrow deposit, earnest money, and other funds you paid at or before closing for any purpose.

$750 in the year paid. You spread the remaining $250 over the life of the mortgage.

Example 2. The facts are the same as in Example 1, except that the person who sold you your home also paid one point ($1,000) to help you get your mortgage. In the year paid, you can deduct $1,750 ($750 of the amount you were charged plus the $1,000 paid by the seller). You spread the remaining $250 over the life of the mortgage. You must reduce the basis of your home by the $1,000 paid by the seller.

Excess points. If you meet all the tests under Exception except that the points paid were more than are generally charged in your area (test 3), you can deduct in the year paid only the points that are generally charged. You must spread any additional points over the life of the mortgage.

Mortgage ending early. If you spread your deduction for points over the life of the mortgage, you can deduct any remaining balance in the year the mortgage ends. A mortgage may end early due to a prepayment, refinancing, foreclosure, or similar event.

Example. Dan paid $3,000 in points in 1996 that he had to spread out over the 15-year life of the mortgage. He had deducted $1,400 of these points through 2002.

Dan prepaid his mortgage in full in 2003. He can deduct the remaining $1,600 of points in 2003.

Exception. If you refinance the mortgage with the same lender, you cannot deduct any remaining points for the year. Instead, deduct them over the term of the new loan.

Form 1098. The mortgage interest statement you receive should show not only the total interest paid during the year, but also your deductible points paid during the year. See *Mortgage Interest Statement*, later.

Where To Deduct Home Mortgage Interest

Enter on line 10 of your Schedule A (Form 1040) the home mortgage interest and points reported to you on Form 1098 (discussed next). If you did not receive a Form 1098, enter your deductible interest on line 11, and any deductible points on line 12. See *Table 1* for a summary of where to deduct home mortgage interest and real estate taxes.

Table 1. **Where To Deduct Interest and Taxes Paid on Your Home**
See the text for information on what expenses are eligible.

IF you are eligible to deduct...	THEN report the amount on Schedule A (Form 1040)...
Real estate taxes	line 6
Home mortgage interest and points reported on Form 1098	line 10
Home mortgage interest *not* reported on Form 1098	line 11
Points *not* reported on Form 1098	line 12

If you paid home mortgage interest to the person from whom you bought your home, show that person's name, address, and social security number (SSN) or employer identification number (EIN) on the dotted lines next to line 11. The seller must give you this number and you must give the seller your SSN. Form W-9, *Request for Taxpayer Identification Number and Certification*, can be used for this purpose. Failure to meet either of these requirements may result in a $50 penalty for each failure.

Mortgage Interest Statement

If you paid $600 or more of mortgage interest (including certain points) during the year on any one mortgage to a mortgage holder in the course of that holder's trade or business, you should receive a **Form 1098** or similar statement from the mortgage holder. The statement will show the total interest paid on your mortgage during the year. If you bought a main home during the year, it also will show the deductible points you paid and any points you can deduct that were paid by the person who sold you your home. See *Points*, earlier.

The interest you paid at settlement should be included on the statement. If it is not, add the interest from the settlement sheet that qualifies as home mortgage interest to the total shown on Form 1098 or similar statement. Put the total on line 10 of Form 1040 (Form 1040) and attach a statement to your return explaining the difference. Write "See attached" to the right of line 10.

A mortgage holder can be a financial institution, a governmental unit, or a cooperative housing corporation. If a statement comes from a cooperative housing corporation, it generally will show your share of interest.

Your mortgage interest statement for 2003 should be sent to you by February 2, 2004. A copy of this form will be sent to the IRS also.

Example. You bought a new home on May 3. You paid no points on the purchase. During the year, you made mortgage payments which included $4,480 deductible interest on your new home. The settlement sheet for the purchase of the home included interest of $620 for 29 days in May. The mortgage statement you receive from the lender includes total interest of $5,100 ($4,480 + $620). You can deduct the $5,100 if you itemize your deductions.

Refund of overpaid interest. If you receive a refund of mortgage interest you overpaid in a prior year, you generally will receive a Form 1098 showing the refund in box 3. Generally, you must include the refund in income in the year you receive it. See *Refund of home mortgage interest*, earlier, under *Home Mortgage Interest*.

More than one borrower. If you and at least one other person (other than your spouse if you file a joint return) were liable for and paid interest on a mortgage that was for your home, and the other person received a Form 1098 showing the interest that was paid during the year, attach a statement to your return explaining this. Show how much of the interest each of you paid, and give the name and address of the person who received the Form 1098. Deduct your share of the interest on line 11 of Schedule A (Form 1040), and write "See attached" to the right of that line.

Mortgage Interest Credit

The mortgage interest credit is intended to help lower-income individuals afford home ownership. If you qualify, you can claim the credit each year for part of the home mortgage interest you pay.

Who qualifies. You may be eligible for the credit if you were issued a *mortgage credit certificate (MCC)* from your state or local government. Generally, an MCC is issued only in connection with a new mortgage for the purchase of your main home.

The MCC will show the certificate credit rate you will use to figure your credit. It also will show the certified indebtedness amount. Only the interest on that amount qualifies for the credit. See *Figuring the Credit*, later.

 You must contact the appropriate government agency about getting an MCC before you get a mortgage and buy your home. Contact your state or local housing finance agency for information about the availability of MCCs in your area.

How to claim the credit. To claim the credit, complete **Form 8396** and attach it to your Form 1040. Include the credit in your total for line 51 of Form 1040; be sure to check box a on that line.

Reducing your home mortgage interest deduction. If you itemize your deductions on Schedule A (Form 1040), you must reduce your home mortgage interest deduction by the amount of the mortgage interest credit shown on line 3 of Form 8396. You must do this even if part of that amount is to be carried forward to 2004.

Selling your home. If you purchase a home after 1990 using an MCC, and you sell that home within 9 years, you may have to recapture (repay) all or part of the benefit you received from the MCC program. For additional information, see *Recapturing (Paying Back) a Federal Mortgage Subsidy*, in Publication 523.

Figuring the Credit

Figure your credit on **Form 8396.**

Mortgage not more than certified indebtedness. If your mortgage loan amount is equal to (or smaller than) the certified indebtedness amount shown on your MCC, enter on line 1 of Form 8396 all the interest you paid on your mortgage during the year.

Mortgage more than certified indebtedness. If your mortgage loan amount is larger than the certified indebtedness amount shown on your MCC, you can figure the credit on only part of the interest you paid. To find the amount to enter on line 1, multiply the total interest you paid during the year on your mortgage by the following fraction.

$$\frac{\text{Certified indebtedness amount on your MCC}}{\text{Original amount of your mortgage}}$$

Example. Emily bought a home this year. Her mortgage loan is $125,000. The certified indebtedness amount on her MCC is $100,000. She paid $7,500 interest this year. Emily figures the interest to enter on line 1 of Form 8396 as follows:

$$\frac{\$100,000}{\$125,000} = 80\% \ (.80)$$

$$\$7,500 \ \times \ .80 \ = \ \$6,000$$

Emily enters $6,000 on line 1 of Form 8396. In each later year, she will figure her credit using only 80% of the interest she pays for that year.

Limits

Two limits may apply to your credit.

- A limit based on the credit rate, and
- A limit based on your tax.

Limit based on credit rate. If the certificate credit rate is higher than 20%, the credit you are allowed cannot be more than $2,000.

Limit based on tax. Your credit (after applying the limit based on the credit rate) cannot be more than your regular tax liability on line 41 of Form 1040, *plus* any alternative minimum tax on line 42 of Form 8396, *minus* certain other credits. Use Form 8396 to figure this limit.

Dividing the Credit

If two or more persons (other than a married couple filing a joint return) hold an interest in the home to which the MCC relates, the credit must be divided based on the interest held by each person.

Example. John and his brother, George, were issued an MCC. They used it to get a mortgage on their main home. John has a 60% ownership interest in the home, and George has a 40% ownership interest in the home. John paid $5,400 mortgage interest this year and George paid $3,600.

The MCC shows a credit rate of 25% and a certified indebtedness amount of $130,000. The loan amount (mortgage) on their home is $120,000. The credit is limited to $2,000 because the credit rate is more than 20%.

Table 2. **Effect of Refinancing on Your Credit**

IF you get a new (reissued) MCC and the amount of your new mortgage is	THEN the interest you claim on Form 8396, line 1, is* ....
Smaller than or equal to the certified indebtedness amount on the new MCC	All the interest paid during the year on your new mortgage.
Larger than the certified indebtedness amount on the new MCC	Interest paid during the year on your new mortgage multiplied by the following fraction. $$\frac{\text{Certified indebtedness amount on your new MCC}}{\text{Original amount of your mortgage}}$$

*The credit using the new MCC cannot be more than the credit using the old MCC. See *New MCC cannot increase your credit.*

John figures the credit by multiplying the mortgage interest he paid this year ($5,400) by the certificate credit rate (25%) for a total of $1,350. His credit is limited to $1,200 ($2,000 × 60%).

George figures the credit by multiplying the mortgage interest he paid in this year ($3,600) by the certificate credit rate (25%) for a total of $900. His credit is limited to $800 ($2,000 × 40%).

Carryforward

If your allowable credit is reduced because of the limit based on your tax, you can carry forward the unused portion of the credit to the next 3 years or until used, whichever comes first.

Example. You receive a mortgage credit certificate from State X. This year, your regular tax liability is $1,100, you owe no alternative minimum tax, and your mortgage interest credit is $1,700. You claim no other credits. Your unused mortgage interest credit for this year is $600 ($1,700 − $1,100). You can carry forward this amount to the next 3 years or until used, whichever comes first.

Credit rate more than 20%. If you are subject to the $2,000 limit because your certificate credit rate is more than 20%, you cannot carry forward any amount more than $2,000 (or your share of the $2,000 if you must divide the credit).

Example. In the earlier example under *Dividing the Credit,* John and George used the entire $2,000 credit. The excess $150 for John ($1,350 − $1,200) and $100 for George ($900 − $800) cannot be carried forward to future years, despite the respective tax liabilities for John and George.

Refinancing

If you refinance your original mortgage loan on which you had been given an MCC, you must get a new MCC to be able to claim the credit on the new loan. The amount of credit you can claim on the new loan may change. Table 2 summarizes how to figure your credit if you refinance your original mortgage loan.

An issuer may reissue an MCC after you refinance your mortgage, but only up to one year after the date of the refinancing. If you did not get a new MCC, you may want to contact the state or local housing finance agency that issued your original MCC for information about whether you can get a reissued MCC.

Year of refinancing. In the year of refinancing, add the applicable amount of interest paid on the old mortgage and the applicable amount of interest paid on the new mortgage, and enter the total on line 1 of Form 8396.

If your new MCC has a credit rate different from the rate on the old MCC, you must attach a statement to Form 8396. The statement must show the calculation for lines 1, 2, and 3 for the part of the year when the old MCC was in effect. It must show a separate calculation for the part of the year when the new MCC was in effect. Combine the amounts from both calculations for line 3, enter the total on line 3 of the form, and write "see attached" on the dotted line.

New MCC cannot increase your credit. The credit that you claim with your new MCC cannot be more than the credit that you could have claimed with your old MCC.

In most cases, the agency that issues your new MCC will make sure that it does not increase your credit. However, if either your old loan or your new loan has a variable (adjustable) interest rate, you will need to check this yourself. In that case, you will need to know the amount of the credit you could have claimed using the old MCC.

There are two methods for figuring the credit you could have claimed. Under one method, you figure the actual credit that would have been allowed. This means you use the credit rate on the old MCC and the interest you would have paid on the old loan.

If your old loan was a variable rate mortgage, you can use another method to determine the credit that you could have claimed. Under this method, you figure the credit using a payment schedule of a hypothetical self-amortizing mortgage with level payments projected to the final maturity date of the old mortgage. The interest rate of the hypothetical mortgage is the annual percentage rate (APR) of the new mortgage for purposes of the Federal Truth in Lending Act. The principal of the hypothetical mortgage is the remaining outstanding balance of the certified mortgage indebtedness shown on the old MCC.

 You must choose one method and use it consistently beginning with the first tax year for which you claim the credit based on the new MCC.

Table 3. **Adjusted Basis**

This table lists examples of some items that generally will increase or decrease your basis in your home. It is not intended to be all-inclusive.

Increases to Basis	Decreases to Basis
Improvements: • Putting an addition on your home • Replacing an entire roof • Paving your driveway • Installing central air conditioning • Rewiring your home Assessments for local improvements (see *Assessments for local benefits,* under *What You Can and Cannot Deduct*) Amounts spent to restore damaged property	• Insurance or other reimbursement for casualty losses • Deductible casualty loss not covered by insurance • Payments received for easement or right-of-way granted • Depreciation allowed or allowable if home is used for business or rental purposes • Value of subsidy for energy conservation measure excluded from income

 As part of your tax records, you should keep your old MCC and the schedule of payments for your old mortgage.

Basis

Basis is your starting point for figuring a gain or loss if you later sell your home, or for figuring depreciation if you later use part of your home for business purposes or for rent.

While you own your home, you may add certain items to your basis. You may subtract certain other items from your basis. These items are called adjustments to basis and are explained later under *Adjusted Basis.*

It is important that you understand these terms when you first acquire your home because you must keep track of your basis and adjusted basis during the period you own your home. You also must keep records of the events that affect basis or adjusted basis. See *Keeping Records,* later.

Figuring Your Basis

How you figure your basis depends on how you acquire your home. If you buy or build your home, your cost is your basis. If you receive your home as a gift, your basis is usually the same as the adjusted basis of the person who gave you the property. If you inherit your home from a decedent, the fair market value at the date of the decedent's death is generally your basis. Each of these topics is discussed later.

Fair market value. This is the price at which property would change hands between a willing buyer and a willing seller, neither being under any compulsion to buy or sell and who both have a reasonable knowledge of all the necessary facts.

Property transferred from a spouse. If your home is transferred to you from your spouse, or from your former spouse as a result of a divorce, your basis is the same as your spouse's (or former spouse's) adjusted basis just before the transfer. Publication 504, *Divorced or Separated Individuals,* fully discusses transfers between spouses.

Cost as Basis

The cost of your home, whether you purchased it or constructed it, is the amount you paid for it, including any debt you assumed.

The cost of your home includes most settlement or closing costs you paid when you bought the home. If you built your home, your cost includes most closing costs paid when you bought the land or settled on your mortgage.

Purchase. The basis of a home you bought is the amount you paid for it. This usually includes your down payment and any debt you assumed. The basis of a cooperative apartment is the amount you paid for your shares in the corporation that owns or controls the property. This amount includes any purchase commissions or other costs of acquiring the shares.

Construction. If you contracted to have your home built on land that you own, your basis in the home is your basis in the land plus the amount you paid to have the home built. This includes the cost of labor and materials, the amount you paid the contractor, any architect's fees, building permit charges, utility meter and connection charges, and legal fees that are directly connected with building your home. If you built all or part of your home yourself, your basis is the total amount it cost you to build it. You cannot include the value of your own labor or any other labor for which you did not pay.

Real estate taxes. Real estate taxes are usually divided so that you and the seller each pay taxes for the part of the property tax year that each owned the home. See the earlier discussion of *Real estate taxes paid at settlement or closing,* under *Real Estate Taxes,* to figure the real estate taxes you paid or are considered to have paid.

If you pay any part of the seller's share of the real estate taxes (the taxes up to the date of sale), and the seller did not reimburse you, add those taxes to your basis in the home. You cannot deduct them as taxes paid.

If the seller paid any of your share of the real estate taxes (the taxes beginning with the date of sale), you can still deduct those taxes. Do not include those taxes in your basis. If you did not reimburse the seller, you must reduce your basis by the amount of those taxes.

Example 1. You bought your home on September 1. The property tax year in your area is the calendar year, and the tax is due on August 15. The real estate taxes on the home you bought were $1,275 for the year and had been paid by the seller on August 15. You did not reimburse the seller for your share of the real estate taxes from September 1 through December 31. You must reduce the basis of your home by the $426 [((122 + 365) × $1,275] the seller paid for you. You can deduct your $426 share of real estate taxes on your return for the year you purchased your home.

Example 2. You bought your home on May 3, 2003. The property tax year in your area is the calendar year. The taxes for the previous year are assessed on January 2 and are due on May 31 and November 30. Under state law, the taxes become a lien on May 31. You agreed to pay all taxes due after the date of sale. The taxes due in 2003 for 2002 were $1,375. The taxes due in 2004 for 2003 will be $1,425.

You cannot deduct any of the taxes paid in 2003 because they relate to the 2002 property tax year and you did not own the home until 2003. Instead, you add the $1,375 to the cost (basis) of your home.

You owned the home in 2003 for 243 days (May 3 to December 31), so you can take a tax deduction on your 2004 return of $949 [((243 + 365) × $1,425] paid in 2004 for 2003. You add the remaining $476 ($1,425 − $949) of taxes paid in 2004 to the cost (basis) of your home.

Settlement or closing costs. If you bought your home, you probably paid settlement or closing costs in addition to the contract price. These costs are divided between you and the seller according to the sales contract, local custom, or understanding of the parties. If you built your home, you probably paid these costs when you bought the land or settled on your mortgage.

The only settlement or closing costs you can deduct are home mortgage interest and certain real estate taxes. You deduct them in the year you buy your home if you itemize your deductions. You can add certain other settlement or closing costs to the basis of your home.

Items added to basis. You can include in your basis the settlement fees and closing costs you paid for buying your home. A fee is for buying the home if you would have had to pay it even if you paid cash for the home.

The following are some of the settlement fees and closing costs that you can include in the original basis of your home.

• Abstract fees (abstract of title fees).

• Charges for installing utility services.

• Legal fees (including fees for the title search and preparation of the sales contract and deed).

• Recording fees.

• Surveys.

• Transfer taxes.

• Owner's title insurance.

• Any amount the seller owes that you agree to pay, such as back taxes or interest, recording or mortgage fees, cost for improvements or repairs, and sales commissions.

Page 8

If the seller actually paid for any item for which you are liable and for which you can take a deduction (such as your share of the real estate taxes for the year of sale), you must reduce your basis by that amount unless you are charged for it in the settlement.

Items not added to basis and not deductible. Here are some settlement and closing costs that cannot deduct *or* add to your basis.

1) Fire insurance premiums.
2) Charges for using utilities or other services related to occupancy of the home before closing.
3) Rent for occupying the home before closing.
4) Charges connected with getting or refinancing a mortgage loan, such as:
   a) FHA mortgage insurance premiums and VA funding fees,
   b) Loan assumption fees,
   c) Cost of a credit report, and
   d) Fee for an appraisal required by a lender.

Points paid by seller. If you bought your home after April 3, 1994, you must reduce your basis by any points paid for your mortgage by the person who sold you your home.

If you bought your home after 1990 but before April 4, 1994, you must reduce your basis by seller-paid points only if you deducted them. See *Points*, earlier, for the rules on deducting points.

Gift

To figure the basis of property you receive as a gift, you must know its adjusted basis (defined later) to the donor just before it was given to you, its FMV at the time it was given to you, and any gift tax paid on it.

Donor's adjusted basis is more than FMV. If someone gave you your home and the donor's adjusted basis, when it was given to you, was more than the fair market value, your basis at the time of receipt is the same as the donor's adjusted basis.

Disposition basis. If the donor's adjusted basis at the time of the gift is more than the FMV, your basis when you dispose of the property will depend on whether you have a gain or a loss.

- If using the donor's adjusted basis results in a loss when you sell the home, you must use the fair market value of the home at the time of the gift as your basis.
- If using the fair market value results in a gain, you have neither a gain nor a loss.

Donor's adjusted basis equal to or less than the FMV. If someone gave you your home after 1976 and the donor's adjusted basis, when it was given to you, was equal to or less than the fair market value, your basis at the time of receipt is the same as the donor's adjusted basis,

plus the part of any federal gift tax paid that is due to the net increase in value of the home.

Part of federal gift tax due to net increase in value. Figure the part of the federal gift tax paid that is due to the net increase in value of the home by multiplying the total federal gift tax paid by a fraction. The numerator (top part) of the fraction is the net increase in the value of the home, and the denominator (bottom part) is the value of the home for gift tax purposes after reduction for any annual exclusion and marital or charitable deduction that applies to the gift. The net increase in the value of the home is its fair market value minus the adjusted basis of the donor.

Publication 551 gives more information, including examples, on figuring your basis when you receive property as a gift.

Inheritance

Your basis in a home you inherited is generally the fair market value of the home on the date of the decedent's death or on the alternate valuation date if the personal representative for the estate chooses to use alternative valuation.

If an estate tax return was filed, your basis is generally the value of the home listed on the estate tax return.

If an estate tax return was *not* filed, your basis is the appraised value of the home at the decedent's date of death for state inheritance or transmission taxes. Publication 551 and Publication 559, *Survivors, Executors, and Administrators,* have more information on the basis of inherited property.

Adjusted Basis

While you own your home, various events may take place that can change the original basis of your home. These events can increase or decrease your original basis. The result is called *adjusted basis.* See *Table 3*, earlier, for a list of some of the items that can adjust your basis.

Improvements. An improvement materially adds to the value of your home, considerably prolongs its useful life, or adapts it to new uses. You must add the cost of any improvements to the basis of your home. You *cannot* deduct these costs.

Improvements include putting a recreation room in your unfinished basement, adding another bathroom or bedroom, putting up a fence, putting in new plumbing or wiring, installing a new roof, and paving your driveway.

Amount added to basis. The amount you add to your basis for improvements is your actual cost. This includes all costs for material and labor, except your own labor, and all expenses related to the improvement. For example, if you had your lot surveyed to put up a fence, the cost of the survey is a part of the cost of the fence.

You also must add to your basis state and local assessments for improvements such as streets and sidewalks if they increase the value of the property. These assessments are discussed earlier under *Real Estate Taxes.*

Repairs versus improvements. A repair keeps your home in an ordinary, efficient operating condition. It does not add to the value of your home or prolong its life. Repairs include repainting your home inside or outside, fixing your gutters or floors, fixing leaks or plastering, and replacing broken window panes. You cannot deduct repair costs and generally cannot add them to the basis of your home.

However, repairs that are done as part of an extensive remodeling or restoration of your home are considered improvements. You add them to the basis of your home.

Records to keep. You can use *Table 4* (at the end of the publication) as a guide to help you keep track of improvements to your home. Also see *Keeping Records,* later.

Energy conservation subsidy. If a public utility gives you (directly or indirectly) a subsidy for the purchase or installation of an energy conservation measure for your home, do not include the value of that subsidy in your income. You must reduce the basis of your home by that value.

An energy conservation measure is an installation or modification primarily designed to reduce consumption of electricity or natural gas or to improve the management of energy demand.

Keeping Records

Keeping full and accurate records is vital to properly report your income and expenses, to support your deductions and credits, and to know the basis or adjusted basis of your home. These records include your purchase contract and settlement papers if you bought the property, or other objective evidence if you acquired it by gift, inheritance, or similar means. You should keep any receipts, canceled checks, and similar evidence for improvements or other additions to the basis. In addition, you should keep track of any decreases to the basis such as those listed in *Table 3.*

How to keep records. How you keep records is up to you, but they must be clear and accurate and must be available to the IRS.

How long to keep records. You must keep your records for as long as they are important for meeting any provision of the federal tax law.

Keep records that support an item of income, a deduction, or a credit, appearing on a return until the period of limitations for the return runs out. (A period of limitations is the period of time after which no legal action can be brought.) For assessment of tax you owe, this is generally 3 years from the date you filed the return. For filing a claim for credit or refund, this is generally 3 years from the date you filed the original return, or 2 years from the date you paid the tax, whichever is later. Returns filed before the due date are treated as filed on the due date.

You may need to keep records relating to the basis of property (discussed earlier) longer than for the period of limitations. Keep those records as long as they are important in figuring the basis of the original or replacement property. Generally, this means for as long as you own the property and, after you dispose of it, for the period of limitations that applies to you.

Table 4. Record of Home Improvements

Keep this for your records. Also, keep receipts or other proof of improvements.

Caution: *Remove from this record any improvements that are no longer part of your main home. For example, if you put wall-to-wall carpeting in your home and later replace it with new wall-to-wall carpeting, remove the cost of the first carpeting.*

(a) Type of Improvement	(b) Date	(c) Amount	(a) Type of Improvement	(b) Date	(c) Amount
Additions:			**Heating & Air Conditioning:**		
Bedroom			Heating system		
Bathroom			Central air conditioning		
Deck			Furnace		
Garage			Duct work		
Porch			Central humidifier		
Patio			Filtration system		
Storage shed			Other		
Fireplace					
Other			**Electrical:**		
			Lighting fixtures		
Lawn & Grounds:			Wiring upgrades		
Landscaping			Other		
Driveway					
Walkway			**Plumbing:**		
Fences			Water heater		
Retaining wall			Soft water system		
Sprinkler system			Filtration system		
Swimming pool			Other		
Exterior lighting					
Other			**Insulation:**		
			Attic		
Communications:			Walls		
Satellite dish			Floors		
Intercom			Pipes and duct work		
Security system			Other		
Other					
			Interior Improvements:		
Miscellaneous:			Built-in appliances		
Storm windows and doors			Kitchen modernization		
Roof			Bathroom modernization		
Central vacuum			Flooring		
Other			Wall-to-wall carpeting		
			Other		

Page 10

How To Get Tax Help

You can get help with unresolved tax issues, order free publications and forms, ask tax questions, and get more information from the IRS in several ways. By selecting the method that is best for you, you will have quick and easy access to tax help.

Contacting your Taxpayer Advocate. If you have attempted to deal with an IRS problem unsuccessfully, you should contact your Taxpayer Advocate.

The Taxpayer Advocate independently represents your interests and concerns within the IRS by protecting your rights and resolving problems that have not been fixed through normal channels. While Taxpayer Advocates cannot change the tax law or make a technical tax decision, they can clear up problems that resulted from previous contacts and ensure that your case is given a complete and impartial review.

To contact your Taxpayer Advocate:

- Call the Taxpayer Advocate toll free at **1–877–777–4778**.
- Call, write, or fax the Taxpayer Advocate office in your area.
- Call **1–800–829–4059** if you are a TTY/TDD user.
- Visit the web site at **www.irs.gov/advocate**.

For more information, see Publication 1546, *The Taxpayer Advocate Service of the IRS.*

Free tax services. To find out what services are available, get Publication 910, *Guide to Free Tax Services.* It contains a list of free tax publications and an index of tax topics. It also describes other free tax information services, including tax education and assistance programs and a list of TeleTax topics.

Internet. You can access the IRS web site 24 hours a day, 7 days a week at **www.irs.gov** to:

- *E-file.* Access commercial tax preparation and *e-file* services available for free to eligible taxpayers.
- Check the amount of advance child tax credit payments you received in 2003.
- Check the status of your 2003 refund. Click on "Where's My Refund" and then on "Go Get My Refund Status." Be sure to wait at least 6 weeks from the date you filed your return (3 weeks if you filed electronically) and have your 2003 tax return available because you will need to know your filing status and the exact whole dollar amount of your refund.
- Download forms, instructions, and publications.
- Order IRS products on-line.
- See answers to frequently asked tax questions.
- Search publications on-line by topic or keyword.
- Figure your withholding allowances using our Form W-4 calculator.
- Send us comments or request help by e-mail.
- Sign up to receive local and national tax news by e-mail.
- Get information on starting and operating a small business.

You can also reach us using File Transfer Protocol at **ftp.irs.gov**.

Fax. You can get over 100 of the most requested forms and instructions 24 hours a day, 7 days a week, by fax. Just call **703–368–9694** from your fax machine. Follow the directions from the prompts. When you order forms, enter the catalog number for the form you need. The items you request will be faxed to you.

For help with transmission problems, call **703–487–4608**.

Long-distance charges may apply.

Phone. Many services are available by phone.

- *Ordering forms, instructions, and publications.* Call **1–800–829–3676** to order current-year forms, instructions, and publications and prior-year forms and instructions. You should receive your order within 10 days.
- *Asking tax questions.* Call the IRS with your tax questions at **1–800–829–1040**.
- *Solving problems.* You can get face-to-face help solving tax problems every business day in IRS Taxpayer Assistance Centers. An employee can explain IRS letters, request adjustments to your account, or help you set up a payment plan. Call your local Taxpayer Assistance Center for an appointment. To find the number, go to **www.irs.gov** or look in the phone book under "United States Government, Internal Revenue Service."
- *TTY/TDD equipment.* If you have access to TTY/TDD equipment, call **1–800–829–4059** to ask tax or account questions or to order forms and publications.
- *TeleTax topics.* Call **1–800–829–4477** to listen to pre-recorded messages covering various tax topics.
- *Refund information.* If you would like to check the status of your 2003 refund, call **1–800–829–4477** for automated refund information and follow the recorded instructions or call **1–800–829–1954**. Be sure to wait at least 6 weeks from the date you filed your return (3 weeks if you filed electronically) and have your 2003 tax return available because you will need to know your filing status and the exact whole dollar amount of your refund.

Evaluating the quality of our telephone services. To ensure that IRS representatives give accurate, courteous, and professional answers, we use several methods to evaluate the quality of our telephone services. One method is for a second IRS representative to sometimes listen in on or record telephone calls. Another is to ask some callers to complete a short survey at the end of the call.

Walk-in. Many products and services are available on a walk-in basis.

- *Products.* You can walk in to many post offices, libraries, and IRS offices to pick up certain forms, instructions, and publications. Some IRS offices, libraries, grocery stores, copy centers, city and county government offices, credit unions, and office supply stores have a collection of products available to print from a CD-ROM or photocopy from reproducible proofs. Also, some IRS offices and libraries have the Internal Revenue Code, regulations, Internal Revenue Bulletins, and Cumulative Bulletins available for research purposes.
- *Services.* You can walk in to your local Taxpayer Assistance Center every business day to ask tax questions or get help with a tax problem. An employee can explain IRS letters, request adjustments to your account, or help you set up a payment plan. You can set up an appointment by calling your local Center and, at the prompt, leaving a message requesting Everyday Tax Solutions help. A representative will call you back within 2 business days to schedule an in-person appointment at your convenience. To find the number, go to **www.irs.gov** or look in the phone book under "United States Government, Internal Revenue Service."

Mail. You can send your order for forms, instructions, and publications to the Distribution Center nearest to you and receive a response within 10 workdays after your request is received. Use the address that applies to your part of the country.

- **Western part of U.S.:**
  Western Area Distribution Center
  Rancho Cordova, CA 95743–0001
- **Central part of U.S.:**
  Central Area Distribution Center
  P.O. Box 8903
  Bloomington, IL 61702–8903
- **Eastern part of U.S. and foreign addresses:**
  Eastern Area Distribution Center
  P.O. Box 85074
  Richmond, VA 23261–5074

CD-ROM for tax products. You can order IRS Publication 1796, *Federal Tax Products on CD-ROM*, and obtain:

- Current-year forms, instructions, and publications.
- Prior-year forms and instructions.
- Frequently requested tax forms that may be filled in electronically, printed out for submission, and saved for recordkeeping.
- Internal Revenue Bulletins.

Buy the CD-ROM from National Technical Information Service (NTIS) on the Internet at www.irs.gov/cdorders for $22 (no handling fee) or call 1-877-233-6767 toll free to buy the CD-ROM for $22 (plus a $5 handling fee). The first release is available in early January and the final release is available in late February.

CD-ROM for small businesses. IRS Publication 3207, *Small Business Resource Guide*, is a must for every small business owner or any taxpayer about to start a business. This handy, interactive CD contains all the business tax forms, instructions and publications needed to successfully manage a business. In addition, the CD provides an abundance of other helpful information, such as how to prepare a business plan, finding financing for your business, and much more. The design of the CD makes finding information easy and quick and incorporates file formats and browsers that can be run on virtually any desktop or laptop computer.

It is available in early April. You can get a free copy by calling 1-800-829-3676 or by visiting the web site at www.irs.gov/smallbiz.

Index

To help us develop a more useful index, please let us know if you have ideas for index entries. See "Comments and Suggestions" in the "Introduction" for the ways you can reach us.

A
Adjusted basis 9
Assessments:
　For local benefits 3
　Homeowners association ... 3
Assistance (*See* Tax help)

B
Basis 8

C
Certificate, mortgage
　credit 6
Comments 2
Construction 8
Cooperatives 3, 4
Cost basis 8
Credit:
　District of Columbia first-time
　　homebuyer 2
　Mortgage interest 6

D
Deduction:
　Home mortgage interest ... 3
　Real estate taxes 2
District of Columbia
　first-time homebuyer
　credit 2

E
Escrow accounts 2

F
Fire insurance premiums ... 9

Form:
　1098 6
　8396 6
Free tax services 11

G
Gift of home 9
Ground rent 3

H
Help (*See* Tax help)
Home:
　Inherited 9
　Mortgage interest 3
　Purchase of 8
　Received as gift 9
Homeowners association
　assessments 3
House payment 2
Housing allowance, minister
　or military 2

I
Improvements 9
Inheritance 9
Insurance 2, 9
Interest:
　Home mortgage 3
　Prepaid 3

K
Keeping records 9

L
Late payment charge 3

Local benefits, assessments
　for 3

M
MCC (Mortgage credit
　certificate) 6
Minister's or military
　housing allowance 2
More information (*See* Tax help)
Mortgage credit certificate
　(MCC) 6
Mortgage insurance
　premiums 9
Mortgage interest:
　Credit 6
　Deduction 3
　Late payment charge ... 3
　Paid at settlement 4
　Refund 3, 6
　Statement 6
Mortgage prepayment
　penalty 3

N
Nondeductible
　payments 2, 9

P
Points 4
Prepaid interest 3
Publications (*See* Tax help)

R
Real estate taxes 2
　Deductible 2

Paid at settlement or
　closing 2, 8
Refund or rebate 3
Recordkeeping 9
Refund of:
　Mortgage interest 3, 6
　Real estate taxes 3
Repairs 9

S
Settlement or closing costs:
　Basis of home 8
　Mortgage interest 4
　Real estate taxes 2, 8
Stamp taxes 3
Statement, mortgage
　interest 6
Suggestions 2

T
Tax help 11
Taxes, real estate 2
Taxpayer Advocate 11
Transfer taxes 3
TTY/TDD information 11

V
VA funding fees 9

W
What you can and cannot
　deduct 2

■

Page 12

246

Index

AARP web site, 181
Accountant's fees, 64
Acquisition costs, 13–14
Acquisition indebtedness, 22–24
Adjusted basis value, gain in excess of, 96–99
Adjusted gross income, 173
Alternative minimum tax, real estate tax prepayment and, 21
Appraisal:
   for casualty loss deduction, 29–31
   fees, purchase, 13
   for rental conversion, 148
Appreciated residence, use of to trade up and get tax-free cash, 142–143
At-risk rules, 173

Basis of home for depreciation, 68
Builder, suit against, proceeds, 73
Business expenses:
   commuting, 47–48
   home office deduction, 38–42
Business owners, eligible for home office deduction, 35–37
Bypass trust, 210

Car loan interest, 53–57
Carryovers:
   capital losses, 96
   divorce and, 129
   home office deduction, 43–45
Cash basis taxpayers, 8
Casualty losses:
   boosting deduction, 29–30
   in disaster areas, 31–33
   figuring loss, 26–28
   guidelines, 24–26
   home office deduction, 41–43
   insurance and, 26–27
Charitable deduction, gift of remainder interest, 148–151
Checklist, tax-planning:
   purchaser's, 16–17
   seller's, 103
Closing costs:
   incidental, 13–14
   real estate tax payment and, 5–6
Commuting costs, 47–49
Condominiums, 73, 83, 93
Contract of sale, real estate tax prorating and, 5–6

Co-op apartments, 73, 83, 93
Credit card interest, 53–57
Credit shelter trust, 210

Damage to home, *see* Casualty losses
Death:
    step-up home value, 96, 107–108
    unrealized gain, 86–87, 90
Deductions:
    casualty loss, 24–33
    interest, *see* Interest
    itemized, 18–19
    real estate taxes, annual, 20–21
    real estate taxes, year of purchase, 4–6
Deferred sale, unrealized gain, 107–108
Delinquent real estate taxes, 5–6, 16
Depreciation:
    home office deduction, 42–46
    residential rental property, 69–72
    vacation home rental property, 168–172
Disabled, home improvements for, 60–61
Disaster losses, 31–33
Distance rule:
    moving expenses, 10–12
    unrealized gain, 85
Divorce:
    $500,000 exclusion, 89
    ownership and use rules, 124–125
    sale prior to, 126–127
    splitting up marital property, avoiding traps, 128–130
    tax traps and, 128–130
    transfer of home to spouse, 125–126, 130
    unforeseen circumstances test, 86
    vacation home and, 127–128
Drought damage, 25

Election out, 65–66
Elevator, 57
Employees, eligible for home office deduction, 33–34
Employment change, unrealized gain, 83–84, 86–87
Equipment:
    home office, 49–50
    vacation home, 170

Equity:
    reverse mortgage, 73, 181–185
    trade-downs, 178–181
    trade-ups, 142–143
Equity stripping, in home equity loans, 56
Estate planning, 186–187
    current law, 186, 188–190
    lifetime exemption, planning for, 190
    need for, 189
    qualified personal residence trust, 195, 199–202
    sale and leaseback, 195–199
    title issues, 12, 187–188, 190
    vacation home, reducing estate tax on, 192–194
Exchange of property to avoid tax:
    investment property, 140–142
    triangular transfer, 136–140
    unrealized gain, 115–116
Exclusive use tests, for home office, 35–36
Expenses:
    home office, 33–50
    maintenance, 67–68, 146–148, 157, 163–164
    moving, 4, 10, 12, 16–17
    purchase of home, 13–14

Fannie Mae web site, 183
Federally declared disaster areas, 31–33
Fire damage to home, *see* Casualty losses
First-time homebuyer IRA distribution, 14–15
First-year deductions:
    checklist for, 16–17
    closing costs, 4, 12–15
    mortgage points, 4, 7–10, 15, 16–17
    moving expenses, 4, 10–12, 16
    real estate taxes, 3, 4–6, 16
    title issues, 4, 12, 14–16
Flipping, in home equity loans, 56
Flood damage to home, *see* Casualty losses
Forms, *see also* Internal Revenue Service forms
    certification for no information reporting, 102

INDEX

Gain on sale, figuring, 107
Gift and leaseback, 197
Ground rents, 108

Health problems, unrealized gain, 84, 85–86
High-priced home, unrealized gain, 104–108
   conversion to rental and exchange, 115–116
   deferred sale, 107–108
   installment sale, 111–114, 117–123
   leasehold carve-out, 108–111
Home equity loans:
   about, 53–54
   business use of, 65–66
   cautions about, 54, 56
   costs of, 53–55
   interest deduction and, 23–24
   in retirement, 178
   tax reduction with, 53, 55
   trade-ups and, 142–143
Home improvements:
   as business, 145–146
   for disabled, 60–61
   loans for, 10
   medically mandated, 57
   mortgage loan, points, 9–11
   records of, 14
   tax benefits and, 107, 143–145
Home office deductions, 19, 33
   commuting costs and, 47–50
   eligibility of business owners, 35–37
   eligibility of employees, 33–35
   figuring deduction, 37–46
   flowchart, 34
   Form 8829, 37–38, 40
   office equipment costs, 49–50
   outside of home work and, 46–48
   Schedule C, use of, 37–38, 39
   "sideline" business, 62–63
   unrealized gain, 93, 101
Home ownership benefits, 3
House hopping, *see* Home improvements
Husband and wife, *see* Marriage

Improvement costs, records of, 14
Imputed income, 152–154

Individual retirement account, first-time homebuyer distribution, 14–15
Installment sale, unrealized gain, 111–114
   loan repayment table, 117–123
Insurance:
   casualty losses, 26–27
   casualty losses, federal disaster areas, 31–33
   premium, not deductible, 22
Interest, *see also* Mortgage interest
   credit and car loan, 53–57
   home equity loan, 23
Internal Revenue Service, avoiding reporting sale to, 99–102
Internal Revenue Service forms:
   Form 8829, 37–38, 40
   reporting sale or exchange of residence, 102
   Schedule A, 21
   Schedule C, 37–38, 39
Investment property, tax-free exchange, 140–142
IRA break for first-time homebuyer, 14–15
Itemizing deductions, 20, 21

Joint ownership:
   estate planning, 187–188, 190
   purchase year, 4, 12, 16

Land, vacant, 93–94
Late payment charge, deduction, 22
Lawsuits against builders, 73
Leaseback, *see* Sale and leaseback
Leasehold carve-out, 108–111
Legal fees, deduction, 13, 73
Level payments self-amortizing note, 114, 117–123
Line of credit, *see* Home equity loans
Loans, *see* Interest; Mortgage; Reverse mortgage
Loopholes:
   appreciated property trade-up, 142–143
   charitable deductions, 148–151
   home improvements, 143–145
   imputed income, 152–154
   land including house and investment property, 140–142

Loopholes (*Continued*)
  loss on sale of home, 146–148
  serial sales, 133–136
  vacation home bought from sale of rental property, 136–140
Losses, *see also* Casualty losses
  carryover for capital losses, 96
  home sale and, 79
  vacation home, 158–161
  vacation home, full-year rental, 156, 165–173

Maintenance expenses:
  home rental and, 67–68
  vacation home rental, 157, 163–164
  ways to deduct, 146–148
Marriage:
  $500,000 unrealized gain, 87–91
  estate tax and, 186, 190–192
  title issues, 4, 12, 14–16
Medical home improvements, 57–60
Mortgage, exchange of property and, 138, 139–140. *See also* Mortgage interest; Mortgage points; Reverse mortgage
Mortgage interest:
  government threat to, 18–19
  home rental and, 67
  late payment charge, 22
  qualified as deduction, 7–12, 17, 21–23
  refinanced loans, 22–24
  vacation home and, 157, 161, 163
  versus service charges, 4
Mortgage points:
  deduction of, 4, 7–12, 15–16, 17
  flowchart, 11
  home improvement loans, 9–11
  refinancing, 24
Moving expenses, 4, 10–12, 16, 213–226
Multiple births, 87

Net lease, 116
Nondeductible points, amortization of, 9
Nonforeign affidavit, 17

Packing, in home equity loans, 56
Passive loss rules, vacation home, 172–173

Personal expenses, home office, 41–42
Personal property, depreciation, 170
Personal use, of vacation home, defined, 160, 168
Points, *see* Mortgage points
Preemptive sale, 106
Prepayments, real estate taxes, 20–21
Principal residence requirement:
  low-tax states and, 94–95
  serial sale strategy, 133–136
  tax traps and divorce, 128–130
  unrealized gain, 91–92, 94–95
Property exchange, *see* Exchange of property to avoid tax
Property split, *see* Leasehold carve-out
Purchase expenses, 13–14
Purchase of home, down payment from IRA, 14–15
Purchase year, *see* First-year deductions

Qualified personal residence trust, 195, 199–202
Qualified terminable interest property (QTIP) trust, 191

Real estate taxes:
  first year of purchase, 3, 4–6, 14–16, 17
  home rental and, 67
  prepayment of, 20–21
  recurring deduction for, 19–22
  vacation home and, 157, 161, 163
Record-keeping:
  adjusted basis of home value, 14, 96–97
  closing costs, 12–16
  gain on home sale, 79–80
  home improvements, 14
Recurring deductions:
  casualty losses, 24–26
  home office expenses, 33–50
  maximizing, 19
  mortgage interest, 21–24
  real estate taxes, 20–21
Refinancing, 22–24
Remainder interest, 148–151. *See also* Retained interest
Renovation, *see* Home improvements

Rentals:
  after trading down, 180
  conversion to, and exchange, to avoid excess gain on sale, 115–116
  deductions for, 98–99
  depressed markets and unrealized gain, 98–99
  employers and home offices, 34–35
  entire home, 68–72
  exchange of property, 141–142
  leasehold carve-out, 108–111
  part of home, 67–68
  to relative, 166
  serial sale strategy to avoid tax, 133–136
  short-term, tax-free income, 51
  tax advice and, 65
  vacation home, entire year, 156, 165–168
  vacation home, fewer than 14 days, 51–52, 156, 157–158
  vacation home, more than 14 days, 156, 158–159
Repairs as permanent improvements, effect on basis, 44
Residency, *see* Principal residence requirement
Retained interest, *see also* Remainder interest
  sale and leaseback, 196–198
  vacation home, 193, 210–211
Retirement homes, exchange of property, 139
Retirement planning, 177–178
  equity trade-down, 178–181
  home as nest egg for, 73
  installment sale, 111–112
  reverse mortgage, 73, 181–185
  trading down tax-free, 178–181
Reverse mortgage, 73, 181–185
  benefits, 182–183
  disadvantages, 185
  refinancing, 184

Sabbaticals, residency requirements and, 82
Sale and leaseback, 195–199
Sale of home:
  $250,000 gain excluded, 79–80
  $500,000 gain excluded, 87–91
  basis for figuring amount of gain, 107
  checklist, 103
  depressed housing market and, 98–99
  divorce and, 124–130
  exceptions to two-year rule, 83–87
  gains in excess of, 96–97
  government rationale for, 77–78
  high-priced homes, 104–123
  home office, 93
  IRS reporting avoidance, 99–102
  married couples, 87–91
  planning for, 78
  preemptive, 107
  principal residence requirement, 91–92
  qualifying for, 80–83
  qualifying for, exceptions, 83–87
  record-keeping for, 79–80
  serial sale to shield unrealized gain on other property, 133–136
  snowbirds, 94–95
  spouses, 87
  vacant land, 93–94
Second home, *see* Vacation home
Second mortgage, 54
Second refinancing, 24
Separation, *see* Divorce
Serial sale strategy, 133–136
Service charges versus interest, mortgage point deduction, 4
"Sideline" business, 61–63
Snowbirds, unrealized gain, 94–95
Special-situation deductions:
  credit card/car loan interest, 53–57
  home equity used for business, 65–66
  medical home improvements, 57–60
  renting part of home, 67–68
  retirement nest egg, 73
  short-term rentals, 51–52
  "sideline" business, 61–63
  tax advice, 64–65
Split gifts, vacation home, 192–194
Standard deduction versus itemizing, 20, 21
Step-up rule, unrealized gain, 96, 107–108
Storm damage to home, *see* Casualty losses
Survey costs, 13
Swimming pools, 58–59

Taxable gain, reducing on future sale, 13–15
Tax advice, deductibility of, 64–65
Tax basis, incidental closing costs, 13–16
Telephone lines:
    home office deduction, 41–42
    for tenants, 68
Termite damage, 235
Time rules, *see also* Two-year ownership/waiting period
    moving expenses, 10–12
    serial sale strategy, 133–136
    unrealized gain, 80–87, 98
Title insurance, 13
Titles:
    estate planning issues, 187–188, 190
    married couple issues, 4, 12, 14–16
Trade-downs, 178–181
    benefits, 180–181
    disadvantages, 180
Trade-ups, 142–143
Transfer and recording taxes, 7, 16
Transportation expenses, 47–49
Triangular transfer, 136–140
Trusts:
    qualified personal residence trust, 195, 199–202
    qualified terminable interest property (QTIP) trust, 191
Two-year ownership/waiting period, for home sale exclusion, 80–83. *See also* Time rules
    $500,000 exclusion, 87
    divorce and, 124–126
    exceptions to, 83–87

rentals and, 98
serial sale strategy, 133–136

Unforeseen circumstances, 86–87
Uniform Settlement Statement, 8

Vacant land, unrealized gain, 93–94
Vacation home, 155–156
    avoiding gain on sale of, 127–128
    deductions for, figuring, 161–165
    depreciation, 168–173
    divorce and, 127–128
    estate planning issues, 192–194
    line of credit and, 54
    maintenance costs, 147
    mid-year change in use, 167
    purchased from sale of rental property, 136–140
    qualified personal residence trust, 195, 199–202
    rented entire year, 156, 165–168
    rented fewer than 14 days, 52, 156, 157–158
    rented more than 14 days, 156, 158–165
    residency requirements, 82–83
    serial sale strategy, 133–136
    short-term rental deduction, 52
    tax-free income, 157
    tax loss not allowed, 158, 160
    tax shelter rules, 172–173
    unrealized gain, 91–92, 127–128
    used exclusively by owner, 156–157

Wills, *see* Estate planning